GAME
OF KINGS

A Year Among the Geeks, Oddballs,
and Geniuses Who Make Up America's
Top High School Chess Team

MICHAEL WEINREB

GOTHAM BOOKS

GOTHAM BOOKS
Published by Penguin Group (USA) Inc.
375 Hudson Street, New York, New York 10014, U.S.A.

Penguin Group (Canada), 90 Eglinton Avenue East, Suite 700, Toronto, Ontario M4P 2Y3, Canada (a division of Pearson Penguin Canada Inc.) • Penguin Books Ltd, 80 Strand, London WC2R 0RL, England • Penguin Ireland, 25 St Stephen's Green, Dublin 2, Ireland (a division of Penguin Books Ltd) • Penguin Group (Australia), 250 Camberwell Road, Camberwell, Victoria 3124, Australia (a division of Pearson Australia Group Pty Ltd) • Penguin Books India Pvt Ltd, 11 Community Centre, Panchsheel Park, New Delhi–110 017, India • Penguin Group (NZ), 67 Apollo Drive, Rosedale, North Shore 0632, Auckland, New Zealand (a division of Pearson New Zealand Ltd) • Penguin Books (South Africa) (Pty) Ltd, 24 Sturdee Avenue, Rosebank, Johannesburg 2196, South Africa

Penguin Books Ltd, Registered Offices: 80 Strand, London WC2R 0RL, England

Published by Gotham Books, a member of Penguin Group (USA) Inc.

Previously published as a Gotham Books hardcover edition
with the title *The Kings of New York*, March 2007

First trade paperback printing, January 2008

10   9   8   7   6   5   4   3   2   1

Gotham Books and the skyscraper logo are trademarks of Penguin Group (USA) Inc.

Copyright © 2007 by Michael Weinreb
All rights reserved

Excerpt on page 254 © New York *Daily News* L.P. Reprinted with permission.

Photo credits:
p. x: Courtesy of Eliot Weiss; p. 20: Courtesy of the author; p. 28: Josh Wendelken, MyChessPhotos.com; p. 56: Christopher Oquendo, MyChessPhotos.com; p. 74: Matthew Logan, MyChessPhotos.com; p. 88: Heidi Oquendo, MyChessPhotos.com; p. 194: Christopher Oquendo, MyChessPhotos.com.

LIBRARY OF CONGRESS CATALOGING–IN–PUBLICATION DATA

Weinreb, Michael.
    The kings of New York : a year among the geeks, oddballs, and geniuses who make up America's top high school chess team / Michael Weinreb.—1st ed.
        p. cm.
    Includes bibliographical references.
    ISBN: 978-1-592-40261-8 (hardcover) ISBN: 978-1-592-40338-7 (paperback) 1. Chess—New York (State)—New York. 2. Chess players—New York (State)—New York. 3. High school students—New York (State)—New York. I. Title.
    GV1325.N49W35 2007
    794.109747'2—dc22   2006027864

Printed in the United States of America
Set in Bembo • Designed by Elke Sigal

While the author has made every effort to provide accurate telephone numbers and Internet addresses at the time of publication, neither the publisher nor the author assumes any responsibility for errors, or for changes that occur after publication. Further, the publisher does not have any control over and does not assume any responsibility for author or third-party Web sites or their content.

Praise for *Game of Kings*:

"Lively, inspiring. . . . With [Michael Weinreb's] vivid portraits and brisk narrative style, he manages to find high drama in a roomful of brilliant young minds pushing little pieces across a 64-square grid."

—*Entertainment Weekly*

"[*Game of Kings*] is supported by well-chosen detail, intelligence, and terrific writing. Weinreb clearly develops an affection for the eclectic members of his team, and because of the skill he brings to his project, so will his readers."

—*Publishers Weekly* (starred review)

"Compelling. . . . Weinreb paces the action expertly. . . . The season's ebbs and flows intermingle with the prosaic details of inner-city adolescence to singularly lyrical effect."

—*Kirkus*

"Entertaining."

—*Newsday*

"Not only among the very best accounts written about chess, but also among the best nonfiction works 2007 has offered."

—*OK Gazette*

"Writing with the deft, propulsive style of a young Frank Deford, Michael Weinreb has captured both the intellectual insanity—and the curious normalcy—of what it's like to be a teenaged super-genius. *Game of Kings* is the *Friday Night Lights* of high school chess."

—Chuck Klosterman, author of *Sex, Drugs, and Cocoa Puffs* and *Chuck Klosterman IV*

"*Game of Kings* is about chess in the same way that Darcy Frey's *The Last Shot* was about basketball. Michael Weinreb's real subjects are the nature of talent, the onset of adolescence, and the kingdom of Brooklyn. This is a wonderful book."

—Mark Kriegel, author of *Pistol: The Life of Pete Maravich* and *Namath: A Biography*

"Michael Weinreb has done a heroic job doing something once thought impossible—making an eminently readable topic out of chess. Part *Word Freak*, part *Season on the Brink*, *Game of Kings* is a gripping inside look at an endearingly quirky subculture."

—L. Jon Wertheim, author of *Transition Game* and *Venus Envy*

"*Game of Kings* isn't so much a book about high school chess as it is an unforgettable journey into the blessing and curse of adolescent genius. With a narrative rich in voice—a gathering of intoxicating characters—Weinreb has delivered nothing short of a generational classic. This is a stunning book. You won't soon forget it."

—Adrian Wojnarowski, author of *The Miracle of St. Anthony*

SAMANTHA WEINMAN

Michael Weinreb's work has appeared in *The New York Times*, the *Boston Globe*, the *Los Angeles Times*, *Newsday*, and *ESPN The Magazine*. In his career as a journalist, he has been named best sportswriter in Ohio by the Associated Press, was nominated for a Pulitzer Prize, and has been cited three times in the *Best American Sports Writing* anthology. He lives in New York City.

In memory of my uncle,

Mark Rosenbloom (1945–2005),

the first chess player I knew

CONTENTS

PROLOGUE *1*

PART ONE ♛ OPENING
ONE: DO THE MATH *11*

TWO: BRUCKNER'S GAMBIT *21*

THREE: FREEDOM OF CHOICE *29*

FOUR: AN ACADEMIC CHALLENGE *43*

FIVE: A GAME UNLIKE ANY OTHER *57*

SIX: THE ORANGUTAN *75*

SEVEN: CHESS AND THE CITY *89*

EIGHT: ALL THE PRESIDENT'S MEN *101*

PART TWO ♛ MIDDLE GAME
NINE: THE THIRTY-NINTH ANNUAL GREATER NEW YORK SCHOLASTIC TEAM
AND INDIVIDUAL CHESS CHAMPIONSHIPS *119*

TEN: THE WOMEN IN THE ROOM *137*

ELEVEN: TIRESOME DAYS AND SLEEPLESS NIGHTS *159*

TWELVE: THE 2005 NEW YORK STATE SCHOLASTIC CHAMPIONSHIPS *169*

THIRTEEN: IT'S IMPOSSIBLE TO CHANGE YOUR DESTINY *195*

PART THREE ♛ ENDGAME
FOURTEEN: SUPERNATIONALS III *213*

FIFTEEN: SUMMERTIME *251*

EPILOGUE *271*

AFTERWORD *279*

ACKNOWLEDGMENTS *283*

GLOSSARY *287*

BIBLIOGRAPHY *291*

WEB SITES *293*

GAME OF KINGS

The Murrow team with President Bush (from left to right): Congressman Anthony Weiner, Senator Charles Schumer, Alex Lenderman, Sal Bercys, Ilya Kotlyanskiy, President George W. Bush, Willy Edgard, Nile Smith, Oscar Santana, Olga Novikova, Dmitriy Minevich, and Eliot Weiss with his two children

PROLOGUE

FOUR DAYS AFTER CHRISTMAS, 2004, IN A PIN-DROP-SILENT HOTEL conference room with a panoramic view of a TGI Friday's and an adult bookstore, Oscar Santana nudges a black pawn forward, sweeps a white rook off the board, and presses the button atop his game clock with a faint click.

"This is *not* chess," mutters the man on the opposite side of the board. His name is Norman, according to the pairings board at the Empire City Open, and Norman is regarding Oscar with a slack jaw and a pair of bugged-out eyes. Norman is also wearing a black winter cap indoors, as if to conceal from the outside world the strings that command his elastic facial features. "This is *not* chess," Norman says again, and he is speaking far too loudly now, his voice piercing the white noise of ticking game clocks and humming air vents and muffled coughs.

Norman is approximately three times Oscar's age, and a good half a foot taller, and his choice of headwear, coupled with his tics and twitches and grimaces and the plaintive noises he emits through his bulbous lips, lends him the appearance of a burglar trying to make an escape through a narrow air shaft. In truth, the board is shrinking on Norman; there are few safe places for his king to escape. His is, as they say in the sport, a *lost game,* and there is no worse feeling in chess than the realization that defeat is imminent and unavoidable.

Norman shakes his head and says something utterly incomprehensible. Oscar just sits there, stone-faced, a pair of silver headphones clapped over his ears, a tinny hip-hop beat creeping out from underneath. Then he moves his rook to Norman's back row, to threaten his queen. The queen is the most potent piece on a chessboard, the only one capable of moving any number of spaces in any direction, horizontal, vertical or diagonal, and if the queen is crippled, if the queen is retreating instead of attacking . . . and especially when Norman is already down a rook, because only a pair of rooks can begin to approach the queen in terms of strength . . . and who the *hell* is this kid, anyway? Norman has no idea. All he knows is that things have gone wrong, that a seventeen-year-old in baggy jeans and FUBU sneakers has surrounded his king and endangered his queen and taken one of his rooks and rendered him into a stammering caricature.

But it's not just Oscar's age, and it's not merely the fact that his official United States Chess Federation rating, which determines the social order in chess, is nearly three hundred points lower than Norman's. More than all of that, it's the *way* this little brace-faced miscreant is beating him, using a bush-league tactic involving a knight and a pawn that even Oscar himself knows is a joke. It's the type of attack that makes very little sense to those with a thorough knowledge of the chessboard. It defies all the conventional wisdom Oscar has picked up over the years: that you should make a concerted effort to control the center of the board in the opening moves of the game, that you should avoid unnecessary sacrifices of your own pieces, and that you should not rely upon tricks, especially against a higher-rated player. Oscar's tactic has holes so gaping that when one of his teammates asks a grandmaster about the possibility of using it, months later, the grandmaster will be tempted to dismiss him from the room for the mere mention of it. It makes little sense to Oscar, as well, but this is what made him try it. He's never been one to surrender to the tyranny of the ordinary.

Across a hall, in the free-form holding pen for competitors and their families known as the Skittles Room, there are stacks of books about the Ruy Lopez and the Sicilian and the Nimzo-Indian and the

Caro-Kann defenses, pages and pages of diagrams and complex notations that resemble an organic chemistry textbook. But this is not the type of knowledge that Oscar concerns himself with. Oscar prefers to accumulate his knowledge through experience. He's never been big on studying lines of attack or complex variations or all those esoteric diagrams found in thick books of strategy authored by the masters of the game.

When Oscar was younger, when he was in middle school and he first learned chess, he became enamored of an elementary opening called the four-move checkmate, which essentially relies upon the fact that your opponent does not know how to play chess. When that began to fail, he memorized a conventional opening for the white pieces called the Ruy Lopez and a defense for the black pieces called the Sicilian (the fact that white moves first necessitates separate strategies for each set of pieces). He memorized just enough moves, maybe eight or ten, to get him through the beginning of a game, and then he came to rely on his wits, which is how Oscar would prefer to play chess. Sure, he could spend a few hours with one of those seminal chess texts like Nimzovich's *My System,* and he could commit the whole thing to memory—he has this type of mind, whether he'll admit it or not—but where's the fun in that? His old middle-school teacher has always told him that he has to keep progressing in his chess career, and this is why, in recent months, he has fallen in love with a completely illogical opening for the white pieces called the Orangutan. No doubt Oscar would have used that here, if he weren't playing with black, so instead he relied on this weird pawn-knight variation, which harkened back so far in Oscar's chess education that Norman could have not have possibly seen it coming. Where the hell did this kid *come from*? "This is *not* serious chess," Norman is saying, but no one is listening, because their cerebrums are otherwise occupied with their own gambits, their own tactics, their own eager attempts to throw their opponents off guard.

This is the first day of the Empire City Open, a minor event at which first place in the under-2000-rated division, Oscar's division, will pay $375. The competitors sit side-by-side at long tables, squinting at their positions and stealing glances at the clocks next to their boards. Behind Oscar, near the window, at a row of boards overlooking the snow-dusted sidewalks of Eighth Avenue, Ilya Kotlyanskiy is recalibrating his vision. He does this most often by sitting up on one knee in his chair and peering over the board from above. Ilya is one of the few people in the room whose pants actually appear to have been pressed before his arrival. His hair is short and worked into neatly tended spikes, and his sweater matches his trousers. This is something that cannot be said for many of the other men in the room (and it is populated almost entirely by men), but then, Ilya has never fit neatly into this world. He has a small face and a prominent nose, and he hasn't eaten all morning, because he has yet to lose today, and Ilya cannot eat a proper meal until he is relaxed. This means that sometimes he'll go all day, through school and work, without ingesting anything except liquids. Right now, Ilya's match remains suspended in what's known as the middle game, the precarious interlude between the opening and endgame when one ill-considered move can destroy the entire setup.

The Empire City Open engulfs an entire floor of a midtown Manhattan hotel, and on every door there are bright yellow signs urging visitors to turn off their cell phones and to keep quiet in the hallway. The pairings boards have been set up on chunks of posterboard near the elevators; interspersed throughout the halls are metal jugs of water with stacks of plastic cups piled high next to them. Parents sit on the floor staring glassy-eyed at paperback novels, waiting for their children to finish inside the room, chasing their offspring as they toddle down the carpeted hallways, shushing them when they raise their voices.

While he waits for Norman to process his defeat, Oscar stands and walks toward Willy Edgard's table on the far side of the room, to look in on his classmate's game. Oscar's gait is slow and measured; if you look closely enough, you can detect a slight limp. It is not something Oscar would ever willingly betray, but it is there, and it's the reason his face has filled out since freshman year, and it's partly why he's spending his time in a room like this in the midst of his winter vacation. These days, given the dearth of private clubs and the prevalence of the

Internet, tournaments like the Empire City Open are the last bastions of face-to-face competitive chess in America. And so they tend to draw all sorts, including those who reside on the extreme edges of the human psyche. Take, for instance, the pairing Oscar is looking in on right now: a bearded Duane Allman doppelgänger wearing a trucker hat and a Humane Society T-shirt, with a bag full of sinus tablets and prescription meds at his feet, going up against a black man with a pile of Don King hair, outfitted in the closest thing to pajamas—white Hanes Beefy-T shirt, shapeless gray sweatpants—a human being can get away with in public.

At the next board over, Willy is playing three hundred points above his head as well, and he's bleeding pawns. He's down four of them, and this loss of material has grown to the point where he most likely can't extricate himself. Willy is one of Oscar's best friends; they met in the chess club at middle school, and they've grown up together ever since. Above the wispy goatee he's taken pains to cultivate, Willy's mouth is a straight line. He's wearing a pair of baggy sweats and a black long-sleeve T-shirt, and he's listening to hip-hop on his CD player, and deep down he harbors dreams of producing his own rhymes someday, if only he can figure a way to get into college, let alone pay for it.

Oscar returns to his table. By now, you can practically see the steam rising from Norman's cap; his face has wrenched itself into one massive contortion. With an hour remaining on his clock, Norman shakes his head one last time, and then he resigns. Oscar offers a customary postgame handshake, and Norman takes it, and Oscar scoops his down-lined North Face jacket from the chair and heads out into the hallway and lets out a quivering sigh.

"Wow," he says. "I don't know how I did that."

The previous spring, a math teacher at Edward R. Murrow High School in Brooklyn had faxed a press release to every newspaper and television station in the metro area, trumpeting his team's most recent national high-school chess championship. This is something he does virtually every spring, since, most years, his team manages to win a championship of one kind or another, at the local or the state or the national level. In this press release, the math teacher, Eliot Weiss, described each of his top players in a single sentence. Next to Willy's name: "One of several who will be helping our team." Next to Ilya: "Most improved chess player." And, next to Oscar: "Adding more knowledge."

Out in the hallway, Oscar talks to a friend of his named Steadroy about another one of his teammates, a Russian sophomore named Alex Lenderman. Nobody really knows what to make of Alex. Most of his teammates call him by his last name. He's barely five feet tall, and painfully shy among strangers, and he has disheveled hair and an inadvertent wisp of facial hair above his lip. More than once, Ilya's helped shoo away the bullies who pick on him in school. Alex is also the second-highest-rated fifteen-year-old chess player in the United States, behind only his own classmate, Salvijus Bercys, and he's playing in the Open Section, the highest-rated section, among grandmasters like Joel Benjamin, the balding former child prodigy who signed an autograph for a young player earlier this afternoon.

"You hear what Lenderman did?" Oscar says. "He won three games against nobody and then he took two byes. He didn't hardly play anyone. He comes up to me, and he says to me, with that quiet little Russian accent, 'I'm in the money.' He was guaranteed money. I guess he figured that was good enough."

Steadroy shakes his head.

"Why aren't you playing?" Oscar says.

"Saving myself up for New Year's," Steadroy says. In a couple of nights, Steadroy explains, there will be an all-night New Year's tournament at the Marshall club, the last of the city's major private chess establishments. The way Steadroy figures it, his youth will serve to his advantage in an all-nighter; the old men will be snoozing in their seats sometime past midnight, and he'll be going strong.

Oscar fishes a deck of cards from his jacket. Everywhere he goes, Oscar carries a deck with him. He has become a devotee of online poker Web sites, an inveterate small-time hustler. In the school cafeteria, he and his friends bet their dollars on a Russian card game called Stupid. Most of the time, Oscar comes out ahead.

Behind him, Ilya bursts out of the elevator, carrying a Starbucks coffee and a sandwich in a paper bag. "I could have won that game," he says, and then he disappears into the Skittles Room. A short time later, Willy emerges, defeated, making excuses for himself.

"Yo, I'm hungry, man," Oscar says. "You should have resigned."

Two flights down on the elevator, and then Willy and Oscar hurtle past clumps of disoriented European tourists and clatter through the revolving doors. A few weeks earlier, they'd stood in the Oval Office for a photo op with the president, served up as shining examples of what a public-school system can produce when it nurtures its minority and immigrant youth, and so on, and so on. But all those plaudits were based on their accomplishments within the game, within an artificial hierarchy contained to nondescript hotel conference rooms and debated on Web sites and online message boards. Out here on the streets, where no one gives a goddamn about the silence and order contained within those sixty-four squares, where most people on Eighth Avenue can't even begin to comprehend the strange beauty of what Oscar has just accomplished, he's scratching together his cash to pay for a Quarter Pounder.

PART ONE

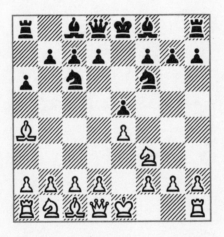

OPENING

ONE

DO THE MATH

ON A DRAB SEPTEMBER AFTERNOON IN BROOKLYN, ON THE FOURTH floor of a sprawling red-brick school building set tight against the elevated subway line, the best fifteen-year-old chess player in the United States struts into a classroom and falls into a litany of complaint. His name is Salvijus Bercys, though he goes by the Americanized truncation of Sal, and he has braces and cowlicked blond hair and a devastatingly thin frame. Sal drops his backpack on a desk with a hollow thud, considers the strangers in his midst, and then turns to Eliot Weiss, the teacher who presides over this room, the teacher who recruited him to this high school, and he says, "How long is this going to take?"

The way Sal figures it, he has no compelling reason still to be in school on this afternoon, in a roomful of clueless neophytes who could not begin to comprehend the complexity of the strategies gestating within his head. This is the introductory Thursday meeting for underclassmen interested in joining the chess team at Edward R. Murrow High School, and Sal is not a beginner, and if you want to know the truth, Sal doesn't have much patience for beginners. Sal is far beyond that phase of his life. Sal has been playing chess for seven years, starting in his native country of Lithuania. In the summer of 2003, he showed up at a tournament called the U.S. Junior Open, held at SUNY-Maritime, a small college in the Bronx. He had arrived in America with his family four weeks earlier, emerging on the New York chess scene virtually out of thin air. Sal scored five out of a possible six points—in chess tournaments, one point is awarded for a victory, half a point for a draw, and no points for a defeat—and finished first in the under-twenty-one division, earning a full scholarship to the University of Texas at Dallas, which he has no intention of using. Sal has been a regular at local tournaments ever since then, his U.S. Chess Federation rating ballooning to above 2400, ascending toward the ranks of masters and grandmasters, nearly eight hundred points ahead of most of his teammates.

"I can't stay," Sal says. "I have to go soon."

Sal is the defending state high-school champion, the number-one ranked player in the country under the age of sixteen, and the best scholastic player on the best scholastic chess team in America. He led Murrow to the national high-school championship last season, and since then his English has improved to the point where he speaks in a sort of boxy slang. He tends toward trendy clothing brands like Diesel and Nike. He is both self-deprecating and arrogant, gregarious and prickly, as the best chess players can be, and the reason he's in a hurry is because he's on his way to a tournament tonight at the Marshall Chess Club. The entry fee is twenty-five dollars instead of the usual twenty, which means Sal could walk away with more money at the end of the evening. A couple of weeks earlier, Sal had come home with a hundred and ten dollars.

And so Sal delivers perfunctory answers to certain questions about his past—he's been playing for seven years, and age doesn't really matter in chess, the way he chooses an opening series of moves is based upon a matter of feel, blah, blah, blah—and then he slips out the door. "Man," he says, "I'm getting old." You see things when your mind is developing that you don't see when you get older, Sal has said, and chess is all about seeing things that no one else sees, which is why it's a sport that's always produced its share of prodigies: another petulant boy from Brooklyn, Bobby Fischer, was fourteen when he won his first national championship.

Within the rubric of the U.S. Chess Federation, Sal is competing at a master level, although it is a monstrous leap from what Sal can do to what the elite grandmasters (the Fischers and the Karpovs and the Kasparovs) can do, which is why even the top echelon of players often maintain a base of humility beneath their bluster. Still, in November, Sal will play at the World Youth Championships in Greece, and a couple of weeks after that, he'll be at the U.S. Championships in San Diego. He'll miss almost a month of school in order to play chess. He's an elite youth player in a sport so often defined by its youth, and while he'd like to think he's too old to be a prodigy, he is the primary reason why Murrow should win another high-school national championship in Nashville next April. This is the goal at Murrow every year. It's been the goal almost every year for the past decade, when, through a combination of geographic fortune and resourcefulness and outright salesmanship, Eliot Weiss began to construct an unlikely and unconventional sort of dynasty.

One by one, the veteran players at Murrow enter and then go their separate ways: Willy and Oscar and a sophomore named Nile Smith have to attend an after-school chess tutoring program in Manhattan, through a nonprofit organization called Chess-in-the-Schools; Ilya has to study for his SATs; Alex Lenderman has to meet his father at home; and the two incoming recruits, the freshmen Dalphe Morantus and Shawn Martinez, are nowhere to be found. Over the course of the year, each will miss significant amounts of class time because of chess, a fact that will confuse and frustrate certain teachers, who simply cannot fathom the notion of this game as a competitive enterprise. They hear about Murrow's chess championships—everyone in school knows *of* them, even if they can't always understand why anyone would bother with such a thing—but it does not earn the team members any special privileges. It is up to Mr. Weiss to serve as their apologist, and he does all he can, even if he cannot always save them from themselves.

After the veterans are gone, after they've all made their brief cameos and bolted out the door, there are only the newbies, lined up in a pair of tidy little rows in the back of the room, playing against each other. There are fourteen altogether, nine boys and five girls, a surprisingly egalitarian mix, and they're fidgeting in their chairs and gnawing at their cuticles and nearly withering their cheap plastic pawns with angst. This is how chess club begins each season: with a fumbling in the dark, with a reliance upon the vague notions of the sport passed on by fathers and brothers and uncles, with all these fresh faces stumbling toward checkmate.

Eliot Weiss has seen this before. He sees the same mistakes from the newbies every fall, and it's his hope that a few of them, perhaps one or two, perhaps three or four, will take it seriously enough to wend their way through the fog to a greater understanding. But for now, it's just the first meeting of a long year. And for now, Mr. Weiss keeps quiet, and he keeps his hands behind his back, and he hovers above the row of boards like a test proctor. He already has his team, his top boards, his core of talent; what might emerge from this room, perhaps a late bloomer who takes to the game the way he once did, is merely a bonus.

Primarily for reasons of neighborhood preservation and economics, Edward R. Murrow High School was built on a swatch of real estate next to the subway line at Avenue M in Midwood, Brooklyn. The school opened in 1974 with a nontraditional curriculum and a selective admissions process. Before that, the land was occupied by a city sanitation dump and a parking lot for an Oldsmobile dealership. Today, the neighborhood surrounding the school is diverse, multilingual, and primarily middle-class. It serves as a sort of ethnic and geographic centerpoint of Brooklyn, and is home to a large enclave of Orthodox Jews and Russian immigrants and blacks and Hispanics and Middle Easterners. On Avenue M, a drugstore advertises Russian Orthopedic Comfort Shoes, and Pete's Pizza Parlor stands across the street from the remains of the Shalom Hunan, a defunct kosher Chinese restaurant. A block away on Avenue L, surrounded by a towering chain-link fence, is the artificial-turf athletic facility for nearby Midwood High, where the city football championship is played each fall. In the park across the street, students from the local yeshiva play games of pickup basketball, shirts untucked, hair bobbing in the wind.

The easiest way to reach the entrance to Murrow from the subway platform at Avenue M is a shortcut through a narrow produce-market parking lot littered with trash and graffiti. You can also walk a block to Avenue L, then turn left and walk two blocks to the main entrance, threading your way through clusters of disabled students and punk-rock revivalists (pink hair, Sex Pistols T-shirts) hanging out near the school parking lot on Fourteenth Street. Inside the main entrance, as is the case at every New York City public school, a security guard sits at a cramped desk signing in visitors and refusing reentry to teenagers who claim to have forgotten their ID cards.

By 2:45 in the afternoon, when the school day officially ends, students at both neighborhood high schools, Midwood and Murrow, overwhelm the streets and flood toward the subway entrance. Midwood's football field stands on an entire city block no more than fifty feet from Murrow's front entrance, a rectangle of turf bounded on one side by metal bleachers and on the other by that twenty-foot-tall chain-link fence, set almost as a line of demarcation between two disparate institutions.

"Visiting Midwood [High School] is like stepping into a school in the early 1950s," wrote author and education historian Diane Ravitch in a 1984 essay. "It is quiet and orderly, and the students seem serious and purposeful."

At Midwood, classes are crowded and competition can be cutthroat; the school also has more than two dozen varsity sports programs. Midwood has lacrosse teams and soccer teams and volleyball teams and swim teams. So if you live in the neighborhood and you want a *traditional* high-school experience, if you want to play football or soccer or baseball or tennis, you go to Midwood. "There are just so many resources and energy you can have," says Saul Bruckner, the principal at Murrow for the first thirty years of its existence. "Maybe this is an excuse, but to field a football team, you need thirty thousand dollars a year. So the teams we have tend to be in the academic arena.

Or as I used to tell the kids who would bug me about it, the principal's a lousy athlete."

Inside, Murrow looks and feels and smells like a typical American high school entering its third decade of life. The walls are painted in unfathomably hideous shades of yellow and orange, and the white tile floors in the hallway are stained gray, and the sinks in the bathroom are clogged with a thick brown detritus of paper towels. The building is a labyrinth of hallways and annexes; Weiss's classroom is on the fourth floor, number 446, a rectangular space near the art department with a pea-green linoleum floor. On the far side of the room, a wall of windows directly overlooks the elevated train; the Q express line rattles desks each time it shimmies past.

The newbies were lured here by the announcement that morning over the school's loudspeaker—*Come join the Edward R. Murrow chess team, the best of its kind in the nation*—but most of them had known about Murrow's team long before the announcement. It has become a signature of the school, a notation in the guidebooks and on the "best-of " lists, a shining example of how Murrow's unique educational system, one that values expansive personal freedoms, allows its students to thrive. There are children in Russia who have yet to set foot on American soil who have heard of Murrow High School in missives from their relatives in Brighton Beach and Sheepshead Bay and Coney Island, in the articles that appear every spring in *Newsday* and the *Daily News* and the *Post*.

There are essentially two chess teams at Murrow: There is the "traveling" team, consisting of the players that Weiss has recruited and helped gain entrance to the school; and there are the club members, who come and go as they please on Thursday afternoons. The club members, if they are serious, are encouraged to attend weekend tournaments in Brooklyn and Manhattan, sponsored by a foundation known as The Right Move. If they show enough dedication, Weiss will, essentially, promote them to the traveling team. At most chess tournaments, only the top four scorers on each team count; therefore, a team can bring sixty or seventy players to a tournament or a team can bring five, and the results could still match up evenly. One year, Weiss brought more than twenty players to the national high-school championship. In other years, he's brought half a dozen or fewer. Much of it depends upon his budget, which used to depend upon public kindness and now depends on a single private donor who wishes to remain anonymous.

And so these fourteen had heard stories in the hallways, and they studied the photographs and the news clippings on the bulletin board as they entered Eliot Weiss's classroom, the one with the JUST DO THE MATH sign on the door. There are photos of past teams with mayors (Bloomberg and Giuliani), with senators (Clinton and Schumer), and with vice president Al Gore. There is a *Daily News* clipping from the previous spring headlined CHESS CHAMPS DO IT AGAIN.

Outside, save the periodic grumbles of the rush-hour trains, there is quiet. Afternoons at Murrow are placid and forgiving. The expansive hallways, a gathering spot for students during the school day, have emptied out. The math club is meeting next door, and a college prep group is gathering down the hall in a science room named after Galileo. Every couple of minutes, someone else knocks on the door to Weiss's room, pokes their head inside, and bears witness to the conga line of chess games being played in the back of the room, on school desks lined with boards made of xeroxed paper sheets and outlined in masking tape. Is this the College Now program? Is this the Arabic Club?

"This is chess," Eliot Weiss says, and most often he invites them to stay, and this either draws them in or pushes them right back out the door.

Twenty-one years earlier, when Weiss initiated the chess club at Murrow, this was all he had in mind. It was a school club like any other school club in any other neighborhood in any other city in America, a safe way to eat up an afternoon and indulge a passion Weiss had fostered since childhood. That's all it is for the fourteen newbies, as well, who are well beyond the age at which serious chess players take up the game. Among them, there is a girl in a pink T-shirt that says DON'T HOLD BACK, DON'T GIVE UP, and another girl with a half-dozen hemp bracelets looped around her wrists. There are four sophomores, one black, one white, one Asian, and one Hispanic, who decided to join this club together, despite having never played chess before. There was a time, shortly after the fall of Communism, when Weiss's club mostly drew Russian and Eastern European immigrants, but that's changed over the years. So he stands today in front of this tossed salad of city ethnicities, all eyes on a Jew from Long Island with a long face and a gray-speckled beard and a crooked necktie knotted over a rust-hued corduroy shirt.

"All right," he says. "Now that you've played each other, I'm going to play all of you at one time."

In chess, this is called a *simul,* short for simultaneous exhibition. It is something of a lark, a display of ego and showmanship by superior players. A year later, in a blatant attempt to attract publicity for her sport, a female grandmaster named Susan Polgar will set the world record by playing a simul against 326 opponents in a Florida shopping mall. In this case, a simul gives Weiss an opportunity to see what the newbies can do, to gauge the skill levels he's dealing with. Weiss is an expert-level player, his skills far above that of the newbies but well below that of his top two players. For the most part, he cannot teach his team members anything they don't already know; he is more of a facilitator than an educator. The club, however, is an entirely different story.

"Now," he says, "who's going to be the first victim?"

And so it goes exactly how you'd expect it to go: The newbies handcuff their attacking pieces and they lock themselves into corners and they fail to protect their kings. Chess is a sport of actions and reactions, and without a rudimentary knowledge of strategy and tactics, the two primary elements of the game, it is virtually impossible to extend the game beyond a couple of dozen moves. There is no such thing as dumb luck. So a girl named Elizabeth chews on her copper hair and attacks too early with her queen and loses it in an instant. And an Asian boy named Rex, one of the four sophomores, who is attending this club on a whim he can't quite articulate, sputters, "I know what you're doing," and Weiss says, "*I* don't even know what I'm doing," and then he finishes the game. A girl named Emily gives away her rook and tucks her head into her chin and stifles a nervous giggle. And Weiss continues to walk up and down the row, snatching away pieces and making harmless little quips and offering postcheckmate handshakes.

After each chess club meeting, the desks are moved back into place for Weiss's Friday classes, and the pieces are sorted into plastic shopping bags and tucked into one of the mustard-colored lockers in the back of the room. "I hope you come back," Weiss says. Many of them will. Some of them will show up on occasion: once a week, once a month, once a semester. Some of them will never show up again. This is the nature of high school, of course; it is certainly the norm at Murrow, where a diversity of interests and activities is encouraged, and where responsibility is self-imposed. At Murrow, you are on your own. You can avail yourself of independent projects and individualized curricula and college prep programs and guidance counselors, and if you so choose, you can decline to attend classes at all. It is a tempting dynamic for a teenager. It is an atmosphere that has made Murrow both one of the most respected public schools in New York City and a place where self-reliance can degenerate into abject failure.

Edward R. Murrow High School

Two

Bruckner's Gambit

THE LEGEND WENT THAT THE MAN HAD COMPILED SOME SORT OF elephantine mental Rolodex, that he could cross-reference and collate an entire databank of several thousand names and faces and class schedules in the space between those prominent ears, that he was perhaps the only school administrator in America who knew more about your adolescent social life than you yourself.

Even now, a year into his retirement, Saul Bruckner still elicits greetings from students making their way onto Avenue M on a brisk spring afternoon. They are taken aback by the sight of their former principal, a hunched and soft-spoken man with a beaklike nose, who has been likened to Kermit the Frog. They stop and they stare, as if their innermost thoughts have been exposed, as if they know the man can see right through them. "Lookin' good, Mr. Bruckner," one girl says, and it is not a greeting you'd ever expect a student to deliver to a principal, not when it's delivered this way, so sincere, so casual. But Bruckner is not an ordinary authority figure. To those who attended Murrow for the first thirty years of its existence, he is a cult figure, the embodiment of all that set their school apart from every other school in New York City.

Bruckner ate breakfast that morning at the Caraville Diner on Avenue M, a short distance from the school. Mostly, he has stayed away since his retirement; the way he figures, the inner workings of Murrow are no longer his problem. He could only get in the way. It was ten-thirty on a brisk day in May and he ordered a dish of soft-serve vanilla frozen yogurt. When a spoonful landed on the sleeve of his sport coat, he dabbed at it with a napkin. He didn't much seem to care if it stained.

Nobody is, nor will ever be, identified more closely with Murrow High School than Bruckner himself. In the school's front hallway, near the security desk, someone has hung a street sign from the Bruckner Expressway, which runs through the Bronx but which now serves as a tribute to their former principal in Brooklyn. Over the years, Bruckner maintained an omnipotent presence at Murrow. He was a perpetual wanderer of the school's grounds, a constant presence in hallways and classrooms, the type who kibitzed ceaselessly with students, who developed that curved spine by picking up garbage and scraps of paper left behind in the hallways. In the beginning, when the school opened, faculty wore name tags. Years passed, but Bruckner never took his off. Until the final few years of his tenure, in addition to his duties as principal, Bruckner also taught an advanced American history class every morning. It was one of Murrow's most popular courses, steeped in current affairs and propelled by Socratic debate.

"He knows everybody by name their freshman year," one student told *The New York Times*.

In truth, though, after three decades at Murrow, after four decades as an educator, much of the history has blurred into an indistinct tableau in Bruckner's mind. Times have changed, and the original philosophy that Murrow was founded upon has been distorted by blatant overcrowding and lack of funding and the inevitability of city politics. This is partly why Bruckner left when he did. Murrow had been founded upon an experiment, and the laboratory was in danger of becoming corrupted. "It's easier to destroy a school," Bruckner says, "than to build one."

♛

Long before Murrow was built, its roots were planted amid the tumult of the late 1960s, amid an era of labor disputes, amid the push-and-pull of civil rights and the issue of integration in New York City public schools. In 1968, battle lines had been drawn over community control of the schools, leading to a series of strikes that called the effectiveness of the entire system into question.

The year after that, Bruckner became the assistant principal at John Dewey High, an experimental school that had been modeled upon the ideas formulated by a group of principals during a retreat in the early 1960s, in an attempt to devise a "dream school." Dewey was the first high school of its kind in New York City, a $12 million human laboratory erected on Stillwell Avenue and Avenue X in Coney Island.

At Dewey, grades did not exist; students were evaluated on a pass/fail system. Most classes were electives and independent study courses, selected by a computer based upon students' interests and aptitudes. The school day was eight hours long. Instead of dividing the year into two semesters, Dewey ran its classes in six "cycles," with the frequent turnover rate designed to keep students engaged and break the anonymity that's often inherent in larger schools. Dewey also had no interscholastic sports. But its most distinctive trait was its atmosphere of personal freedom: Each student was granted "independent" time that they could utilize as they saw fit, by studying a foreign language or designing an individualized program or by hanging out in the hallways and doing absolutely nothing.

Bruckner stayed at Dewey for five years before the political infighting between the teachers' union and the administration drove him away. By then, he'd been recruited to oversee the inception of a new high school in central Brooklyn that was to operate under a similar system to Dewey's, with some minor tweaks. The residents of that neighborhood, many of them Orthodox Jews, were skeptical. Midwood had always been seen as a sort of suburb in the heart of the city, and they didn't want a massive (and, of course, *integrated*) school to destroy the character of their neighborhood. So they pushed for an experimental curriculum similar to Dewey's, with an emphasis on independent study and electives and no interscholastic sports. They formed an advisory committee of parents who suggested, among other things, that the school construct a planetarium within the building.

The building was supposed to open at the beginning of the school year in 1974, but an electricians' strike forced Murrow to hold its first couple of months of classes in an annex at Midwood High School. The neighborhood remained skeptical; Bruckner counted only two welcome signs on the windows of nearby homes and businesses. They moved into the new building in November. It still wasn't finished. The photography program operated out of a closet and a bathroom. A business teacher was forced to conduct a typing class without type-writers. The theater program held its first show, *The Fantasticks*, in the gym because there were no seats in the auditorium. There were seven hundred students in the school, and most of them had never been granted freedoms this expansive, and what happened was exactly what you think would happen.

Creative disorder, some called it, in an attempt to devise a politically correct term for what happens when all hell breaks loose. "I was not a happy camper," Bruckner says.

And he didn't know how to rectify the situation. One day around Christmastime, a nun who was also a school principal came to visit the school, to witness the manifestation of progressive educational theory. And Bruckner exposed her to this *creative disorder,* and he pleaded with her, as if entering a confessional booth. "Sister," he said, "I'm respon-sible for all of this. Where do I go next?"

The reply is one that Bruckner still remembers, thirty years later.

"It'll calm down," she said.

♛

It took some time for the sister's prophecy to reach fruition. In 1975, a man named Ron Weiss (no relation to Eliot Weiss) requested a hard-ship transfer from a school on the Upper West Side and became a math teacher at Murrow. He knew nothing about the school or its sys-tem. He showed up that first day and he saw students strolling from room to room without hall passes, and he saw them clustered in the hallway with no bells to mark the beginning and end of class, and he began to think he had made one of the worst mistakes of his life. This, he thought, is how anarchy manifests itself. This is a riot waiting to happen. Classes were held four times a week instead of five, which meant cramming more material into each lesson, which meant more labor for teachers. On his second day, he called his supervisor and requested to be transferred back to Manhattan.

Too late, he was told.

"I thought this would never last," he says now, after having spent much of the past three decades as an assistant principal under Bruckner. "I thought, 'You'll never make this work.' But soon enough, within that chaos, we began to see that there was something special going on here."

The students at Murrow adjusted to their freedoms. The atmosphere was like a college campus; you had a great amount of leeway to do what you wanted, to study what you wanted, but if you did nothing you'd find yourself falling hopelessly behind. Those who didn't adjust soon realized they weren't cut out for this type of program, and either transferred out or were asked to leave. The theater program, a staple of the school from the beginning, thrived. Theater, Bruckner likes to say, is the closest thing Murrow has to a football team: among its graduates are an Oscar-winning actor (Marisa Tomei) and an acclaimed director (Darren Aronofsky).

Within a few years, under Bruckner's guidance, Murrow had found its niche. It was producing Intel science contest winners and National Merit Scholars and aspiring lawyers and budding astronomers. Murrow, with its four cycles of classes (instead of two semesters) and its simple grading system (E for Excellent, G for Good, S for Satisfactory, and N for No Credit) and its OPTA, or optional time, structured into the school day, soon built a better reputation than Dewey and Midwood and virtually every other public school in Brooklyn. The special education program also became one of the best in the city, in part, Bruckner says, because special ed kids weren't quarantined from the school's general population.

There is no tracking at Murrow. Anyone can enroll in any class.

When the education editor of *The Christian Science Monitor* showed up at Murrow in 1980, she bet Bruckner that she'd be able to determine which students in a class were special ed. After she failed, she wrote that Murrow had "one of the most sensitive and concerned high school administrations I've ever visited."

By then, Murrow was regularly landing on local and national lists of best high schools. It was championed by Diane Ravitch, back in 1984, as the prototypical example of "a good school." As of 2001, ninety-two percent of Murrow graduates were going on to college. The experiment was a success, recognized as a "School of Excellence" by the U.S. Department of Education. More and more students applied for admission each year. In the 2004–05 school year, nearly ten thousand kids applied for nine hundred seats. "Student morale is undoubtedly lifted by awareness of the difficulty of gaining entry into Murrow," Ravitch wrote.

There are certain admissions quotas: Students who live in a zone immediately surrounding the school are automatically accepted, a provision meant to quell fears in the community when Murrow opened. Those who score in the top two percent of the citywide reading exam and list Murrow as their first choice of high schools are also guaranteed admission. Of the remaining students, fifty percent are selected randomly, and fifty percent are chosen by the school. In each category, sixteen percent of those who are chosen are reading at an above average level, sixteen percent are reading below average, and sixty-eight percent are reading within the average range.

What that brings together, ideally, is a diverse and disparate mix, a school where cliques (such as those formed by athletic teams) are discouraged and a curriculums are tailored to students' interests. Not that it always lives up to the ideal. "In essence," Ron Weiss says, "it also attracts kids who don't belong here. As many kids as are successful, there are a number that are unsuccessful."

Because of its unique properties, because it is so reliant upon the quality of the individual student, Murrow is a fragile environment. For years, Bruckner and his constant wanderings held it together. But in recent years, the old guard have been feeling the vibrations of change within the school hallways. Enrollment has grown and grown, up to four thousand students, and has reached a certain tipping point. If the school is too big, goes Bruckner's theory, if the administration is no longer granted a wide berth of leeway in accepting students, all of the Murrow system's assets are nullified. Students begin to slip through the cracks. In the last few years, Murrow has begun to accept transfer students from underperforming city schools, casualties of the No Child Left Behind Act. The decline has been subtle, but undeniable: As overall enrollment has increased, the graduation rate has slipped, from eighty-six percent to eighty-two percent. In 2003, a fourteen-year-old student was stabbed in the back in a school hallway; in 2004, the number of seniors attending college dipped below ninety percent for the first time. Certain liberties, like the freedom to wear hats or do-rags or hang out in the school's courtyard (and maybe sneak a cigarette) have been curtailed by the new principal, Anthony Lodico. (Then again, not everyone would consider this to be such a detriment: ". . . the previous administration overlooked smoking and cutting class," one teacher wrote on InsideSchools.org, an independent Web site that rates city schools. "Now," the teacher wrote, "kids don't get lost.")

There are exceptions, of course, those constants that continue to set Murrow apart. There is the theater program, still going strong, and a "virtual enterprise" business club that won first place in a national competition in 2004. And, of course, there is the chess team, which Bruckner has had little to do with over the years, and which has become largely self-sufficient by now, a product, almost entirely, of decades of labor by an enterprising math teacher with a vision of his own.

Ilya Kotlyanskiy

THREE

FREEDOM OF CHOICE

THE PARENTS EMERGE FROM A PALLID OCTOBER MORNING CLUTCHING double lattes and rumpled sections of the Sunday *Times,* and they stake out territory wherever they can: in the hallway, in an adjacent classroom, on hard-backed seats pulled up to cramped tables in the kitchen that serves as a holding area. Those who have nowhere else to go, those who lose out in this game of musical chairs, take up residence on the linoleum floor, which affords them the best view through the glass-paneled doors of the cafeteria, marked with skeins of yellow police tape and signs reminding them that, for the next few hours, they are confined to this perimeter:

NO PARENTS, COACHES ALLOWED INSIDE.

This is one of the first chess tournaments of the school year sponsored by The Right Move, a nonprofit organization founded and bankrolled mostly by Fred Goldhirsch, a Staten Island real-estate developer and a onetime board member of the now-defunct Manhattan Chess Club. The Right Move tournaments are free and open to every student in New York City, and they're held on Sunday mornings at alternating sites. This one is taking place at the cafeteria of Brandeis High in Manhattan, a dank and sour-smelling room with faux-wood walls and sticky floors, located on the first floor of a brick school building nestled within the gentrified confines of the Upper West Side.

There is a certain underlying paranoia present at most chess tournaments: There are fears of elaborate cheating schemes involving laptop computers and listening devices, fears of extraneous noise, fears of directors and organizers conspiring to affect the results, fears of attractive women, fears of opponents' diet soft drinks encroaching upon the board, and, in this case, at the Right Move, there are fears of adults morphing into the overbearing beasts who have succeeded in wringing all the pleasure out of competitive youth sports. This concern is nothing new. It's been true for several decades, ever since parents began falling into fisticuffs over their children's competitive endeavors. In the 1980s, it grew so ugly that certain tournaments began barring parents from the room.

Because of this, tournament officials do not take their jobs lightly. One of them is currently stationed in the row between the tables, a man with a shiny pink scalp and cherubic face who is known as Brother John. His full name is John McManus; he is a vice president of the Right Move, and once founded the chess team at St. Raymond's, a Catholic school in the Bronx that has developed a reputation for producing Division I basketball talent. At its peak, St. Raymond's finished nineteenth at the high-school nationals, and fourth in New York City, behind the traditional powers: Dalton, Stuyvesant, and Murrow. Then Brother John left to teach at a school for troubled boys in Albany, and because nobody at St. Ray's cared about chess the way Brother John cared about chess, the program died. These days, Brother John commutes nearly three hours each way to be here at the Right Move tournaments on Sunday mornings, to spread the gospel of chess.

Because it is free and because it is open to anyone, the Right Move pulls in a diverse crowd of participants. Some are public-school students who have come to the game through school-sponsored initiatives; some are private-school students from exclusive uptown enclaves who have just begun studying with their own personal teachers. They come from Harlem, where an African-American chess master named Maurice

Ashley founded the city's first successful public-school chess program, and they come from the Upper East Side, from Dalton, the city's most accomplished private-school team. There are young boys scampering around in Space Ghost T-shirts and there is a teenager named Conrad wearing a Sid Vicious–inspired spiked-collar-and-wristbands ensemble. There is a beginner's section (where a couple of the Murrow newbies, Renwick and Adalberto, have shown up to play), a youth section, and an open section, where Willy Edgard, Ilya Kotlyanskiy, Nile Smith, and Oscar Santana—four of Murrow's top eight—are registered. Because these tournaments are held mostly as a public service, the prize money is paltry, at best, which keeps most of the best young players in the city, including Murrow's top two boards, Sal and Alex, from showing up.

This is fine with Willy and Oscar and Ilya and Nile. They can use the money, even if it's usually twenty or thirty bucks for first place, even if it's just a nine-way split of, say, twenty-seven dollars, and even if they come home with a cheap trophy that's worth more than the check they're carrying in their pocket.

"Aw, man," Willy says. He and Oscar are standing in the hallway between rounds, examining the pairing sheets. "I hope we don't have to play each other."

He turns to Oscar, whose oversized headphones are nestled around the neck of a hooded sweatshirt. "Naw," Oscar says. "It won't happen."

It happened once before, at a Right Move tournament, and the resolution remains in dispute. What happened, Willy says, is that he assumed they were going to play it out until it became an obvious draw, until no one had an obvious advantage, and then they'd raise their hands and show the tournament director the position of the pieces and he'd credit them both with half a point. But they got about twenty-five moves into it and Willy looked at Oscar and said, "Draw?"

And, according to the legend, Oscar said, "No way." And he went on to win the game. But Willy doesn't really count that as a defeat.

"It was a mix-up," Willy says. "That's all it was. A mix-up." He's wearing baggy jeans and a pair of Nikes, his typical Sunday-morning uniform, and a divot of pubescent hairs trail from his chin in a rough outline of a goatee. Willy's been coming to these tournaments all through junior high and high school, and now that he's a senior, he's among the best players in the field. There are a few of them, bunched up around 1600 or 1700 in USCF rating, a level well below master, but one that can be attained with a certain amount of training and skill. Usually, at least three or four of the top five come from Murrow. Usually, unless he sleeps through the morning, Willy is among them.

♛

The father of the modern chess ratings system, the man whose derivations would help define the self-worth of generation of chess players, was a Hungarian physics professor named Arpad Elo, an eight-time Wisconsin state champion who helped found the United States Chess Federation in 1939. Twenty years after its inception, the USCF asked Elo to chair a committee formed to improve its unreliable and often inaccurate ratings system; what he came up with, a few modifications, has become the standard, known in common parlance as the ELO ratings, after its founder. One's ELO number is based on an algorithm that incorporates past performance and the opponent's rating, and the probability of victory, and adds and subtracts points based on these factors. It should be simple, but it was devised by a physics professor, after all, and only a physics professor could attempt to simplify his own calculation by describing it as "the measurement of the position of a cork bobbing up and down on the surface of agitated water with a yard stick tied to a rope and which is swaying in the wind."

What emerges from this equation, the sum total of this esoteric metaphor, is a number that can range from zero to 2400 and beyond, with beginners often starting at around five or six hundred and grandmasters like Fischer and Kasparov stretching the upper echelon into the 2800s, each on the opposite ends of a caste system that looks something like this:

2400 and above—Senior Master
2200–2399—Master

2000–2199—Expert
1800–1999—Class A
1600–1799—Class B
1400–1599—Class C
1200–1399—Class D
1000–1199—Class E

"It is a measuring tool, not a device of reward or punishment," Professor Elo once said of the system, according to his *New York Times* obituary. "It is a means to compare performances, assess relative strength, not a carrot waved before a rabbit, or a piece of candy given to a child for good behavior."

And yet it is impossible to ignore the numbers, or to attend a chess tournament without hearing the numbers bandied back and forth. In time, your number becomes your defining trait; whatever it may be, it can always be improved upon. There will always be someone who is precisely and measurably better than you are, which means there is always something more to be done.

♛

What Willy would really like to do more than anything, at this point in his life, is find a way to get out of Bedford-Stuyvesant. His is the classic New York immigrant story: He came to New York from the Caribbean island of Martinique with his mother and his younger sister when he was seven years old. He left his father behind and hasn't seen him since. Now that he's nearing his nineteenth birthday, he's started to cultivate his own notions of flight. Willy would like to go to college in Paris. He has relatives there, and they've suggested to him that he apply to the American University of Paris, and because Martinique is a French territory, and Willy has a French passport, he could go to school for free. He likes the sound of that: a faraway place, a getaway, without the financial burden on his mother, Irene, who works at a factory and a hair salon to support her children. Willy is given to creative reverie; at times during tournaments, even when he's supposed to be focused on the game, he seems to have drifted onto some far-off cumulus cloud, accompanied by the lyrics of the latest popular rap CD. When he says maybe he'd like to study music production, he says it with a certain conviction, as if he sees no reason why he couldn't become the next Kanye West, and if Oscar or Nile want to bust on him for it, that's fine.

"He's such a good liar," Nile says one day, "I actually start believing him after a while."

Willy took up chess in the second grade at P.S. 23 in Bed-Stuy, when a representative from a nonprofit organization known as Chess-in-the-Schools walked into one of his classes and said he was looking for kids to play chess. No one volunteered, because what inner-city boy is going to risk his livelihood by volunteering to play chess in front of his peers? So the man pulled names out of a hat, and Willy was chosen.

This was how Willy began playing chess, and after that, he never stopped. Something clicked. Willy is no better than an average student, but here was something he could grasp, something he could improve upon, something at which he could achieve tangible success. He started playing in tournaments nearly every weekend. He started taking home trophies. He went to middle school at I.S. 318 in South Williamsburg, which, with the help of Chess-in-the-Schools, had begun to incorporate the game into its curriculum. Here he met Oscar, and together they helped 318 win the first of a string of middle-school national championships, and eventually, with Weiss's help, they gained entrance to Murrow, a considerable upgrade over the local schools they would have attended if not for chess.

Willy is not what is known as a "book" player. He doesn't do a great deal of studying; he does not memorize specific lines and perfect certain tactics. He has a rudimentary knowledge of a few openings, and beyond that, he relies mostly on instinct. He does not overthink. "I just play," he says. "I have no idea. I used to study, like, lines for the French Defense. Now, I'll just study the first five or ten moves, and then I'll play anything that feels right or looks right to me at that moment."

At tournaments like this one, where many of his opponents are rated two hundred or three hundred points lower, Willy will try to trick them into speeding up the game. Each player has thirty minutes on his side of the clock (known as Game/30) at Right Move tournaments, a fairly brisk pace, and by making his moves without much premeditation, Willy can often con his opponents into doing the same thing. It becomes almost like a five-minute speed game or a one-minute "blitz" game, in which reflex supplants the cognitive depth that characterizes games at elite and professional tournaments, where each side often has two hours of time on the clock.

Willy has won each of the first three rounds this morning, and when he defeats a considerably younger boy in the fourth round, he wins sole possession of first place and a sixty-dollar check, enough to buy a birthday gift for a friend and have a few dollars left over to throw around in the card games at school (Oscar finishes in fifth, out of the money, and Ilya and Nile finish near the middle of the field of forty-four). Willy's trying to spend less of his time playing cards and more of his time attending class, but it isn't always easy, and over the years, he's fallen behind in his work. He turns nineteen in the spring. He'd like to finish school and move on already. But the temptation to skip is always there, lingering. If you skip at Murrow, no one is there to discipline you. Mr. Bruckner, the longtime conscience of the school, has vanished. Even Mr. Weiss, without whom Willy would have never gotten into Murrow, has his own responsibilities, his own classes to teach, his own family to look after. Mr. Weiss does his best, but he can't do everything.

The other day, a freshman named Shawn Martinez, another I.S. 318 graduate with a rating over 1900 who will most likely man Murrow's No. 3 board at nationals, called Willy and said, "Yo, I just hung out in the lunchroom all *day* playing cards."

"You know," Willy says now, while waiting for his trophy and his paycheck, "somebody told me before I got to Murrow that it was easy to pass if you went to class. But Shawn, he's about to fall into the same boat I was in. Colleges don't take into consideration that the freedom gets addictive."

Most weekdays, Ilya Kotlyanskiy begins his day by waking up early and riding a city bus for forty-five minutes, from Bay Ridge to Midwood, from an apartment on the second floor of a split-level house on Bay Twenty-second Street to the sprawling red-brick high school on Avenue M where he was accepted after passing a musical exam on the violin. Murrow was not his first choice, but since he couldn't score high enough on the admission tests to get into Bronx Science or Stuyvesant, he figures Murrow is the best he can do. It is only his junior year, but already Ilya is preoccupied with grades and test scores, with polishing his résumé and his extracurriculars so he can somehow get into a college like Columbia or New York University. He can't imagine that happening. Ilya is harder on himself than anyone else, and he assumes that since he attends a public school in New York City, and since he didn't get into an elite public school like Stuyvesant, what chance does he really have?

If it happens, if he somehow gets into a good college, well, then, he is of two minds: In his heart, he would like to be a scientist, because he has an abiding interest in physics. If he could go anywhere, he says one day, he would be at MIT.

Of all the trophies Ilya has brought home to his parents' modest apartment in Bay Ridge, he is proudest of the one that sits atop a curio cabinet, set apart from all the others. This one is not a chess trophy. It is a physics trophy. He won it for devising a way to drop an egg off the fourth floor of a building without breaking it. The solution involved a basketball and some sort of cushioning mechanism.

But Ilya has another aspiration, which often overshadows his ardor for science: He would like to make piles and piles of money, or at least, he would like to make enough to live a comfortable life. And because Ilya is still somewhat naive about the vast possibilities open to American citizens, he cannot imagine how he can possibly reconcile these two desires. You can either do what you love or you can do what is best for yourself or your family. You cannot possibly do both. So Ilya takes business classes at Murrow, and he figures when he gets to college, he'll major in something with more practical applications, something that will earn him the sort of cash his parents don't have.

Ilya is short, though not as short as either his mother or his father, and he has deep-set brown eyes and a distinctive nose that lends his face a weary air of maturity. His father, Alex, whose thick mustache cannot disguise that same melancholy disposition, works as a civil engineer with the Department of Transportation. His mother, Nelli, a tiny woman with amber hair, is a nurse at Long Island College Hospital. Ilya was born in Odessa, a coastal Ukrainian city with a population of more than a million people, and the family came to America when Ilya was almost five years old, after they were sponsored by relatives in Dallas through a Jewish organization. At the time, his father (who had grown up in the industrial town of Kamenets-Podolskiy, and gone to college in Moscow) was working for a large factory that, amid the collapse of the Communist system, was on the verge of closing. Corruption was rampant. The rich were getting richer, and the underclass was growing.

Ilya remembers small things about his home country; certain streets, certain scenes. He also remembers it wasn't always the kindest place for a Jewish boy to grow up. He remembers that when certain people in Odessa found out you were Jewish, they didn't hesitate to ostracize you.

Ilya is the best student on the Murrow chess team. In fact, it's not even close. He is also its best-dressed member, its most skilled musician, and its official captain, despite the fact that he is, with a rating hovering around 1650, the fourth- or fifth-best player on the team. "I won sixty dollars at a tournament in the Catskills in October of 2003," he says. "Then I started taking chess more seriously. That was one of my first major tournament successes, I should say. I got it together that time."

He is the captain because he is, by a distant margin, the most mature person among this bunch. In many ways, Ilya is more driven at age sixteen than most thirty-two-year-olds, and he is far too busy to be drawn in by Murrow's temptations toward truancy and idleness. He goes to school, he goes to orchestra practice, and then he works an internship at Washington Mutual Bank that carries with it all the drudgeries of an actual job. Ilya doesn't particularly like this work, but it means experience, and it means money, and both of those things are more important to Ilya than idle time.

His family's apartment, on a quiet street near Gravesend Bay one block from a police station and a neighborhood pub, is modest and clean. Next to a television set in the living room and below a picture of Ilya with his friend from the Stuyvesant chess team, Anna Ginzburg, a parakeet prances around in its cage. There are photographs of the Kotlyanskiys' only son all over the place, and on a table near the kitchen, his chess trophies are stacked together like the skyline of a small city. Taped to the wall above them are certificates of achievement and photos of Ilya with various local dignitaries and politicians. Here is Ilya with the Brooklyn borough president, Marty Markowitz. Here is Ilya with Mayor Bloomberg. In a few weeks, Ilya will travel to Washington, D.C., and pose with the president in the oval office, all because of chess. His father doesn't play, but his father's father, Simon, was a master-level competitor in the Soviet Union. "My parents like it," he says. "It's much better than doing drugs in the street."

Shortly after he moved to America, Ilya went to a drugstore with his grandmother and she let him pick out a board game to play, because there was little else for a small child with no grasp of English to do except play board games. He needed something simple, something that didn't require a detailed examination of the instructions. So he chose a chess set. And his grandfather on his mother's side, Anatoly, also a master-level player, taught him the game. Soon after that, Ilya began taking lessons at a chess school on Ocean Parkway, run by a former United States women's champion named Angelina Belakovskaya. Now, he'll often take private lessons, whenever he can afford to pay for them, although they've been put on hold this fall while he prepares for the SAT.

Ilya also plays the violin in the school's orchestra, which is, ostensibly, how he found his way to Murrow. He had already heard about the chess team, and he learned that a certain number of students are accepted to the school each year after passing a music exam. Ilya played an arrangement, then went through a few scales for one of the music teachers. It was good enough, even though Ilya wasn't sure it would be. He was accepted. Mr. Weiss took him onto the chess team, and soon began taking him to tournaments.

Sometimes, Ilya will go on his own to tournaments upstate and in Philadelphia and at Foxwoods Casino in Connecticut, traveling with the friends he's met who attend nearby Lincoln High School or Brooklyn Tech or Stuyvesant. They'll get four or five or six or seven people and pile into a hotel room, sharing beds and staying up all night playing cards; somebody's father or mother will drive them in one direction, and somebody else's mother or father will drive them home. Often, Ilya's father, a man so small and quiet he tends to fold into the scenery, is one of the drivers.

These tournaments are the only breaks Ilya tends to take from the daily drudgery of school and work. Even there, he considers himself an abject failure if he comes home empty-handed. "I still can't really get over it, all that money and five hours of travel one way for nothing," he e-mails after a poor performance at one tournament. Once, at a relatively meaningless tournament played near Bethesda Fountain in Central Park, Ilya sat on a concrete bench near the Poet's Walk, alone and forlorn, near tears.

"I had the game won," he said. "And I lost it."

Ilya doesn't speak much about his home country, partly because he remembers very little, but one day, he mentions his sister. She was a year older. She fell ill and died in a Ukrainian hospital because she couldn't get the proper medical care. It was a hard country, Ilya says, and it was even harder for a family of Jews. Perhaps because of what his parents had been through, perhaps because he spoke English only haltingly in those early years in Brooklyn, Ilya was an especially sensitive boy, subject to torment and ridicule at school.

Once, in the second grade, a classmate who had been bullying Ilya threw a basketball at his head and left him with a concussion. That was the breaking point. Ilya decided he was going to retaliate in the most direct way possible: He was going to kill him. The next day, Ilya approached him at lunch and offered him a Snickers bar. "Let's just be friends," Ilya said. So they shook hands and Ilya left him and went to watch. He'd put a pin in the candy bar; someone pointed it out to the boy before he could eat it. He was spared. So was Ilya.

"I don't regret it at all," he says.

♛

One Thursday in November, on the eve of Animated Character T-shirt Day at Murrow, the yearbook photographer shows up to shoot the chess club. A few of the regulars wander into the room, including Sal, who has just returned from a trip to Crete for the World Youth Championships, where he competed in the under-sixteen division. He finished in forty-eighth place out of 116 competitors. For Sal, this was a terrible performance. At one point, after he lost a game, he went to the cafeteria to get something to eat. When the waitress asked what he wanted, he asked her, "Do you serve scrambled brain?"

"I played like crap," he says. And this is pretty much the end of the discussion.

Next week, Sal will leave for the U.S. Championships in San Diego. Most of the field of sixty-four qualifies at various tournaments throughout the year, but because Sal is one of the best young players in America, because he's held his own against grandmasters and international masters in and around New York City, he's been awarded a wild-card berth.

Because of this, Sal is more fidgety than usual. He doesn't have time to pose for a yearbook photo; he doesn't have time for anything or anyone except school and chess, although when a girl who's become a regular club attendee, a girl who also does some modeling work part-time, begins to ask him about his experiences, Sal mellows a little. She asks him about his trip. She asks Sal if he's, like, some kind of genius or something.

"Yeah," Sal says. "I'm a genius, all right. I'm a stupid, lazy genius."

Like everyone else, she just can't figure Sal. She can't figure if he's ever serious with anyone, and she can't determine if his constant wise-cracking reeks of self-importance or self-flagellation or some improbable combination of the two. (It takes time to realize that most chess players, like many artists, are constantly bounding between these opposing poles.) So while Mr. Weiss attempts to round up his group of newbies and veterans and arrange them in the hallway so that the yearbook photographer can capture them for posterity with her digital camera, it is Ilya, the closest thing Sal has to a friend on the chess team, who admits he's grown weary of Sal's bizarre proclamations, of a personality that is both ingratiating and recalcitrant.

"He's very different from the other people," Ilya says. "He doesn't play anyone unless he thinks they're as good as him."

"Can we do this picture already?" Sal is saying.

"Who are we missing?" Mr. Weiss says.

"Well, now we're missing the photographer," Sal says.

Ilya rolls his eyes. "Sal thinks he's Fischer, I guess," he says.

There are two cliques within the Murrow chess team: There are the five boys who came up through I.S. 318 and through Chess-in-the-Schools, one Haitian (Dalphe), one Caribbean islander (Willy), two Puerto Ricans (Oscar and Shawn), and one African-American (Nile). And there are the Russians: Sal and Alex and Ilya, who is the closest thing to an ambassador between the camps. This is true despite the fact that Ilya has little in common with anyone else, that he is far more mature, far more adult in his demeanor, far more forward-thinking than any of the others. At times, his teammates mock him behind his back. They don't understand the way he dresses, and they don't understand why he'd prefer to sleep or study sometimes between tournament rounds rather than engage in marathon games of poker or Stupid all the time. He is not a prodigy like Sal or Alex, and he is not a product of CIS like the others. He is the odd man out, but he is also the glue, and he is the one team member Mr. Weiss trusts to remember certain basic facts that tend to traverse posthaste between the ears of teenagers: dates, times, meeting places.

"It's Mr. Weiss who really keeps the team together," Ilya says. "There's a reason why other schools fall apart and Murrow stays together. Mr. Weiss does that. He takes care of finances. He keeps our team spirit up. He finds the right players. He knows who the good players are who are going to graduate from junior high in one or two years. He even helps us out with school. He'll go talk to teachers about our grades. He's how the team survives."

But why? Why would Mr. Weiss bother to do all those things when there's nothing in it for him?

"I wonder about that sometimes myself," Ilya says.

FOUR

An Academic Challenge

Eliot Weiss, the son of a bookkeeper and an airport postal worker, grew up in the East New York section of Brooklyn, on a street called Pennsylvania Avenue. He was a product of public schools himself: He attended Jefferson High and studied math at Brooklyn College for free, back when city students could attend city universities without paying tuition. He used to play chess even then, with his college classmates, but this was not his first love. Back before he found himself in this classroom at Murrow, transcribing equations rife with meaty variables and posing conundrums like *Find all values of x for which f(x) has any relative minimum or relative maximum points,* Eliot Weiss determined his angles on the ice.

In a filing cabinet topped with a plump stack of calculus textbooks, Weiss keeps a mimeographed program from a semiprofessional hockey game, circa 1977. Inside, there is a blurred photo of a goaltender with pads and a crossed stick, betraying a vaguely bemused expression. The hair is swept low across his narrow forehead. The face is framed by a neatly clipped beard. Underneath the photo, it reads:

Eliot Weiss—Goalie—Brooklyn College, 4 yrs.; New York Rovers,
Mid-Eastern League, 1 year; New Jersey Rockets, 1/2 year;
Newark Sabers, Ironbound, 1/2 years.

Weiss bears a certain resemblance to Paul Krugman, the renowned economist and columnist at *The New York Times,* and the walls of his classroom are adorned with cartoon paeans to great moments in math theory (Golden Ratio, Mayan Numerals). So it is easy to cultivate a notion that the man who presides over this room, a man who chose to spend his career at a school that shuns interscholastic sports, a man who cleans his chalkboards every afternoon and leaves behind strings of quadratic equations encircled in "Do Not Erase" cartoon bubbles, a man who wears cardigan sweaters and plays chess online for fun and has a cell phone that plays the *Jeopardy!* theme song, should be gawky and uncoordinated.

But in his younger days, back when he was single and unfettered, after he'd gotten his master's degree in math from Brooklyn College, and before he'd married a social worker and moved to Long Island and settled into his place in the nuclear family (one son, one daughter), Weiss clung to more whimsical odd jobs than a Dickens character. He taught math during the day and played hockey in the evenings. He sold beer at Madison Square Garden. For nine years, he drove a taxi at night. He was a ski instructor in Vermont; he led summer tours in Europe.

And yet what he wanted, more than anything, as the seventies came to an end, was to find steady work as a math teacher. In 1979, while living off unemployment, he decided to take a proactive approach. That August, Weiss walked through the open front doors at Murrow, prepared to beg. He'd heard about the Murrow system. He'd heard of the school's reputation. He figured this would be a good place to work. The building was deserted, except for the man sitting in the principal's office. So Weiss marched right in and introduced himself and offered his résumé. "I'd like to teach here," he said.

And Saul Bruckner, being who he was, being a man who believed in the value of chutzpah, did not consider this an odd request at all. He looked over Weiss's résumé and told him, "This is good." He said, "We need math teachers." He gave Weiss a letter of recommendation, and he gave Weiss his home phone number, and he told him to take the letter to the offices of the Board of Education. Which is what Weiss did.

Because of the politics of the era, because of the whims of a school board determined to hire minorities to teach at predominantly white schools and whites to teach at minority schools, Weiss's request was turned down. He called Bruckner at home from the board's office. He asked if Bruckner would speak directly to the board president. Weiss pleaded, and he begged, but nothing could be done. So he wound up teaching that year at Marine Park Junior High School, and the following August, he went back to Murrow, and back to Bruckner, and he asked once more.

Another letter. Another visit to the Board of Ed. Again, the board turned it down. Weiss spent a year as trainer for fifth-grade math teachers. He went back again in August of 1981, got another letter, made another visit, and finally got approved.

Through it all, Weiss had continued to play chess. Never competitively, never on a team, but merely for his own amusement. Eventually, his rating settled at somewhere around 2000. And since no one else at Murrow High School, home of the Chinese Cultural Club and the Game Show Club, had thought to start a chess club, he took the same sort of initiative that had brought him to Murrow in the first place. He figured he might as well start it himself.

The Edward R. Murrow High School chess club held its first meeting in the fall of 1983, soon after Weiss gave up his nighttime cab-driving shift, around the time Diane Ravitch visited Murrow and later wrote, in her *American Scholar* essay, that "the school's philosophy is that no student should be discouraged from taking on an academic challenge." Back then, the dominant chess program in Brooklyn was the one at James Madison High School, where a young prodigy named Joel Benjamin had chosen to attend. Benjamin's father was the coach at Madison, and in 1981, Joel became the first player to win back-to-back individual championships at the high-school nationals in Philadelphia. That year, Madison lost the team title by half a point to Stuyvesant, an exclusive public school in Manhattan that draws some of the best students in the city.

Weiss had no intention of competing with chess programs like these, or the ones at private schools like Dalton, on the Upper East Side. He had no real intention of his little club competing at all. They were a small group, and they spent their time reviewing games from magazines and newspaper columns and studying strategies and playing against each other. But the landscape of Brooklyn began shifting in the mid-1980s, driven by the imminent fall of Communism and the mass influx of Russian and Eastern European immigrants to communities like Brighton Beach and Bay Ridge and Midwood. The best and the brightest couldn't afford to attend private school and didn't want to attend subpar public schools in their neighborhood. They needed a school that would both accommodate them and challenge them. By the late 1980s, many of them had found Murrow. And in turn, Weiss had found them. In 1987, the club had twenty-five members, and they began to compete against local schools like Canarsie and Midwood and Sheepshead Bay and Midwood and Westinghouse.

Murrow won its first city championship in 1989. They've never finished lower than second since then.

♛

"You should have an idea what to do, instead of just moving the pieces randomly to get a good position," Mr. Weiss says at the second chess club meeting of the year. He's wearing a yellow sweater vest over a dress shirt, and every so often he'll indulge in stale jokes that mostly go unacknowledged by his audience, which this week numbers about a dozen. ("Is that your boyfriend?" he says, after a girl's cell phone rings.) He is gifted with a dry sense of humor and a lack of pretense, qualities honed over more than twenty years of teaching. If he's focused on playing a game or instructing an opening, he falls into a such a thick halo of concentration that he'll fail to acknowledge a student's request to use the bathroom.

"If you have a bad opening," he says, "you can't win the game." He explains that opening with the wrong pawn, with a pawn toward the end of the board instead of one of the two near the center, will only muddy one's chances, and that even a novice player must understand that control of the center of the board is crucial. This is the thesis behind nearly all of the popular openings memorized and utilized by every level of player; white most often opens by moving one of the two center pawns forward two squares, to the locations known in modern notation as d4 and e4:

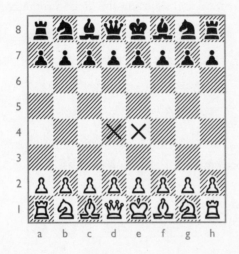

Black then counters by attempting to negate that advantage, perhaps by moving one of his pawns out in a counterattack, or by moving out one of his knights from the back row (pawns, because of their relative weakness, are merely referred to by their proper name, while the rooks, pawns, knights, and queen are called *pieces*— the sum of one's army is called *material*). Most often, Mr. Weiss explains, knights, because of their ability to jump from place to place, are developed before bishops, even though their relative value is the same:

> Pawns are worth one unit
> Knights are worth three units
> Bishops are worth three units
> Rooks are worth five units
> Queens are worth nine units

So it makes no sense to exchange, say, a knight for a pawn, and it makes no sense to protect a pawn from capture with a queen, and it makes much more sense to castle early in the game. "Does everyone know what castling is?" Mr. Weiss says, and everyone nods, even though it is clear from the blankness of their stares that some of them have no idea. They don't know you can move two pieces at once, shifting the rook in one direction and shuttling the king into the corner in order

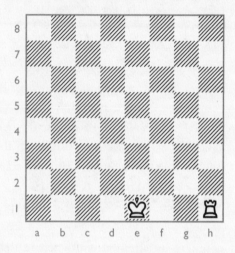

to play offense and defense at once, to both provide a safe place for the king to hide and to bring out a rook so it can attack more effectively.

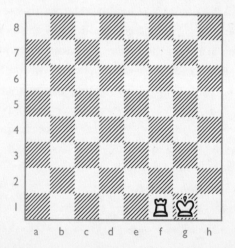

From there, the opening gives way to the middle game, the stage of back and forths, of exchanges and tactics and positioning. This is the stage when tactics like forks (attacking two of your opponent's pieces at once with the same piece) and pins (a straight-line attack along a rank, file, or diagonal, in which one threatens an opponent's piece that happens to be shielding another piece, forcing it to stay in place: Imagine your rook on the same file as your opponent's queen, with only a knight positioned in-between—that knight is *pinned*) become so crucial. Now is when one must determine the lines and angles of attack (from the queen's side? From the king's side?) while maintaining a defensive presence (is my own king shielded?). The middle game is where theory and memorization of certain lines of attack often give way to innovation and improvisation, where thought must be given to the value of every exchange of material, and where the board slowly begins to simplify, until the queens are usually off the board and there are only a few pieces left, and the middle game transitions into the endgame.

By then, one player often has an edge, and it is this player's job to exploit this edge, to turn an advantage in material or an advantage in position into a victory, while the player with lesser material or a less-developed position does all he can to stave off defeat. Often, beginners don't even make it this far, as the newbies are aware, from their early flailings. Often, experts and masters and grandmasters find themselves falling into inextricably drawn positions by this point: No one can win, and only a blunder can cause defeat, and it becomes a matter of simple fortitude. But there are other times when one player or the other has the slightest edge, perhaps a single pawn in a more advantageous place, and these pawns are advanced toward the opponent's back rank in the hope of transforming one into a queen, and using this queen to entrap the opponent's king, once and for all, and induce checkmate.

"Questions?" Mr. Weiss says.

There is much hesitation among the newbies; mostly, they just want to get to playing. Before they can, Weiss tells them about the first

Right Move tournament of the season, that Sunday at Brandeis. The tournaments are free; they're an optimal starting point for unrated beginners. Win a couple of games at a Right Move tournament (as most everyone does eventually, if only by inertia), and the foundation pays for a yearly membership in the United States Chess Federation. "The fact is," Weiss says, "you don't have to be a great player to play tournament chess. The more you play, the more you'll learn."

Murrow's first national championship came in 1992, at a national tournament held in the unlikely hamlet of Lexington, Kentucky. In truth, it might have come earlier than that, because Weiss had already formed a stockpile of talent. What he didn't have was the means. Back then, even Bruckner, who never played the game, wasn't sold on the net worth of the school possessing a nationally renowned chess team. So Weiss, who was teaching as an adjunct lecturer at Brooklyn College and working with the United Federation of Teachers in the evenings and raising two young children, had to spend a certain amount of his spare time begging.

In 1991, he thought he'd finally found the backing to send the team to its first national tournament in Atlanta, courtesy of one of his former students, a graduate of the Class of 1983, who had financed the team's trip to Albany, where it won the school's first-ever state championship. The alumnus had promised to take care of everything at nationals. He had promised to put up the team in a first-class hotel, to pay for limousines, to take care of it all, and Weiss had little doubt his team, stacked with high-rated Eastern European immigrants, could win a championship. On the day of their scheduled departure, the team waited outside the school with its bags packed and ready; the alumnus never showed up. He called Weiss and told him he couldn't book the flights on time; they weren't going. A team from Cleveland won the championship. Weiss, who had already called for a substitute, had to slink back into his classroom and start teaching again. "I was very depressed for a long time after that," he says. "I realized I shouldn't rely on anybody. I should just do this myself."

The following year, aided by a two-thousand-dollar donation from Brooklyn Union Gas, Murrow raised enough to make it to Lexington. They finished one point ahead of Dalton, which has long had one of the strongest developmental chess programs in the country, an institution that will never be short on finances. At Dalton, students begin learning the game in the first grade and advance in skill every year toward graduation. At Murrow, however, Weiss had managed to recruit a small group of immigrants, many of whom could outplay him, and merely helped to facilitate their travel and entry fees. In truth, this is still Weiss's primary role: He is the chief administrator, the planner, and the organizer. He procures the talent, and then wrangles the money to allow it to succeed. For his efforts, he receives no money, beyond a couple hours of overtime pay here and there.

In those early days, in order to raise money, the team sold refrigerator magnets and miniature chess sets and lapel pins and sweatshirts and T-shirts and homemade chocolate valentine lollipops. They solicited donations from teachers and administrators. The school didn't have any money to contribute; the Board of Education gave on occasion, when it could, without any guarantees. Murrow was a school without sports teams, after all, and a budget that would have normally gone toward football helmets and basketball uniforms was already apportioned toward other things.

So in 1993, when the Murrow administration and the Board of Ed told Weiss it simply didn't have the money to send the team to Dallas to defend its title, he sprang into action. He did what he's since learned to do quite well: He alerted the media. On December 30, 1992, *Newsday* ran a story headlined "Pawns of the Budget," in which Weiss responded to a board member's comment that "there are too many needs in the classroom" with this: "They have money for condoms and other things but not for something the kids could really use."

Three weeks later, when the *Times* ran a story of its own, the money had come through, thanks to a "last-minute budget surplus." And that team, comprised entirely of immigrants from what had been the Soviet Union, led by individual national champion Alex Sidelnikov and Latvian Anna Khan, a future U.S. women's champion, won again. The margin of victory was four points, large enough that all of its top competitors could have sat out the final round and Murrow still would have won first place.

♛

"So," asks a girl named Elizabeth. "How do we get on the *actual* chess team?"

"Well," Weiss says, "I pick people. If you want to go to the local tournaments around here and go to the city championships, I might just let you go. They only take the top four scorers, so you're not going to hurt the team if you don't play well."

"What about the nationals?" someone asks.

"That's a little different," Weiss says. "The state tournament is in Saratoga—that's upstate—at the end of February. The nationals are four days in April in Tennessee. If you show me you're really interested, if you play in tournaments and show up every week, I might be able to take you."

"Is there a limit?"

"No limit at all," Weiss says. "I've taken as many as twenty-three people to nationals. Last year, only eight went. So it all depends."

When the question-and-answer session is complete, they get down to playing. The games are still sloppy and haphazard, devoid of precision and depth of thought. Queens are blundered away. Rooks become trapped in corners. No one seems to care. They switch partners and try it again. The four sophomores, Rex and Robert and Adalberto and Renwick, are here again, playing against each other in round-robin fashion. None of them had played chess before last week; they heard about the team, about its history, about the championships, and they showed up together. They figured they had nothing to lose.

After failing to compete in the state tournament due to a lack of funds, Murrow won its third straight national championship in Dearborn, Michigan, in 1994, behind an immigrant from Uzbekistan, Alex Kaliksteyn, who won all seven of his matches. This time, the margin of victory was three and a half points. It was the first time any school had won both the team and individual championships two years in a row. "The word *dynasty* does not completely describe Edward R. Murrow High School's preeminence in high school chess," wrote longtime tournament organizer Steve Immitt in an article detailing the history of the high-school nationals. "Complete hegemony is more accurate."

The newspapers had caught on by now, and Weiss had caught on to the engine that drove the newspapers. A nationally recognized high-school chess team in need of funds, supported by a local congressman and ignored by the board of education, was optimal fodder for a tabloid-driven city in search of David-versus-Goliath stories. At times, forced publicity was the team's only hope. And Weiss was nothing if not persistent. A *New York Post* story in early March of 1994 was headlined "HS Team: Send a check, mate," and detailed how Murrow, aided in its fund-raising efforts by City Councilman Dan Feldman, was still $2,000 short of the $6,554 it needed to make it to Detroit. Eventually, a Russian television network donated additional monies, and in early May, the *Post* ran another story, headlined "Check it out: B'klyn HS team tops in chess."

Murrow didn't make it to Chicago for the nationals after finishing second to Stuyvesant for the city championship in 1995; the money didn't come through, and Dalton won both the team and individual titles at the nationals. And in 1996, Weiss once again found himself in a position of begging, pleading, appealing to *Newsday* after the team wound up more than $2,300 short of the money needed to compete at the state tournament in White Plains and the national tournament in Somerset, New Jersey. "We're having a tough time with this," he said. "This team has been a source of pride for our school, for the city."

This time, the money *did* come through, although Murrow finished eighth, far behind Philadelphia's Julia Masterman High School, led by a young master named Greg Shahade. Murrow's hegemonic run had come to an end. And yet Weiss kept at it, and in 1997, the owner of a Long Island City construction company donated $7,000 after reading a story in the *Daily News,* telling the paper he "didn't think it was fair" that Murrow didn't get to go to nationals. They finished twelfth that year at the first-ever "Supernationals," a quadrennial gathering in which the elementary, junior-high, and high-school nationals are melded into one event; in the two years after that, 1998 and 1999, Murrow failed to win a city or state championship, and came in fortieth and twenty-third at the nationals. And yet Weiss kept on appealing for funds, and kept on building up his team for a future he could never quite guarantee.

♛

It could be argued that nothing has served as a more potent advertisement for Murrow High School in the past two decades than Eliot Weiss and his one-man publicity machine, which has produced countless headlines not just in the *Post* and the *Times* and the *Daily News* and *Newsday,* but in community newspapers read by parents of prospective students, papers like the *Bay News* and *Brooklyn Skyline* and the *Kings Courier.* It took Bruckner a few years to determine the value of such publicity, but once he did, he encouraged Weiss's experiment. A certain percentage of incoming students are chosen by the school itself; if those students happen to be slightly below par academically, but also happen to have USCF chess ratings in excess of 1500, or 1700, or 1900, then, well, isn't this indicative of a certain unfulfilled potential? Doesn't that make them, as Diane Ravitch once wrote, the perfect fit for a school whose students "have been persuaded that Murrow is a very special school and they are very special students?"

This may sound ridiculous, like the genesis of a comedy sketch: a high-school chess coach engaging in recruiting. And yet there is no other way to characterize it. Weiss finds out about prospective students at tournaments like the Right Move, and he pitches them on the merits of Murrow. They learn about him. He learns about them. There is nothing untoward about it. There are no grand promises, no guarantees of playing time or special treatment as there might be in football or basketball. All Weiss is doing is attempting to improve the makeup of his traveling team, which, in turn, improves the reputation of his school. Each national championship Murrow wins earns a place in the school's promotional material. Each article about Murrow's latest title spreads the gospel of the school across the five boroughs and beyond.

A school like Abraham Lincoln High, in Brooklyn's Coney Island neighborhood, has earned a reputation as a basketball powerhouse, and yet this does nothing to enhance its standing academically. But given Murrow's mission statement, given the purpose ascribed to it by Saul Bruckner himself, there could be no more well-suited public face than a formidable chess team. With each championship, with each headline, Murrow becomes known as a school populated by quirky geniuses, a school that embodies all the stereotypes of a sport whose most celebrated American practitioner was both brilliant and inscrutable.

Alex Lenderman (left)

FIVE

A GAME UNLIKE ANY OTHER

IN THE SUMMER OF 1972, BOBBY FISCHER PLAYED BORIS SPASSKY IN A series of games for the world chess championship in Reykjavík, Iceland, and for the first time in the history of the United States, the game became part of the zeitgeist. It became a televised drama and a geopolitical metaphor and a cult of personality centered around a twenty-nine-year-old boy from Brooklyn who had neither the tact nor the stability to deal with this sudden burst of fame, whose name would become shorthand for a brand of mania that is unique to his sport.

Bobby Fischer was raised by his mother in a small apartment near Prospect Park, a short distance from where, two years after Fischer-Spassky, the experiment in secondary education known as Edward R. Murrow High School would open its doors. Fischer had become terminally obsessed with the game at the age of six, and entered his first tournament at age nine, and when he wasn't at home, buried in chess literature, he spent most of his time at one oasis or another, at the Marshall Club in Greenwich Village or the Manhattan Chess Club on West Forty-sixth Street or at the outdoor tables in Washington Square Park. This evolution took place despite the growing dismay of his mother, who consulted experts and pleaded with psychiatrists and eventually gave up and left her boy to fend for himself in their Brooklyn apartment, surrounded by his books and his boards.

By the time Fischer was fourteen, when he was on the verge of both dropping out of Erasmus Hall High School and winning his first U.S. Championship, he was well known in the community as a freak of nature, as the most talented young player to have graced the streets of New York City since a nine-year-old Polish boy named Samuel Reshevsky had toured the United States in 1920. In 1956, while playing at the Lessing J. Rosenwald Tournament at the Manhattan Chess Club, Fischer sacrificed his queen on the seventeenth move, a tactic so stunning and innovative that a magazine called *Chess Review* referred to it as "the game of the century."

"He admitted that in his younger days he cried whenever he lost at chess and sometimes he remained despondent for days," wrote author Gay Talese, then of *The New York Times,* in June of 1957, in a profile headlined "Another Child Prodigy Stirs Chess World." "But he does not cry any more, possibly because he does not lose often these days, or maybe he is just getting old."

In chess, a sport rife with prodigies, "getting old" is often measured by the same accelerated lifespan we associate with gymnasts and tennis players. The vast majority of talented young players peak at a certain age, and then forsake the diminishing returns of a nuanced study of the Nimzo-Indian Defense for certain outside obsessions brought on by puberty. But Fischer was the exception to every rule. He never displayed much of an interest in women. He was a savant, with an IQ reportedly in the 180s, and even if there was no real living to be made by a chess player in the United States, Fischer had little interest in making a living in anything beyond chess. "Though school tests have shown him to have generally superior intelligence, he does no better than average in his studies, displaying little interest in most of the subjects taught and being restless in class," a *New Yorker* correspondent reported in September 1957. "His teachers are amazed when they hear of his chess victories—not so much at his mental powers that they hadn't suspected as at his being able to sit still for the five hours a tournament game may last. 'In my class, Bobby couldn't sit still for five *minutes,*' one of them says."

And yet not since a player named Paul Morphy emerged from New Orleans in the mid-1800s had America produced a player with this sort of talent, and the fact that, according to legend, Morphy wound up dead in a bathtub at age forty-seven, surrounded by women's shoes, hardly figured into the calculus. Fischer got better and better, and fell deeper and deeper into himself and his ego. (". . . a highly emotional, tense combatant whose cockiness often disconcerts the older masters," Talese wrote of the fourteen-year-old Fischer.) All of which led up to 1972, when, in the preliminary matches leading up to the World Championships, Fischer dominated some of the best players in the world, winning six straight games from formidable Russian grandmaster (and classical pianist) Mark Taimanov and six more in a row from a Dane named Bent Larsen on his way to earning the right to face Spassky. In a sport in which draws are commonplace and losses are inevitable, this type of feat was unprecedented, the chess equivalent of DiMaggio's fifty-six-game hit streak.

Fischer's opponent, Boris Vasilievich Spassky, was from Leningrad, and had been nurtured by the infrastructure of a country where superiority in chess was viewed as a verification that the Communist system worked. He was attended to in Iceland by a small army of advisors and government overseers. Fischer was essentially on his own. He made absurd demands throughout the match, continually threatening to pull out altogether if they weren't met, until finally Henry Kissinger urged him to continue playing in service of his country. Fischer ordered cameras to be barred from the room, along with children, and stiletto-heeled shoes, and all spectators sitting in the first seven rows. His behavior was theatrical and it was absurdist and damned if it wasn't fascinating. He demanded a large purse for his appearance, and at the last minute, he decided it wasn't enough and demanded more. "I am only interested in chess and money," he told an Italian newspaper.

The Fischer-Spassky games (Fischer wound up winning, 12 1/2 to 8 1/2) became front-page news in America. They were broadcast on public television and moderated by national master Shelby Lyman and another young and shaggy-haired chess master from Brooklyn named Bruce Pandolfini, who at the time was working at the Strand, a used bookstore in Manhattan. "That summer of 1972, chess became monumental, a game unlike any other," wrote Fred Waitzkin in his memoir, *Searching for Bobby Fischer,* "and everyone wanted to play. . . . Mothers pulled their sons out of Little League and ferried them to chess lessons."

Chess clubs sprouted throughout New York City; youth programs proliferated. Fischer was on the covers of *Sports Illustrated, Life, Time,* and *Newsweek,* and he appeared on talk shows with Dick Cavett and Johnny Carson. "The chess epidemic infected all generations and classes: the old played the young, business suits looked across the board at blue collars," wrote David Edmonds and John Eidinow in their book about the match, *Bobby Fischer Goes to War.* "African Americans took up the game in increasing numbers. . . . Kibitzing decamped from the obscure club to the park bench. . . ." Pandolfini himself became a minor celebrity—a few days after the broadcast began, he was walking on Sixth Avenue when a gorgeous woman leapt out of a limousine and shouted, "Bruce! Bruce Pandolfini! Oh, wow!"—and eventually he parlayed it into a career as a renowned instructor and a prolific writer of instructional chess books, of which more than a million copies have sold.

♛

"Chess has its own mythology—about the game's origins, its proponents and players, and even its very purpose," Pandolfini writes in the aptly titled *Pandolfini's Ultimate Guide to Chess.* "But no one really knows who invented chess."

The legends have persisted over centuries, like the one about Sissa, the Brahmin philosopher who supposedly created the game to teach a despotic king that he couldn't rule without the support of all of his subjects, or the one about the wise men in a Persian kingdom who invented the game to placate a Persian queen, to re-create the battle that had killed her son and show that he had died honorably. Stories like these, apocryphal though they may be, seem to support the widely held theory that the game's origins can be traced back to fifth- or sixth-century India (although there are certain historians who would argue for China), to a primitive ancestor called *chaturanga,* meaning "army composed of four members": elephants (bishops), horses (knights), chariots (rooks), and foot soldiers (pawns). Its popularity spread westward to Persia and Arabia and eventually to Europe around the year 1000, imported from the northern shore of Africa, most notably into Spain by the Moors. At the same time the game spread eastward into Asia, spawning numerous variations, and eventually into Russia (perhaps via Genghis Khan and his Mongols, when they overran the country in the twelfth century, but more likely sooner than that). In Czarist Russia, the game was banned by the Christian church, but this only inflamed its popularity, both among the commoners and among royalty, including Ivan the Terrible, who supposedly died in front of a chessboard. In time, chess became a unifying force: "Russia, by the early eighteenth century, was a kind of focal center, a boiling stew of chess ingredients from all over the world," wrote author J. C. Hallman. Along came Mikhail Chigorin, who played for the world championship twice in the late 1800s, and who became the first Russian to devote his life to chess. After the Bolshevik Revolution, chess continued to anchor this fledgling culture. It became a method for appeasing the masses in their leisure time, and for establishing and expanding the intellectual culture of the governmental system. Chess came under the jurisdiction of the Supreme Council for Physical Culture; the game was taught in schools to all children who achieved good grades. By the 1970s, by the time of Spassky's rise to prominence in the midst of the cold war, accomplishment in chess in the Soviet Union became an *imperative;* to lose, and especially to lose to an American who had grown up without any proper teaching, without any governmental infrastructure, was simply unfathomable.

♛

Bobby Fischer vanished into the ether in the mid-1970s and then reemerged as a paranoid xenophobe (he reportedly had the fillings in his teeth removed in fear that his enemies might be using them as antennas to beam messages) and a raging anti-Semite. He won more than three million dollars in a bland 1992 rematch against Spassky in Yugoslavia in the midst of its civil war—in direct defiance of an executive order from the U.S. Treasury Department—and then vanished again as a wanted man, only to surface to tell a Filipino radio station that the events of September 11, 2001, were "wonderful news." And yet, for all of his follies, it is nearly impossible to discuss American chess (and, it could be argued, chess in general) without referencing the looming presence of Fischer. It is impossible not to attach Fischer's personal life to his chess, but it is his chess that remains seminal: Grandmasters still marvel at the history, and the theory, the brashness of his tactics; his book, *My 60 Memorable Games,* is considered a classic. "There was a clarity to what he was doing on the board," Pandolfini says. "You could see it happening, but you were helpless to stop it."

To compare a young player to Fischer is to compare a CYO basketball star to Michael Jordan. It is both impossible and entirely unfair, and it occurs without fail every few years, when some prepubescent talent, almost always male, emerges at a precocious age. It is easy to get caught up in such hope.

And so it was easy to read Talese's story and study the accompanying picture of a boy with a long face and a blond military cut hunched over a chessboard and make the connection to another fourteen-year-old ranked No. 1 in his age group in the United States, and to the odd admission he had made a few months earlier.

"I'm getting old," Sal had said.

♛

In December, in the month before the New York City Scholastic Championships, Salvijus Bercys (with a U.S. Chess Federation rating of 2419) remains the top-ranked fifteen-year-old chess player in America, by a margin of seventy-one points. This is according to the system that determines the numerical (and in turn, social) hierarchy in American chess, a system so convoluted that to attempt to explain it would require that one obtain an advanced degree in mathematics from an Ivy League institution, as well as the assistance of several Austrian quantum physicists and a small battalion of robots. Here, for instance, is an excerpt from a USCF press release that attempts to describe recent innovations in the ratings system:

> To approximate one's rating using the standard formulas, a player needs to know (or approximate) the number of games played in tournaments, only if less than 50. Let N be the number of previous games, but set N to 50 if the number of games is 50 or more. Then, if the player has a pre-tournament rating less than 2200, the player computes:

$$N_r = 50/\sqrt{1 + (2200 - R_{pre})^2/100000}.$$

So even though many of the top players in this country couldn't even begin to explain the precise rationale behind their own ratings, these numbers dictate the tenor of virtually every important game. They are both signifiers of one's identity, and the game's equivalent of Las Vegas point spreads. And even though Sal is currently struggling through his sophomore-year math classes at Murrow, he knows this much: He maintains a seventy-one-point margin over the closest competitor in his age group, who also happens to be his teammate, Alex Lenderman. By all accounts, Sal and Alex dislike each other immensely, although this does not stop them from carpooling to major tournaments and sharing hotel rooms when they're on the road and playing endless blitz matches between rounds.

Sal and Alex look nothing alike, and they play nothing alike, and they act nothing alike. Sal is an inimitable personality, blond and brash and given to absurdist statements and odd proclamations. Alex has disheveled black hair and an overbite. He is small in every possible way: He is short and thin and narrow-waisted, and he often wears baggy sweatshirts and oversized boots that make him look like he's drowning in fabric, and sometimes when he tucks in his shirt, his pants can't help but take a slow ride toward his collarbone. And yet when Alex speaks, which is not particularly often, he does it in a cracked bass familiar to every boy who has ever struggled through the uneven onset of puberty. Sometimes, the things he says, shrouded in that husky voice and a vestigial Russian accent, are very strange indeed, almost savantlike in their precision. "Thirteen percent of my life is spent on ICC (the Internet Chess Club)," he says one day. Granted, the ICC software calculates this number for each member, but even if it didn't, Alex would have figured it out for himself. He likes math and he imagines himself becoming a statistician someday. At home, he plays along with *Wheel of Fortune* and *Jeopardy!* and *The Price Is Right* and he watches Yankee games with his father. Sometimes, just for fun, he will calculate the probability of, say, the Yankees winning a game after losing three straight. He enjoys probabilities, far more than most boys his age enjoy baseball. He is also a member of the math club at Murrow. But most of the time, when he is not eating or sleeping or studying, he is playing chess. This much can be quantified.

Alex was an Eliot Weiss recruit coming out of Intermediate School 228 in Gravesend, where, along with a classmate named Aleksandr Pelekhaty (who wound up at Brooklyn Tech), he led the school to a junior-high national championship. Around that time, Mr. Weiss first made contact with him. "They wanted me at Murrow," Alex says. "I felt Stuyvesant was too hard for me to get in. In Stuyvesant, I might have screwed up with my grades. It's too hard. I didn't want to overwhelm myself."

Alex's mother is from St. Petersburg, and his father is from the Ukraine, and they came here together when Alex was five years old, in part, Alex says, so that he wouldn't have to go into the army. Which, when you watch Alex wandering around a chess tournament like a lost child in a shopping mall, carrying his pieces in a worn plastic bag from a Spanish department store, is a scenario that is almost impossible to imagine.

Every summer, Alex spends a few weeks at his grandfather's house in Germany, in a town called Sollingen, not far from Düsseldorf.

When he was ten, his grandfather, Iosif Katz, a decent chess player with a rating of about 1600, taught him the game. Alex started playing against a computer, beating the lowest level, then a higher level, then the highest level. "It was addictive," he says. "It was fun, even when I lost. Although I used to cry when I lost."

When he was eleven, Alex played in his first money tournament at the now-defunct Manhattan Chess Club. He beat several higher-rated players, and he won (he remembers the number precisely, of course) fifty-three dollars. His father sent him to a chess school in Brighton Beach, and Alex's rating jumped to 1800, and under the tutelage of a coach named Mikhail Trossman, he reached 2300. Now he's at such a high level that he can no longer afford one of the few coaches who could handle him; the best ones charge at least sixty dollars an hour, and the Lendermans, who live in Borough Park and also have a younger son, can't afford to pay that much. Alex's father works at a document-scanning company in Manhattan. His mother is a computer programmer. "Lessons might be worth it for rich people," Alex says. "Most people who take lessons are billionaires."

Together, Sal and Alex—neither of whom takes private lessons—led Murrow to the national championship in 2004, with Sal scoring six points out of a possible seven and Alex scoring five and a half out of seven, and Murrow's top four players accounting for 20.5 points, a full point and a half ahead of both the University School, a private academy in Fort Lauderdale with a yearly tuition of more than ten thousand dollars, and Stuyvesant High School, which produces as many National Merit Scholars as any school in the nation. And it is Sal and Alex who are the two top boards on the best high-school chess team in the nation, and who are both on their way to becoming International Masters, one of the highest titles in the sport. Together, Sal and Alex could very well lead Murrow to four consecutive national championships, and they have managed to turn schools like Stuyvesant, with an entire roster bound for highbrow universities, into intellectual underdogs.

Still, this is not something they celebrate particularly often.

Once you graduate into the small community of elite American chess players, as Alex and Sal have done, the game begins to change. It becomes more serious and more daunting, a thing to be revered and deconstructed and properly prepared for. Scholastic tournaments, *trophy* tournaments devoid of cash prizes, are nothing more than diversions from the regular circuit of higher-level events. One of the best players in Murrow's history, Irina Krush, played so much competitive chess during her senior year of high school that she couldn't even remember where the national scholastic tournament took place (it was in Kansas City). "Honestly," she says, "they weren't that important in the context of my career."

And so this upcoming season—the city championship in January, the state championship in early March, and the nationals in April—means something entirely different for Sal and Alex than it does for the six others on the Murrow traveling team. A trophy? What good is a trophy? Sal and Alex do this because it is an obligation. They do this because it is what their teammates expect of them, and it is what Mr. Weiss expects of them for speaking to their teachers when they flub a math quiz. "There is no money involved at nationals," Alex says. "There is still pressure, but not as much as there is at a money tournament."

When Sal and Alex have gone up against each other in tournament play, Sal has won all three times. These days, they refuse to play each other in any official capacity, and on those rare occasions when a tournament director forces them into a match, they'll conspire to take an easy draw. Neither one will say outright that he dislikes the other, but beneath the enmity, they appear to have forged a grudging respect, which is what allows them to coexist.

Alex still thinks Sal is the better player, that Sal understands the game more completely, that he's a more skilled positional player, that's he's more in control. (Alex likes to think of himself as a "wild" player, which is hard to imagine, given his persona.) Sal may not dispute Alex's notions when you ask him, but somewhere in that cluttered mind of his, he realizes that Alex is one good tournament away from eclipsing him. He also recognizes that Alex's father is often willing to drive him to tournaments, because Alex's father accompanies his son to virtually every competitive event, lurking in the dark corners of the room for hours at a time, staring over Alex's shoulder with a meaty hand clutched under his chin, and holding hushed conversations in Russian with other parents in the Skittles Room.

It is never hard to find David Lenderman at a chess tournament, because there is nothing small about him. He is built like a professional wrestler. He is stout from neck to waist and has a bottom-heavy face and thick brown mustache, and it is hard to believe that someone as fragile-looking as Alex could have emerged from the genes of such a massive figure. Because of the physical disparities, because of his constant presence at tournaments, people who don't know him make assumptions about Alex's father, but Alex was never forced into playing chess. It simply seems as if, perhaps more than anyone else at Murrow, his brain has been wired for such things.

"The best players on our team," Ilya says one day, "are a little bit strange."

♛

But then, maybe you have to veer toward the bizarre in order to play chess at this level, to spend your free time amid a gathering of idiosyncratic masters and grandmasters, in tournaments played in drab hotel ballrooms, with the winners, in many cases, earning enough money to cover their expenses and the rest of the top ten players winning barely enough cash to pay for a sirloin dinner at an Outback Steakhouse. Is it a sign of abnormality to labor so hard, to ponder so deeply, for little or nothing in return? If so, then perhaps this is the definition of strange: four days holed up at, say, a Ramada in rural Vermont for something called the Green Mountain Open, when one honest mistake, one simple blunder, could make the difference between a $450 first-place prize and a lost weekend.

There are eighty-five billion ways to play the first four moves of a chess game, and it has been said that there are more variations in a single chess game than there are atoms in the universe. These sorts of daunting truths may lead to sharper math skills and a deeper understanding of one's self, but they have not rendered chess a lucrative pursuit in this country. Virtually no one in America can make enough money to survive on their own simply by playing chess. There are a couple of relatively well-paying tournaments each season, but the rest are mostly played for pocket change, and the regulars at these events tend to hold down more *respectable* day jobs, as aspiring physicians and teachers (often of chess, which doesn't pay much better than playing does) and professional gamblers. And Fischer, for all his bluster, for all his press clippings, for all his bottom-line capitalistic urges, did nothing to change the model. After the high drama of 1972, after the initial buzz subsided, Fischer vanished and then reappeared and then became a late-night punch-line, and chess once again won more renown as a metaphor than as a profession.

So here in this country, in this day and age, even someone as gifted and naturally inclined toward chess as Alex Lenderman is not crazy enough to imagine that he can make a living at this thing. His winnings are not so bad for a fifteen-year-old boy, not so bad when they're applied to the family's bills and the grocery shopping, a hundred dollars here, a hundred dollars there. "Even when I'm sixty, I'll still be playing chess," he says. "But I'll have a job too. Chess players just don't earn enough money."

♛

For his nineteenth-place finish out of sixty-four at the U.S. Chess Championship in San Diego in early December, at one of the richest tournaments in America, Sal takes home a check for $3,250. He once again contends that this is a disappointing end for him, despite the fact that all three of his losses came to players with ratings above 2600. But you get the sense he doesn't mean it this time. Still, when a *Daily News* reporter interviews him at school a few days later while working on a story about the team, he is mostly recalcitrant. It is Sal being Sal, elusive and deflective and charming all at once. He has no need for interviews. They bore him.

The *News* also sends a photographer, who shoots a staged photo of Sal and Alex playing each other in a game that is not really a game, but merely a stage prop, because if this were the real thing, well, then, Sal and Alex wouldn't be doing this in the first place. "*This* is a photo?" Sal says. "This is *hardly* a photo."

The rain is falling in thick sheets in midtown Manhattan, and out on the sidewalk the suits are dodging lake-sized puddles, their umbrellas twisted into baroque sculptures above their heads. And in the lobby of a polished office building on Third Avenue, an officious-looking young woman in a pressed skirt and a white blouse is squinting through the glass into the late-afternoon haze and growing ever more impatient. "Who are you waiting for?" her male colleague asks.

"My chess team," she says, adopting the false possessive embraced by speechmakers and politicians, by important people like her boss. "They were supposed to be here fifteen minutes ago."

"Well," says her male colleague. He appears to be suppressing a chuckle. "A chess team. I guess you'll recognize them when you see them."

Not long after that, they watch as a dozen men, women, teenagers, and children, an odd assortment of colors and races dressed up in low-cost formalwear, in hand-me-down ties and ill-fitting sweaters, come rushing along the sidewalk and sprint directly past the building. They look nothing like the gawky stereotype the officious-looking woman's male colleague had in mind, but they still stand out among the midtown hordes like a wayward vaudeville act. They've got the wrong address, and by the time they find their way inside, they're both damp and late, and fortunately for them, the senator is running late as well. The officious-looking young woman introduces herself to Eliot Weiss and his wife and they head toward the elevators, hurtling down to a room in the basement where Hillary Clinton is preparing to pose for a few hundred early-December photo ops with local heroes, proud citizens, and, all the way from Midwood, Brooklyn, the defending national chess champions.

In the elevator, Oscar launches into a harangue.

"Hey," he says. "Let's say someone owes me twenty-seven dollars. *Hypothetically*. Let's say I owe someone twenty-seven dollars, and Willy here"—he slaps Willy on the shoulder—"owes me fourteen dollars."

Willy rolls his eyes. Clearly this argument has been raging for miles, aboveground and underground, on the forty-minute ride from Midwood to midtown, on the Q train and the 6 train, over the Manhattan Bridge and through the Lower East Side and along Lexington Avenue. Clearly, this all relates to debts stemming from card games, and clearly, Oscar is not making any sense.

"So let's say I tell Willy here to pay this person thirteen, and this person pays me fourteen," Oscar says.

"That *still* doesn't make any sense," says Sal, wedging his way into the discussion, but at this point Oscar is on a roll, and when Oscar is on a roll, momentum often trumps logic.

"Wait, wait," Oscar says. "Yes, it does. Let me finish."

"No, it doesn't," Willy says. He's pleading now. He's insistent. He can't take much more of this. "I *told* you, Oscar, it ain't right. It don't make no sense."

Oscar is wearing a sweater vest and a skinny *Wall Street*–era tie and a pair of black loafers. Most of the others are have put on shirts and ties, as well, except for Sal, who's dressed in a fleece jacket and a pair of jeans. Shawn Martinez, one of the freshmen, is not here, but the other freshman, Dalphe Morantus, has showed up wearing an oversized oxford shirt that makes him look smaller than he already is. It is easy to mistake Dalphe for someone's little brother. Happens all the time. He has a boyish face and dimples and huge expressive eyes. One of the seniors from last year's team, a well-dressed Ukrainian named Dmitriy Minevich, has also come along. He's at Pace University now, in lower Manhattan, studying business, and he watches, as Willy and

Oscar go back and forth and then fall into another argument about what might happen at this year's national tournament (both in terms of results and hotel-room arrangements), and what actually did happen at last year's nationals, which is the reason why they're here in the first place. It wasn't like this last year. "This team," Dmitriy says, "is much less mature."

They've been herded into a conference room in the bowels of the building, into a line behind dozens of people, all waiting to be funneled into an adjacent room for pictures with the senator. They've been told to keep the noise down, out of respect for the senator, but the argument about the twenty-seven dollars is still raging and Sal is complaining ("I haven't eaten in like, ten hours and twenty-three minutes," he says) and the Weisses' two children, who have accompanied them to this photo op, who accompany them to most of the team's tournaments, are growing restless.

It's not that they haven't grown accustomed to these types of events by now. It's all part of the process of winning. They've met their local congressman so many times that it's become a dull postseason routine. They've had proclamations issued in their honor and they've been feted at City Hall meetings.

Feb. 8, 1996, press release, "Mayor Honors New York City champions": "Applauding the team, Mayor Giuliani said, 'I am pleased to extend my congratulations to the Edward R. Murrow High School Chess Team for your outstanding achievements in the international chess community. Your commitment to the game, your self-discipline . . ." *blah, blah, blah, etc. . . .*

May 18, 2000, Brooklyn city proclamation: "Whereas, the Borough of Brooklyn has produced some of the best chess players in the world, and it is most fitting that we recognize these individuals and groups that have risen to the highest ranks of success in competition . . ." *and so on, and so on. . . .*

May 5, 2004, City Council proclamation: "Whereas: Under the astute direction of Coach Eliot Weiss, the team was led to victory by players Dmitry (sic) Minevich, Olga Novikova, Alex Linderman (sic), Ilya Kotiyanskiy (sic), Oscar Santana, Willy Edgard, and Nile Smith . . ."

But now, thanks to the persistence of Mr. Weiss, after phone calls to a congressman named Anthony Weiner (who, a few months later, would make an unsuccessful run for mayor) and follow-up calls every two weeks to the scheduling people in Washington, they've attained a new watershed in political photo-ops: In five days, they're going to the White House to meet the American president, George W. Bush, who will honor them for their 2004 national championship. So the Clinton meeting is a mere warm-up. And it is taking far longer than they would have liked. Because, in truth, these meetings are as much for Mr. Weiss as they are for the team. As far as Sal is concerned, he'd rather be at McDonald's.

Five more minutes, says one of Clinton's handlers, once again urging them toward silence.

"They said five more minutes ten minutes ago," Sal says.

"Listen," Oscar says. "It's simple. I give Willy fourteen dollars, and you give me thirteen."

"*Oscar,*" Willy says. "Just give it up."

And then the line begins to move. They can see the flashbulbs popping in the other room. The assembly line is created: A photo, a handshake, and then move on. When it is Murrow's turn with the senator, they pose for a group photo, and for individual photos, and Hillary Clinton expresses her pride, and Mr. Weiss tells the senator they're heading to the White House the next week. "Any advice?" he says.

What she tells them, according to the officious young woman who aids Hillary Clinton in her public affairs, is supposed to be off the record, as are all comments uttered by the senator to her constituents on this day. But since she does not mention this until after the fact, here is the advice Hillary Rodham Clinton imparts to seven teenaged boys who represent her constituency, seven teenaged boys who are regarded as a spectacular photo-op by the political establishment (who can go wrong posing with a *chess team*?), seven teenaged boys who have just spent the past hour arguing over outstanding poker debts and reciting R-rated rap lyrics and negotiating sleeping arrangements at a hotel in Nashville in April:

"Challenge him to a game of chess," she says.

When they've been swept from the room, when Eliot Weiss's latest crusade for political recognition has been fulfilled, the arguments rage on. Facts remain malleable; it's as if nothing at all has happened in the interim. Oscar's versions of past events and Willy's versions of the same event vary wildly from what Nile and Ilya and Sal might have seen. In the lobby, Alex Lenderman gets a call from his parents, who would like him to come home as soon as possible. And out on the sidewalk, amid the wind and the drizzle and the last miserable dregs of a December afternoon, Oscar takes a brief respite from pleading out of his debts to ask something else of Willy.

"Yo," he says. "You think George Bush even *plays* chess?"

Oscar Santana

SIX

THE ORANGUTAN

THE FACTS ARE THESE:

Oscar Santana is seventeen years old, and he is in the twelfth grade at Murrow High School, and he lives in a fourth-floor apartment in Bedford-Stuyvesant, near the G train station at Classon Avenue, above a mini-market and across the street from the Lafayette Houses, a sprawling complex of city projects. Oscar Santana should not be confused with Oskar Santana, who is twelve years old and in the seventh grade at Intermediate School 318 in Williamsburg, and lives in the same apartment, and happens to be Oscar Santana's brother. Both have registered in separate divisions for the upcoming Right Move tournament at Brooklyn College, which is held on a brisk Sunday morning inside an expansive cafeteria on the school's Flatbush campus. Furthermore, neither Oscar Santana nor Oskar Santana should be mistaken for their father, Oscar Santana (or "Big Oscar"), who lives in the same apartment, along with a wife and a daughter (whose name, mercifully, is Talitha) and several varieties of domesticated birds, who roam freely about the kitchen and living-room floor.

The Santanas are Puerto Rican, and this whole name thing is in keeping with a Hispanic tradition, according to Big Oscar, who is built like a freezer, short and rectangular, the type of man who looks as if he could strangle a bear but is so genial that it's hard to imagine him stepping on a cockroach. "It's like how George Foreman named all five of his sons George," Big Oscar says one day while sitting in his modest living room, waiting for Oscar (and Oskar) to come home from school. (That George Foreman is actually from Texas does not seem to bother him.) The confusion is mitigated through nicknames: The littlest Oskar is referred to as "Machi," which means "little man" in Spanish, and the midsized version of Oscar is referred to by his mother as "Osky."

Oscar (that is to say, "Osky"), who has a plump face and wire-rimmed glasses and a grin that exposes a mouthful of dental work, tends to make an indelible impression on the adults who negotiate beyond his reticent veneer. This is not always easy. Once, when his parents found out Oscar hadn't been attending one of his classes at Murrow, they asked him what was wrong. "I don't think the teacher likes me," Oscar told them.

"At times, Oscar can close himself off to people," says his father, wringing a pair of massive hands. "He has to know you. If he don't know you, he'll close up like a nutshell. That's when he can get in trouble. He's extremely smart, but I tell him, I say, 'Oscar, sometimes you gotta talk.' "

Oscar shows up at the Right Move tournament in Brooklyn wearing his typical school uniform, an untucked blue oxford shirt and ridiculously baggy jeans and white sneakers, with a pair of Sony headphones draped around his neck. His brother, who is thin and hyperactive and almond-skinned and looks only vaguely like Oscar, is hanging around with him, trying desperately to look cool, which is funny, because Oskar is a handsome boy, and this is, after all, a chess tournament. Oskar is not a particularly talented chess player (he is far too hyperactive), but it is immediately apparent that Oskar idolizes Oscar, who with a victory in his fourth and final game of the day against a lower-rated junior-high schooler, can finish with three points and in a tie for third place in the open division. It should be an easy victory, but Oscar tends not to do things the easy way, which is what has prompted him to embrace an opening known as the Orangutan.

"People don't know how to play the Orangutan," Oscar says. "People fear the Orangutan."

The Orangutan is, in fact, as odd and loopy an opening as its name suggests (other unconventional and more recently developed openings named after zoo animals include the Hippopotamus, the Elephant, and the Hedgehog). A conventional chess opening begins with white moving one of the two center pawns, known in chess notation as 1.d4 or 1.e4, in order to gain control of the center of the board. This is the first theoretical tenet every chess player learns: The opening is a fight for control of the center squares of the board. Whoever wins that fight has a distinct advantage, which is why nearly every serious opening for white begins with one of those two moves.

In the Orangutan, white opens the game by moving the knight's pawn from b2 to b4:

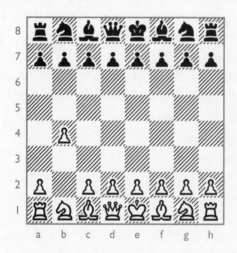

A single opening move like this, something as radical and unexpected as 1.b4, changes the entire dynamic of the game. The balance of the board is upended, the center remains wide open for one's opponent, and chaos and confusion ensue, which is the way Oscar would prefer it.

This name, the Orangutan, traces its roots back to New York in

1924, to an idiosyncratic Polish grandmaster named Savielly Tartakower, who was visiting the Bronx Zoo on a day off during a tournament called the New York International. Tartakower passed the monkey cages, where an orangutan moved closer as he approached. This orangutan's name, according to Tartakower, was Susan. It was then that he had a brainstorm: He showed Susan a chess set. He asked her what opening he should play in the next round. Somehow, Tartakower insisted, the orangutan told him to play b4, and because the climbing movement of the pawn to b4, and eventually to the b5 square, reminded him of Susan's movements, the name stuck. Tartakower played the Orangutan to a draw, and while other masters and grandmasters have dabbled in the possibilities, the opening remains a novelty, an irregularity, its strength lying largely in the element of surprise.

Oscar used to rely on the Ruy Lopez opening, which begins with 1.e4 and makes perfect theoretical sense and allows for early castling (another basic theoretical tenet), but then he learned the intricacies of the Orangutan from an international master named Yury Lapshun, and he now plays it virtually every chance he gets. Often, it will get him into trouble, but this is Oscar Santana we're talking about, and Oscar has a way of squirming out of even the most serious kinds of trouble.

♛

The biggest mess Oscar ever happened into came earlier this fall, when he realized he was about to face up to a subpar report card during his first cycle of classes at Murrow. By all accounts, Oscar has a sharp intellect, but his grades have never reflected that, and this is not something his father has much tolerance toward. Oscar also has a certain aptitude toward computers; at one point, he was given a very old Dell desktop, and with the help of his next-door neighbor, he dismantled it, incorporated parts of it into his current computer, and souped the whole thing up into a superior machine. His parents couldn't quite understand how he did it, but when they came home one day, there were the Dell and Oscar's old computer on the living-room table, melded into a single formidable machine, capable of running the latest Windows incarnation at full speed and logging on to the World Wide Web at all hours of the night.

So after Oscar realized his upcoming report card would not play well with his father, he hatched a scheme worthy of a Hollywood film. (In fact, it *was* a scheme worthy of a Hollywood film, back in 1983, several years before Oscar's birth, when a teenaged Matthew Broderick did the same thing in *War Games*.) Somehow, Oscar hacked his way into the New York City Board of Education's computer, and he changed his grades manually. Then he brought home a perfect report card: Straight As. His parents were shocked. They had no idea what had happened. They thought maybe Oscar had finally applied himself. They thought that maybe their constant admonishments, their insistence that Oscar do his homework before falling into hours of online chess and poker games, had finally been heeded.

Problem was, Oscar hadn't thought out his plan to the end. His parents insisted on attending the next open-school night, to verify the causes of this miraculous turnaround, this little gift from the heavens. Oscar went with them. When they got there, he told them none of his teachers were around that night. So they went to the principal's office, which is about the time that Oscar's scheme finally unraveled altogether. When school officials found out what Oscar had done, the Santanas say, they didn't just want to expel Oscar. They wanted to charge Oscar with a felony. But Mr. Weiss put up an argument for Oscar, and Oscar's parents put up an argument for him, that he was on the chess team, that he was a quiet boy who didn't mean to hurt anyone, and somehow, because this is Oscar, because he has a magical ability to wend his way out of trouble, the school decided to give him another chance. His parents didn't know what to feel. They wanted to knock him around and shake him and hug him, all at the same time. They wanted to know how someone so demonstrably smart could do something so unbelievably stupid. They wanted him to use his powers for good, instead of using them to subvert the system, just this once.

"Look, Oscar," said his mother, Rosa, a thin woman who offsets her husband's formidable physical presence. "If you're able to break into the Board of Education's computer, you should be able to do your classwork. If you're able to break into the Board of Education's computer, then you're not dumb."

For his part, Oscar won't say much of anything about it. It was a gamble, after all, and it didn't work. Sometimes, in chess, in school, in poker, in life, that happens.

♛

Big Oscar and Rosa first met when they were still children growing up in Williamsburg. Years later, after Oscar had divorced his first wife, he met up with Rosa again, and now they've been married for eighteen years. They lived in Florida for a short time but then they came back here, back to New York and to the apartment on DeKalb Avenue in Bedford-Stuyvesant where they've lived for the past nine years. It's not much, but it's home. There are no locks or buzzers on the building's front door. The address is written by hand in what looks like a black permanent marker above the entrance. The stairs are steep and unforgiving, but the apartment itself, in a neighborhood that is slowly giving way to gentrification, is a bargain: seven small rooms, set up railroad-style, including four modest bedrooms, for slightly over one thousand dollars a month, with just enough room for a computer desk, atop which lies Oscar's Frankensteinian creation, and a leather couch in the living room. It's tight, what with five people and four birds, but given that the only income is from Big Oscar's disability checks, this is about the outer limit of what they can afford. And they've come to like it here, as the neighborhood has changed.

In the old days, they could look out the living-room window and watch people getting held up in the middle of the street, and there was a steady spate of shootings and drug deals taking place at the Lafayette Houses. Now, just recently, a man had come and bought the old factory across the street and turned the whole thing into luxury lofts. The Santanas aren't worried about the gentrification of Bed-Stuy forcing them out of the neighborhood. At least, not yet. They figure as long as their rent stays steady, these changes can only be positive for their children. Talitha is only nine years old, but a teacher has already singled her out for her artistry, telling the Santanas she has a keen eye for detail. On Saturdays, she takes classes at the Pratt Institute, which happens to be near their apartment, which is another blessing that Rosa says a prayer of thanks for every day.

"The Lord is good," Rosa says, and she says it as often as she can.

The Santana family disease is called osteonecrosis, which means, literally, "dead bone." It's what happens when the blood stops flowing to a joint, and the cells within the bone and the marrow begin to die, and an almost unbearable pain sets in and doesn't go away. Big Oscar got osteonecrosis in his knee, and was honorably discharged from the Marines because of it, and his body hasn't been the same since. He started taking cortisone injections, which he says triggered diabetes. The only cure is a joint replacement, but Big Oscar can't exactly afford to splurge and buy himself a new knee. He used to work for a bank, and then for a brokerage firm, and then he was a supervisor at Mount Sinai Hospital, but now he has trouble doing much of anything, so he lives off the disability.

And then the younger Oscar somehow contracted this disease, as well, in his hip, early in his teenage years. Oscar, who used to love playing handball, would start coming back from the courts in so much pain that he'd have to pop several painkillers and coat his hip in Icy Hot in order to make it through the night. The doctors told him he'd probably need a hip replacement at some point, but not yet, Oscar says, not while his body is still developing. So he deals with the pain by remaining mostly sedentary, by mastering those things that don't cause his hip any further pain. His parents have told him to go on disability when he turns eighteen, but Oscar insists he wants to work.

Around the time his hip fell into its slow and inevitable demise, Oscar started playing chess. He was in the sixth grade, in his first year at I.S. 318, and he asked his parents to take him to a tournament at a Catholic church on Stuyvesant Street. Chess? His parents had no idea what this was about, what the game entailed, or how Oscar had picked up the habit. Chess? They figured it had to be a phase. "We didn't hardly pay no mind to it," Big Oscar says.

So they dropped him off, and when they came to pick him up, one of his friends came over and said, "Oscar got first place." And then Oscar started bringing home trophies on a regular basis: A half dozen, a dozen, twenty-five, fifty, seventy-five, until the Santanas no longer had any idea what to do with them, until they had no space for them in their living room and had to start storing some in garbage bags and throwing the others away. Oscar started staying up all night, logging on to chess Web sites, playing against faraway opponents on Yahoo! and on the Internet Chess Club, studying tactics and positions and attempting to improve his game for reasons even he couldn't begin to explicate. It all made sense, though. Oscar has a personality suited for the game. Not only is he a risk-taker, he's also a singular philosopher, a font of charisma, the kind of kid who does his math homework and marks down the answers and refuses to show his work, and when the teacher asks why, he tells his mother, "Why should I show them how I did it?"

♛

On certain occasions, the grandmasters and elite players will make an appearance at the Right Move tournaments at Brooklyn, men like Leonid Yudasin, men who are hoping to make a few extra dollars either by playing simultaneous games against inferior opponents for twenty dollars per try or by playing in blitz tournaments like the one that's going on today. Yudasin is an Orthodox Jew, and he's wearing a black yarmulke and a matching suit. His USCF rating is somewhere around 2700, among the top players in the country, and at one point, a dozen people are clustered around one of his games, trying to figure out what the hell is going on. "I feel like an idiot," someone whispers, "but I don't have a clue who this guy is."

There are other elites playing in the blitz tournament this morning, like Gata Kamsky, a former child prodigy with a famously overbearing father who quit playing competitively to attend medical school, and Polish champions Kamil Milton and Alex Wojtkiewicz and Russians Yury Shulman and Yury Lapshun. This is not especially unusual. The amount of chess talent concentrated within a few dozen square miles in New York City, largely because of the influx of Russian and Eastern European immigrants, is staggering. No other region in America comes close. Of those, many choose to reside in Sheepshead Bay and Coney Island and Bay Ridge, in neighborhoods whose signage is primarily in Cyrillic, and they play games or teach classes to young immigrants in the back rooms of clubs in Brighton Beach.

Amid this fog of pale faces and thick consonants, a teenager with coffee-colored skin is wandering about in a replica Allen Iverson jersey, like a nearsighted man trying to spot a taxi. He is a big boy, two hundred thirty pounds of flesh and urban-themed apparel, and his eyelids appear almost stuck together, and he has a bewildered look plastered on his plump mug. He appears to be on the verge of curling up in the corner and hibernating for the winter. The boy's name is Shawn Martinez, and he is a freshman at Murrow, and his rating is slightly above 1900, which makes him the team's No. 3 board, the strongest player on the team besides Sal and Alex. Among a team of independent spirits, Shawn may be the most individualistic of them all. He spends his nights at home in Crown Heights, parked in front of the computer, playing chess, and he spends much of his school day avoiding class in the school cafeteria, playing cards and listening to music and wasting time however possible. As far as he's concerned, the Right Move tournaments are no longer worthy of his time or his effort. But Shawn also fancies himself a pretty damn good blitz player, and so this tournament has drawn him out of his cocoon.

Blitz games are furious and expeditious and sloppy, the chess equivalent of a playground pickup game. In blitz (during which each player puts either three or five minutes on his clock), and especially during a subset of blitz called bullet (in which sixty seconds are put on the clock for each player), the action becomes a blur, fingers moving to pieces, fingers pounding the hammer atop the clock, eyes darting about the board, pieces shifting, pieces falling, captured pieces dropping to the ground with a steady tumble. Blitz is as much about reflex as it is about strategy, and in blitz, if you happen to nudge a piece to a more favorable square and get away with it, or if you happen to capture a piece illegally and your opponent doesn't notice, well, then so be it. Blitz is the game favored by the hustlers in Washington Square Park. It's street chess, and this is what Shawn likes about it, because there's a certain edge to it that slow play simply can't replicate. Also, in blitz, at the right moment, a 1900-rated player can beat a grandmaster, and this evens the score between someone like Shawn, who picked up the game only a few years ago, and this clique of men who learned how to castle shortly after emerging from the womb.

Because of the way he looks, because of his sleepy visage and his slow drawl and the extra weight he carries, people have never taken Shawn to be much of an intellectual threat. That's why chess matters to him as much as anything else in his life. That's why, if the game's being played his way, he's willing to take on anybody, anywhere, at any time. "He's a really sensitive kid," says Jennifer Shahade, one of his teachers at Intermediate School 318, where Shawn stumbled into the game entirely by chance. "You can tell he cares so much about winning and losing."

Shawn and Oscar have a symbiotic relationship, if only because they are both Puerto Rican, the only two Hispanic players on Murrow's eight-man roster. Sometimes, when they play a two-on-two variation of Bughouse, in which a pair of games are played simultaneously and teammates can trade captured pieces and reuse them, Shawn and Oscar will be teammates, and they'll communicate entirely in Spanish. It doesn't matter that they've both spent virtually their entire lives in New York City; they share a certain brotherhood, a direct connection to each other in a city that remains divided by ethnicity.

This Sunday's tournament is not exactly a showcase for Oscar, who blunders with the Orangutan and finishes fifth in the Open Section, and it's not a breakthrough for Shawn, either, who loses his final two blitz games and finishes twenty-second out of forty-one in the tournament. It's not a great day for the newbies, either, as the four sophomores who joined the club cold turkey in the fall—Rex, Renwick, Robert, and Adalberto—win a total of two games among them. "This stuff is *hard*," says Renwick, who's mostly been practicing in the free chess forums on Yahoo! But on this day, the stars are two of Murrow's other top boards, Ilya and Willy, who are both undefeated heading into the fourth and final round. That's when something disconcerting occurs: There is a direct intercession of emotion upon the proceedings.

Willy's opponent in the last round is an eighth-grader, a cherubic-looking boy wearing a yellow button-down shirt and a braided belt. Late in the endgame, with only a few pieces on the board, the boy offers his hand. A draw. Willy pushes one side of his earphones back from his head, purses his lips, and then he shakes his head, refusing the draw. After another series of moves, the boy tries again. Willy gives him the same placid look, settles into another track off the latest Eminem disc, and refuses once more. So then the boy raises his hand, in an attempt to summon a tournament director, someone, anyone, to review the notation of moves he's been keeping, to mandate a draw, which can be done if the game is void of any winning possibilities (a "dead draw") and the clock is the only factor in determining a victor. Meantime, the game goes on; the boy's clock continues to run toward zero. What once seemed a dead position suddenly turns to Willy's advantage. The boy drops his hand to his side. Willy makes a few more moves, and then he somehow squeezes out a win, and his opponent screws up his face and begins to cry. The boy lets out a series of thick, heaving sobs, and it seems as if he might never stop, and his wails begin to pierce the cone of silence within the cafeteria, which only renders the moment more awkward. A series of conferences ensues: with the boy's father, with one of the tournament directors, with several of the other tournament directors.

Willy's expression doesn't change. It never does, really; even when he *is* rattled, he maintains a preternatural cool. "He talks so slow and relaxed," one of his friends' parents told me. "Cool, calm, collected, intelligent: That's Willy." That doesn't always translate to the board, of course. Like at nationals last year, when that kid got up near him and began a sprint toward the bathroom but couldn't hold it in and puked right next to Willy's feet. That threw him off so bad he didn't win a game the rest of the day. "Or that time at nationals when you lost to that kid because you said he looked like Michael Jackson," Oscar says.

"Naw," Willy says. "That ain't what happened."

"Yeah it was," Oscar says.

"Naw," Willy says. "That ain't it at all. You guys don't *listen* to me at all."

♛

One thing Willy does not discuss often, if at all, is his sister. Laura was a chess player, too, and had come up through I.S. 318 and the Chess-in-the-Schools program, just like Willy, and the previous May had finished in the top ten in the sixteen-and-under division at an all-girls chess tournament in Chicago. In the seventh grade, she was a straight-A student, but in the eighth grade, her struggles began, and she chose not to go to Murrow so she wouldn't have to share a school hallway with her brother.

In November, her mother filed a missing persons report. *Date of Last Contact: November 24, 2004. "Before she ran, Laura was seen in the area of Nostrand Ave."*

She resurfaced shortly after that, and eventually came back home, but their relationship remains distant, and it's something Willy doesn't discuss. At home, his bedroom is on a separate floor, and his mother is at work almost all the time, and he mostly keeps to himself. "I don't know what Laura does," he says.

So it was a harsh way for the boy to lose a game, but such is life, and such is the learning process, and now Willy has finished the day undefeated, as has Ilya, which means they'll each take home thirty-five dollars.

"Kid had a draw, and he didn't take it," Willy says while waiting for his check. The case for the Eminem CD is splayed open on the table, near his elbow, next to his Discman. "He should have stopped the clock when he called the tournament director."

Nobody seems to know much of anything about the boy Willy defeated. It's a funny thing—the same faces show up at the Right Move tournaments virtually every week, and they spend hours together, sitting three feet from each other's faces and kibitzing between games all morning long, and yet most of their knowledge of each other is based on generalizations and assumptions. And so one of the competitors in the open section, a student at another Brooklyn public school who happens to be listening in on the conversation, delivers a response in a low, sharp whisper, which is based entirely upon speculation. It is based upon the simple fact that the boy's father has accompanied him to this tournament, because among the public-school contingent, parental attendance is such a rarity.

"Fucking rich kids," he says.

Nile Smith

SEVEN

CHESS AND THE CITY

THE FOUNDER OF THE RIGHT MOVE CHESS FOUNDATION (MOTTO: "Free Chess for Youth") lives in a luxury apartment building on East Fifty-seventh Street with crystal chandeliers and seventeenth-century Flemish tapestries in the lobby. His home is on the forty-second floor, and he has a terrace with an unobstructed view of the Fifty-ninth Street Bridge, which is what sold on him on this location in the first place.

"This country's been very good to me," Fred Goldhirsch says, and he takes a seat in a black leather Eames lounge chair in his living room. He is thin and gray and slightly stooped and still speaks with a trace of an Eastern European accent. In 1938, in the midst of the Anschluss, the Nazi annexation of Austria, SS soldiers burst into his family's home and ransacked it and left him huddled in a heap on the floor. He was thirteen years old and he was Jewish, and a sponsorship from relatives in America that same year almost certainly saved his life.

Goldhirsch fled the country with his parents, and they settled in the Bronx, where he worked as a caddy at a golf course. When he was eighteen, even though he was on the youngish side, he found a way to enlist in the army and went back to Europe. He fought at Normandy and the Battle of the Bulge. He spent those years hoping to come across the SS officer who had once bullied him in his own house (to no avail), then played soccer for the army's Third Division team in

Czechoslovakia while waiting to be shipped home in 1945. When he came back, he took up work as a civil engineer for the city, helping to plan and build a cluster of project homes on Staten Island. The job itself was miserable, but the industry was booming, so he decided to try building his own homes, in Queens and on Staten Island. Soon he was building entire developments.

It should come as no surprise that once Goldhirsch built up a considerable amount of wealth, he started giving back. He sent his daughters to Marymount, an exclusive Catholic school on the Upper East Side, and he convinced the sisters there to begin a program to educate their students about the Holocaust. As he got older, and his body began to break down, and he could no longer play soccer and tennis, he turned to chess, a game he'd learned back in Austria. He joined the Manhattan Chess Club, where, by the late 1980s, he'd become a board member. The club was struggling to make ends meet, and Goldhirsch suggested teaching some classes to youth and turning it into a charitable foundation, a 501(c)(3). This suggestion met with a great deal of resistance, and in late 1990, along with his cofounder, Norman Friedman, Goldhirsch broke his foundation out as a separate entity, and they started offering free chess classes for underprivileged city youths at the club.

They advertised in chess magazines, and they sent notices to schools, and still they only drew about twenty kids. They started handing out free subway tokens, figuring that maybe their pupils couldn't afford the cost of transportation. The attendance was still low. Finally, at the end of the first year, they ran a tournament. The number of participants tripled; it was as if they had come from out of nowhere. So the Right Move started running tournaments every month during the school year, and they negotiated with schools for space, and most weeks they draw around a hundred kids to the tournament in Manhattan (they also hold satellite tournaments in neighborhoods like Bedford-Stuyvesant and Brownsville, and offer limited programs in a few schools). The foundation's budget is about a hundred and twenty thousand dollars (most of it Goldhirsch's own money, since he does little fund-raising), and is run entirely out of Goldhirsch's apart-ment/office, where he maintains a part-time secretary to help him run his businesses. A few years back, Eliot Weiss signed on as a member of the board of directors for the Right Move, and since then he's used these tournaments as both a source of supplementary income (the di-rectors are paid a nominal amount for running the tournaments) and as a recruiting tool for Murrow.

Everybody plays for free at the Right Move tournaments, and nobody is turned away, regardless of rating or school affiliation or household income, and in a city where the lines of ethnicity and class grow ever deeper, they draw students from Catholic schools and Jew-ish yeshivas and public schools and private academies, many of whom make the hour-long commute to the Upper West Side on sparsely populated Sunday-morning subway trains. (One day a boy arrived late, well after the first round had started, and approached John Mc-Manus, the Catholic schoolteacher, and told him a murder on the subway had kept him from arriving on time. "I'm not even sure I'd want to play after dealing with something like that," McManus says.) Some participants are members of teams preparing for the city and state and national championships, like Murrow, like Hunter; others simply have nowhere else to play competitive chess. "We were the first ones to offer free tournaments for youth," Goldhirsch says. "Now there are other organizations doing it, and sometimes we get a few less kids. But what's that they say about imitation being the greatest form of flattery?"

In fact, this is still a relatively recent phenomenon, the notion of chess as charity, as an educational tool, as a cultural equalizer in under-privileged neighborhoods. The first stirrings came in the wake of the Fischer-Spassky match, and they came largely from one man, a gawky figure who fell so hard for the game at the age of thirteen that he checked every single chess book out of the Brooklyn Public Library and skipped school for a month so he could read them all.

In the beginning, there was Bruce Pandolfini, and there was virtually no one else. Even now, three decades after he became the first professional chess instructor in New York City, he will assert himself, with a certain amount of neurotic calculation, as the reigning world champion of pedagogy. "I've given more private lessons than anyone on the planet," he says. "And I'm willing to bet on that."

Pandolfini lives on the fifth floor of a prewar building on the Upper West Side, in an apartment that resembles the stockroom of a used bookstore. Here is an abbreviated sampling from one of a number of piles of books stacked next to his couch: *Pride and Prejudice, The Concise Columbia Dictionary of Quotations, The Oxford Book of Aphorisms,* and *Moby-Dick.* On one midsummer day, a Faulkner novel lay in the center of his coffee table, and copies of his own books, more than two dozen, none of which he is particularly proud of, were scattered on bookshelves lining the walls: There was *Chess Target Practice* and *The Chess Doctor* and *Chess Openings: Traps and Zaps* and *More Chess Openings: Traps and Zaps 2* and *Bobby Fischer's Outrageous Chess Moves* and *Power Mates* and *The Weapons of Chess* and *Pandolfini's Chess Complete* and *Pandolfini's Endgame Course.*

The chess community in New York City is an insular web of names and faces, all of whom tend to gather at select locations and share the same gossip. It's rare, in most cases, to find more than a degree or two of separation. But even within this cabal, Pandolfini himself is a Zelig-like figure, a man who first gained renown as a PBS television analyst during the Fischer-Spassky match. He has since become famous as a teacher, a coach, a regular columnist for *Chess Life* magazine, and a fictional character, played by Ben Kingsley in *Searching for Bobby Fischer,* one that happened to share his name and occupation but few of his character traits.

In real life, Bruce Pandolfini looks as much like Ben Kingsley as he looks like Elizabeth Taylor. His signature feature remains his hair, which at the time of the Fischer-Spassky match had grown (by his own admission) to hippie length, and while it is much shorter now, it is still tinted red and marred by kinky disorderliness, and is accompanied by a whimsical hyphen of a mustache.

Setting up a meeting with Pandolfini can be a prolonged ordeal. This is not because he is intentionally elusive, nor is it because he is unfriendly or disinterested or aloof, as Kingsley portrayed him in the movie. It is simply because Pandolfini is perpetually disorganized. He forgets things. Sometimes he shows up for lessons an hour late; most of the time, he doesn't answer his home telephone. "His forgetfulness is entirely democratic: he neglects to return the phone calls of grand-masters and patzers alike," wrote Fred Waitzkin. "It is a quirk of nature that this man, who can play ten simultaneous chess games blindfolded and has total recall of tens of thousands of chess positions, has such difficulty remembering appointments, publication dates, and the departure times of airline flights."

It is not an overstatement to say the modern notion of professional chess teaching originated with Pandolfini, in part because he had the charisma to handle the role, and in part because he found himself in the right place at the right time, in the wake of the Fischer-Spassky match in 1972. Five hours a day of commentary on PBS had rendered him something of an intellectual celebrity, thanks to Shelby Lyman, who had offered him the job, and Pandolfini took advantage of his status. Hundreds of people called the station searching for a teacher; Pandolfini took on fifteen of them, charging fifteen dollars an hour.

Before the summer of 1972, no one had really thought of teaching chess to make a living, since most of America hadn't thought much of chess at all. The game was taught by parents to children, and by a few masters and grandmasters scattered here and there, many of them immigrants, who gave instructions for little or no money in return. But afterward, there was a sudden demand for teachers, and because Pandolfini was already a brand name among them, he began to make more money than he ever could have imagined. That he was making money at all—just a couple years before this he had dropped out of graduate school at the University of Arizona so he could play at a chess tournament in Reno, at which he won fifty dollars—seemed something of a miracle. "I wouldn't say I was a good teacher," he says. "I just worked very hard."

The first formal chess class he taught was at the New School University in downtown Manhattan. It was an adult education class, and he had no idea what he was doing. And he stood there in front of a hundred people—some of them novices, a few of them grandmasters who had shown up out of pure curiosity, because this was the only chess class anyone could take, anywhere, as far as they knew—and he had no idea how to tailor his message for such a widespread audience. So he prattled on about the history and about how the principles of the game had been developed. Some of his students were women who had never played the game before, who wanted to learn so they could relate to their husbands and boyfriends, and some of them wanted to learn surreptitiously because they were tired of those husbands and boyfriends using chess as a way to keep them down. It was fascinating, all these people wanting to learn his game, and it was only the beginning, because after that even more people began clamoring for private lessons. Pandolfini taught from seven in the morning until one the next morning. He taught children and adults, he taught the deaf and the blind and the disabled, and he taught prisoners, and he taught rock stars. He took on every obligation, and charged well over a hundred dollars an hour to those who could afford it, and gave ten thousand dollars in free lessons to a student who couldn't afford to pay him anything. He was afraid to say no to anyone, for fear that the money would dry up, that this would be his only chance to spread the gospel.

But for Pandolfini, the money never dried up, even after Fischer had disappeared into the ether, and even after chess had once again been relegated to back rooms and private clubs and to a shaded corner of Washington Square Park. Unlike many of the others, expert players who had turned to teaching simply because it was the only way to make money, Pandolfini seemed born for this avocation. In the mid-1980s he began writing books, and in a genre where incoherence often seems like a virtue, his titles stood out. Most are geared toward children and beginners, and they are written in a voice that manages to be both welcoming and authoritative, grounded in the Socratic method. *Pandolfini's Ultimate Guide to Chess* consists entirely of an imaginary conversation between a student and a teacher.

Since he began teaching, he hasn't played competitive chess. It's one or the other, he figures, and because of the role of the subconscious mind, it's impossible to balance both. If you're a tournament player and you start to spend more time teaching, especially if you have a shallow ego (and how many chess players *don't* have shallow egos?), you'll find yourself in competition with your student. If you're a teacher and you start playing competitively, you'll be passive and nonantagonistic. "People can never truly make up for their mindsets," Pandolfini says, and shortly after that, he has to be reminded of what he was just talking about.

♛

In 1985, Pandolfini was serving as the manager of the Manhattan Chess Club and was approached by a man named Faneuil Adams, a direct descendant of Samuel Adams who was also an executive with the Mobil oil company. Adams had a surplus of funds he was willing to put toward improving the dismal state of tournament chess. He came to Pandolfini, and Pandolfini steered him toward scholastic chess. Pandolfini had an absurd ambition, which was to teach everyone in America, an entire generation, the rules and moves of chess. He figured you accomplished this by starting with young people; this was what he was best at, and this was the argument he presented to Fan Adams. "He realized that was a more interesting way to go," Pandolfini says.

So they began to pitch. They went to the Board of Education, and the board didn't really understand what they were proposing, even though it would cost them nothing to wager with Fan Adams's money. It was Pandolfini's job to sell them on chess, and this is something he was born to do, something he had been doing virtually his entire life. He stood in boardrooms and conference rooms, in front of audiences of a hundred or more, and he explained to them how chess could really and truly be utilized as an educational tool. He cited studies and quoted research reports, and when they continued to resist, when they asked for specifics, he pulled out a chessboard and he asked them: How many squares do you see here?

There is an easy answer, of course, which is sixty-four. But what does that prove? The real answer, Pandolfini told them, the answer that a particularly imaginative student might come up with, is that there are infinite answers to this question. The four squares in the center make up another square. Each quarter of the board is a separate square. Each square can be parsed into separate squares, on and on and on and on, ad infinitum. His point was simple: Chess is eminently adaptable. It can be fused and plugged into an infinite number of problems. It is a tool within a tool within a tool, and not just in terms of mathematics and spatial relations, but in terms of *art*. For instance, what's one of the major ways to solve a chess puzzle, Pandolfini asked them. Simple. Switch around the order of the moves; do the second idea first, and do the first idea second. And isn't that kind of pliancy, the ability to juggle two disparate ideas at once, as F. Scott Fitzgerald once said, the chief characteristic of a creative mind?

It took them some time to see these things. Once they did, Pandolfini and Adams thought they had won. But not before Pandolfini had to make one last pitch, to a man who served as the "head of critical thinking" in New York City, a position that may or may not exist anymore.

They met in private. Pandolfini began by espousing the usual argument for chess, that children who play chess tend to do better in school, that a direct correlation has been proven in study after study. To which the man said, "Isn't it true that kids getting special attention in any way *whatsoever* will do better in school?" He was "some big Harvard guy," Pandolfini says. "He kept hitting me with one thing after another. I didn't find out until later that his real passion was for bridge. He wanted to bring bridge into the schools, which was the reason for his objections."

After that, Pandolfini went back to Adams. He told him he didn't think they were going to get the approval. He figured the deal was dead.

The next week Pandolfini was out at dinner with a friend, and he saw the Harvard man sitting at another table. He didn't know what to do, whether to bother saying hello, whether he'd just embarrass himself further by saying anything, whether the Harvard man would even remember him. But he did it. He went up and said hello, and he said, I'm not sure if you remember me, and the Harvard man said, "I remember you very well, Mr. Pandolfini." Then he said to his lunch companion, "This is Bruce Pandolfini. He's the only one I will allow to bring chess into the New York City school system. He's the only one who could answer every one of my questions."

The program was formed under the auspices of the American Chess Foundation, a relatively small, decades-old philanthropic group that had been formed in the 1950s by men on Wall Street to underwrite certain professional players, and which held its meetings in the living rooms of its board members. Pandolfini and Adams's scholastic reincarnation of the ACF began its work in poor neighborhoods, in places like the Bronx and Harlem, under teachers like Doug Bellizzi and Maurice Ashley (who would go on to become the first African-American grandmaster). In 1987, the program had expanded to six schools, and by the early 1990s, chess was being taught in thirty-five schools, and began producing potent results, the sort of rags-to-riches stories that piqued the attention of the media. In 1991, Ashley's team at J.H.S. 43 on 129th Street and Amsterdam Avenue in Central Harlem (which was then a hub of the crack trade) tied for first at the Junior High School national championships, defeating Dalton, where Bruce Pandolfini had landed temporarily as head coach. "Juxtaposing chess with inner-city youth came as a shock to many in the press who were intimidated by the game," Ashley wrote in his 2005 book, *Chess for Success.* "One of the most common questions I was asked, often with a look of befuddled wonder, was, 'How do you motivate these kids to play chess?' I could hear the echo of the underlying assumptions: that chess was akin to rocket science and that minority kids would prefer to play basketball."

Perhaps because it seemed such an improbable tale of success, the sort of feel-good story that makes for the perfect kicker on the local news, Ashley's team (known as the Raging Rooks) became a minor sensation. They made television appearances, they did a live radio interview at the Apollo Theater, and they were invited to a victory party at the Upper East Side town house of *Penthouse* publisher Bob Guccione, who helped pay for their trip to nationals. Their story appeared on the front page of *The New York Times*. Two of Ashley's best players eventually got scholarships to private schools, and afterward, the money began coming to the American Chess Foundation in waves. Ted Field, of the Marshall Field family, held a benefit dinner at the Plaza Hotel that raised two hundred thousand dollars. A philanthropist named Lewis Cullman donated a million dollars, and became chairman of the board.

By 1994, the program had reached a thousand students. Five years later, that number was thirty-eight thousand, and the name had been changed from the American Chess Foundation to Chess-in-the-Schools. CIS became a massive operation incorporating nearly four dozen teachers and twenty administrative positions, a specific curriculum, teaching materials, tournaments, in-school programs, after-school programs, and sponsorship money for teams to travel to national tournaments. By 2003, the contributions to CIS had reached three and a half million dollars (which was spread among 160 public schools, all in underprivileged neighborhoods), Pandolfini had moved on to other things, and an experienced fund-raiser and entirely inexperienced chess player, Marley Kaplan, had been hired to head the program.

Kaplan is a small dark-haired woman who could probably recite the CIS fund-raising spiel in her sleep. Because of her background, because she is not a chess player, she has evoked a certain amount of resentment among some of the chess teachers and administrators who form the core of the program. They are thankful to have jobs, and disdainful of the inevitable bureaucracy.

For reasons that seem mostly due to that bureaucracy, CIS has no relationship with the Right Move foundation (at one point, Goldhirsch says, his people started offering some classes in city schools and CIS objected, saying the Right Move was "infringing on their territory"). Despite all of that, CIS has become an unquestioned success, the first of its kind, and its formula has been replicated in other cities. All of its schools are Title I (a government designation reserved for schools populated mostly by underprivileged children), and nearly all are elementary and junior-high schools like I.S. 318, the school that produced five members of Murrow's team.

Every Thursday afternoon during the school year, CIS also holds an alumni program, a loose amalgam of tutoring and mentoring and instruction and college preparation for its high-school-aged students. The best thing about the Thursday afternoon meetings, if you ask Willy or Oscar or Nile, is the presence of some of the city's top teachers, like Jennifer Shahade and her brother Greg, and like Miron Sher, a Russian grandmaster. The worst part is the constant prodding from Sarah Pitari, a young administrator who handles the "college bound" portion of the program (she also holds separate academic sessions), whose job is to push CIS's former students toward higher education. It can be a lonely job, complicated by indifference from both students and their parents, by the fact that many of them would rather while away their hours playing blitz than even think about taking the SATs. So go Sarah's interactions with Willy and Oscar, who have failed so many classes over their years at Murrow that their chances of graduating on time are looking slimmer and slimmer, and there is only so much Sarah can do without holding their hands and leading them into class by herself.

"Murrow doesn't need us," Kaplan says. She's sitting in a conference room at the CIS headquarters on Eighth Avenue, a neatly apportioned full-floor loft that resembles the headquarters of a midsized dot-com operation. An enlarged photo of Bill Clinton visiting the offices looms on the wall behind her. One gets the feeling that Kaplan has spent a great deal of time in this very room, making studied pitches to corporate sponsors. But because its mission is to serve poor neighborhoods, Murrow simply doesn't fit into their plans. "They're not a Title One school," she says. "And they already have a chess program. They don't need us."

It doesn't matter, of course, that the majority of the chess players on Murrow's team are kids who attended Title I schools, and it doesn't matter that the only reason they're attending Murrow in the first place is because CIS led them to this point through chess. CIS offers its older members a lifeline through the alumni program. Whether they decide to take advantage of it is up to them, really.

And the lack of a relationship certainly doesn't matter to Eliot Weiss, who, because of his ties to the Right Move, has made clear his disdain for the bureaucracy of Chess-in-the-Schools, and who, in these past few months, has been doggedly pursuing a mission of his own.

EIGHT

♕

ALL THE PRESIDENT'S MEN

THIS WHOLE TRIP HAD BEEN HIS GRANDEST PUBLICITY CAMPAIGN OF ALL, the product of a stream of phone calls and faxes and letters written to congressmen and senators and community relations officers, to anyone on Pennsylvania Avenue who would listen to him without hanging up the phone: *I coach a chess team, you see . . .*

They had already met with councilmen and assemblymen and representatives and senators and governors. But this . . . this was the last great frontier of the political meet-and-greet; if he could pull this one off, well, then he had done it all. If he could do this, at the age of fifty-one, after more than twenty years of selling lapel pins and holding bake sales to keep this team alive, maybe he could start thinking about retirement. To win an audience with the president of the United States, even *this* president—it was worth the effort, the calls made in the after-school hours from the wall phone in his classroom, speaking over and over to Melissa from the White House and Nathan from the White House and Lisa from the White House. Every two weeks, he called again, and was passed along to someone else. This did not deter him. They *were* the national champions, after all, weren't they? And didn't the perks of a national championship in virtually every other sport include an audience with the president? Didn't the president meet with people who had done much less than what these boys had done? It was still a long shot, he knew, but this was Mr. Weiss's trope, the pitch he kept on making. And perhaps it wasn't entirely altruistic—maybe, in the moment, he appreciated these visits more than his players did—but someday, he knew, they would look back at the photographs and realize what they had accomplished, and how lucky they had been just to get there.

♛

The woman who saved Eliot Weiss from beggary and public appeals doesn't have a surname. For months, he won't even reveal her first name, only that she had started funding the program a few years back, fulfilling every request Mr. Weiss made to her, and had been doing it ever since. Nobody except Mr. Weiss knows Rita's last name, and Rita is hesitant to mention it even off the record.

Rita is a diminutive Upper East Side society lady in her late seventies, with tufted gray hair and sharp blue eyes. On the day the city championships are held, Rita usually makes her annual appearance before the team. Most of the time, she shows up between rounds, on her way to a Sunday theater matinee with her brother and a friend. ("I have no idea what we're ever going to see," she says. "I just go along.")

Here is what can be revealed about Rita: She was born and raised in New York, and majored in math at NYU. She became a high-school teacher (she taught, for a while, at DeWitt Clinton, in the Bronx) and also worked at several colleges. She married, had two children, and after her husband died, she decided to funnel some of the money he'd left behind toward philanthropic causes. She started giving to a ballet school in London where many of the kids can't afford to pay for lessons.

And then one day a few years back, Rita was in a taxi on her way uptown, and the driver had the radio on, and a news station was broadcasting a report, no doubt cribbed from one of the daily newspapers, about a high-school chess team in need of money in order to play at the national tournament, which that year was being held in California. They were talking about holding small fund-raisers here and there, about selling brownies and cookies and muffins and candy, and Rita thought, "How much money can you make from a bake sale?"

So she called the radio station and got the name of the high school; she'd never heard of Murrow, but she called the principal and the principal put her in touch with Mr. Weiss and she told him, "I'll pay for your trip." Soon after, she had rescued him from fifteen years of public pleading, and she has paid for every trip and every possible expense since then, to state tournaments and national tournaments, and if it were to happen, she would pay for their trip to Washington, D.C., to visit the president. Even now, though, Mr. Weiss refuses to ask her for money outright, so that every time they speak, Rita has to say, "What do you need money for? What's coming up?"

The whole business of kids playing chess fascinates Rita. She's never played before, and her late husband dabbled in the game a little, but he wasn't very good. But these children, my word! She could stand here for hours and watch them play, except that, really, this isn't her place. She prefers to be invisible, to write her checks and slip off to her Sunday matinee virtually unnoticed, after delivering a brief statement to the team, which goes something like this:

"Thank you for winning. Because I don't like to lose."

♛

And then one day, just like that, the White House called Eliot Weiss back.

So on a Wednesday in mid-December, a month after George W. Bush won reelection over John Kerry despite losing the New York City vote by a three-to-one margin, the Murrow chess team and its entourage (Weiss's son and daughter), accompanied by a Democratic senator, Charles Schumer, and a Democratic congressman, Anthony Weiner—two more men Mr. Weiss had needled and needled while attempting to set up this day—trundled into the Oval Office to meet the forty-third president of the United States of America. It was an abbreviated visit, of course, part of a three-day tour of D.C., complete with trips to the Smithsonian and the National Mall, and how it went really depended upon your point of view. Perhaps this is why, in the photos of that moment, pictures that would eventually wind up on the plaster walls of apartment buildings in minority-dominated neighborhoods where the man at the center would not be particularly welcome, the top boards on the top chess team in the nation wear expressions that can be described only as uncomfortable, verging on bored.

Still, for the briefest of moments, the doors to the Oval Office closed and they were alone, or at least, as alone as a group of multiethnic teenagers from Brooklyn could ever get with the president of the United States. He made small talk. He asked them where they were from. *Puerto Rico,* Oscar told him, and then, the way Oscar tells it, "He just gave me a blank stare." Then the president—the president of the United States!—asked Ilya what it was like to captain a winning team, and Ilya didn't really know what he was supposed to say. Nobody did, not Willy (who had boasted to a reporter from the *Bay News* that he was going to ask "about his No Child Left Behind Act and how he came up with the idea"), not Alex, not even Sal. And certainly not Nile Smith, who wore a suit that appeared about three sizes too large, the pants drooping at his thighs like a pair of carpenter jeans, and who, in the photo that appeared in the *Daily News* the next day, is the only one who has his eyes cast toward the floor. It was an act born not of defiance, but of pure and overwhelming shyness.

Nile and his family live on the fourth floor of a five-story walk-up in a mostly black section of Crown Heights, a Brooklyn neighborhood that gained a certain amount of notoriety in 1991, when in the midst of a series of racially charged riots a Hasidic Jew named Yankel Rosenbaum was stabbed to death by a sixteen-year-old African-American boy, Lemrick Nelson Jr. It was a crime that exposed the city's underlying racial tension for a new generation, and arguably paved the way for a Republican, Rudy Giuliani, to become the mayor of New York City.

Nile's apartment is part of the Sterling/St. John's houses, a city-subsidized co-op a few blocks from the Utica Avenue subway stop, near a business strip occupied mostly by Caribbean restaurants and African braiding and nail salons with names like "Hair It Is." On a Saturday afternoon, a cluster of people are gathered on and around the front steps of Nile's building, including one woman who appears to be standing sentry at the door.

Nile is easy to misjudge, especially when that judgment is based strictly on appearance. Most days, he wears his hair in cornrows, and he wears do-rags and baseball caps with the purchase labels still affixed to the brim, and he favors oversized athletic jerseys and baggy jeans and Nike sneakers. He can go hours without uttering a single word. People who don't play chess tend to have a preconceived notion of what a chess player looks like, and Nile is not it. (You wonder if, upon bursting into the Oval Office that day expecting to find the geeks he'd avoided at Yale and instead coming upon a group comprised largely of underrepresented minorities—blacks, Puerto Ricans, Eastern European immigrants—treading on the presidential seal, George W. Bush felt the same way.)

Nile answers the door to his apartment wearing a pair of bright red cutoff sweatpants and a white T-shirt that appears to have suffered a long and difficult existence. His forehead is beaded with sweat. His father, Ken, is standing behind him, shirtless—they've been lifting weights all day long and their phone service was shut off and Nile's AOL Internet service was too expensive to maintain, so they've essentially been isolated from the outside world.

Nile's father is broad-shouldered and has a shaved head and a thin goatee. His wife is on the job (she cleans aircraft at John F. Kennedy Airport, which is where Ken used to work as a baggage handler), and in the meantime, the boys have reconfigured the living room into a home gym, outfitted with a weight bench and an old stationary bike and treadmill that Ken acquired through a friend of his. The couches have been pushed into a corner near the television set. The floor is plain white linoleum; on a wall above where the stationary bike stands now, there is a pencil sketch of Malcolm X and another of Martin

Luther King, with *I Have a Dream* written underneath. They're taking a break, and Nile—who was named after the river—has already destroyed his father in a game of chess, and now he's eating pizza and studying music videos.

Ken is trying to build Nile's upper body. He thinks Nile has the same frame as he once did, that he can build up quickly if he puts his mind to it. "He's gonna be so big, and so strong," Ken says. "But it's gonna take time. I tell him it takes ten years to get that kind of build." He'd like to see Nile build up his body in the same way he's built up his mind through chess. These days, Ken works at a print shop in midtown Manhattan, and he's laminated workouts from the pages of *Men's Health* magazine, and they're working through those. At the moment, Nile is just lifting with an empty bar, so he can get acquainted with the mechanics and the range of motion. When asked how he feels about this regimen, Nile gives a noncommittal shrug.

Ken's older brother, Charles, was a strong chess player, and Ken used to go to the Village to watch him play. He was never as good as Charles, whose rating was around 2000, and whose nickname was "Dark Angel." "He used to take care of a girl whose family owned a chess shop," Ken says. At one point, he invested in a one-hundred-dollar Aztec Indian chessboard, the same one he uses to lose to his son these days. "I'll try to do something unorthodox, and he'll notice anything on the board, and his dad will be talking and talking over the board, while he's quiet," Ken says. "And then the game'll be over. He'll beat me in two or three moves."

Ken is absolutely sure that Nile used to watch him play when he was too young to understand the game, and that this is where he first picked up chess, although Nile insists he didn't learn until he started attending I.S. 318 in Williamsburg, and took classes with the chess teacher there, Elizabeth Vicary, the same woman who discovered Willy and Oscar and Shawn and Dalphe. Ken, in fact, went to 318, as well, as did his brother (who has since moved to Alabama) and his sister, Cookie, who went to Howard University and now works at a museum in California. Their mother worked at the post office.

Nile's mother and father met in Brooklyn. She was from Bush-wick, and she was on her way to a typing school, and he started talk-ing to her, and "the rest is history." Since then, Ken has held a variety of jobs. He was a messenger and he worked in a mailroom and he worked as a receptionist at an employee benefits agency in Manhattan, where the money was better than anything he'd made before or since. He spent twelve years there, and wore a suit to work every day, and used to work out for free at the employee health club. Times have got-ten harder since then, but he's doing his best. For a while, when Nile was younger, they lived in the Lindsay Park co-ops in Williamsburg, right near I.S. 318, and then, a few years ago, they moved here, though Ken's still not sure about this neighborhood. (He worries often about his car, a 1985 BMW 725i that he keeps parked on the street.) At one point while he's sitting in the living room, someone in an adjacent building throws a towel out the window, and for a second, Ken won-ders if there's a body inside. "There's always people hanging out on our stoop," he says (later that evening, they're playing games of dice). "But I've gotten used to it by now. I figure there's no park near here, so they don't have no place else to go."

Unlike many of his teammates, Nile, who's a sophomore, is a con-scientious student. He goes to virtually every one of his classes, and he studies for his tests, and he's thinking about becoming a stockbroker someday. He's got a head for math, which is perhaps why he was able to pick up chess so quickly. One of his first teachers at I.S. 318, Jen Shahade, noticed it right away: He started playing later, but he caught on faster than most of the other kids. "Sometimes," she says, "you can just see it." Now, even though he has only about three years of expe-rience, Nile's a strong tactical player with a rating around 1600, al-though he has a tendency to get intimidated against higher-rated players, when he has a feeling they can read his thoughts. At last year's seven-round national tournament, he scored three points, which felt like something of a disappointment.

Nile first won money playing chess on December 1, 2002. He knows this date because the check remains uncashed, placed next to his other trophies and a series of laminated photographs and newspaper articles, on an end table in the corner of the living room, near the portrait of Martin Luther King Jr. The check, from the Right Move, is for $3.57. It sat on the table for more than a year, and at some point Ken figured what the hell, he'd try to cash it, but the bank didn't let him. "Then he started bringing home more checks," Ken says. "And I realized he could make money from this."

But it was about something more than that. Ken had never really left Brooklyn, had never even been on a plane despite all that time spent at the airport, and here was his son, fifteen years old, spending a week in Milwaukee, a week in Dallas, a week in Florida, all for chess. One day a few weeks earlier, Nile had brought home the photo of himself with Hillary Clinton. Ken brought it to the print shop to get it laminated, and they could hardly believe it. Ken's son with a United States senator? Turn it over, they told him. Let's see the backing. Let's see if that's a real photo or just a novelty.

♛

From the *Daily News,* December 16, 2004:

By Kenneth Bazinet
Daily News Washington Bureau

WASHINGTON—Eight chess champs from Brooklyn's Edward R. Murrow High School were applauded by President Bush yesterday.

. . . Bragging about Kotlyanskiy, Rep. Anthony D. Weiner (D-Brooklyn) said outside the White House, "He can think through 10, 12 or 15 moves in his head."

"No, he can't," Oscar says. "Ain't nobody can do that."

"Even Kasparov can't do that," Willy says.

A month later, on a frigid Sunday afternoon in mid-January, at the last Right Move tournament before the city championships, they're still wringing laughs out of this one. This qualifies as politically inspired hyperbole of the type Weiner will unveil in great shovelfuls during his unsuccessful bid for the Democratic mayoral nomination nine months from now. It's the sort of assumption that the uninformed tend to make about elite chess players, as if they have the power to calculate every possibility of a game from beginning to end. Grandmasters, in certain cases, can think ahead eight or nine moves on a specific line or tactic. Players of Ilya's caliber, if they can see three moves ahead—your next move, your opponent's next move, and your ensuing move—are often in good shape. The rest of the game is often dictated by feel; once you know the fundamentals of the game, you see a position and you can eliminate the moves that don't make sense. Bruce Pandolfini calls the three-move maxim "The Rule of the Three." If you can do that, you can be a 1600- to 1800-rated player, no problem, which is what Ilya and Oscar and Willy and Nile and Dalphe all are. It does not require a great amount of genius, but it does require an ability to focus and think ahead and consider the consequences of one's actions. "It's very simple," Pandolfini says. "It's nothing profound. It's not what people think."

♛

The Oval Office was fine, Oscar says, but it was hardly the highlight of the trip. There were other things going on, and these are the things Oscar would prefer to recount. Like the fact that he won some money. Enough money, in fact, to sustain his existence while in D.C. He left town with ten dollars in his pocket (his parents had nothing more to give him), and he spent six of that on a Subway sandwich and the other four on a new deck of cards. Then, on the short flight from New York to Washington, he won twenty-two dollars from one of his teammates, then took a bundle more while he was there. He's also accumulated a couple of hundred dollars in winnings through a friend's account on a poker Web site, and it's all so easy, and so much more lucrative than chess could ever be.

The crowd at the Right Move is more dense than usual this week, because it's almost crunch time, because this is one of the last opportunities to prepare for the cities, which are in two weeks. Willy splits the one-hundred-dollar first-place prize in the sixty-six-person open division with two others: a senior at Molloy, a Catholic school, and Eugene Belilovsky, a squat boy with a 1759 rating who's the No. 3 board at Stuyvesant, which is the only school with even the slightest chance of upending Murrow at the cities. (Stuyvesant finished third at the high-school nationals in 2004.)

The four newbies, the sophomores who joined chess club this year—Rex, Renwick, Robert, and Adalberto—are also here, making their final preparations for the city championships. They've never played in a *real* tournament before; they have no idea what to expect. They'll play in the junior-varsity division at cities, but they're still feeling a little bit lost, like outsiders crashing an exclusive party. They've come to the game so late, years after most of their teammates fell into it, and they've had only the most basic of instruction from Mr. Weiss, who usually leaves them to their own devices on Thursday afternoons, who's usually busy washing his chalkboards or grading papers or heading down to the computer room to do some programming work, for which he gets paid a little extra cash to supplement his teacher's salary.

"I'm still playing chess on Yahoo! a little, but that's about it," Renwick says. Clearly, so has Rex, a tall Asian boy with a perpetual look of bewilderment, who wins three of his four games and becomes the first of the newbies to win a medal at a Right Move tournament (sixth place, under-800 division). Still, the four of them have seen the veterans, and they've seen Alex and Sal, the top boards, the masterly duo, and they cannot imagine playing at such a level, and they have no idea how to go about catching up.

———

The sign appears at Murrow sometime in late December, on walls and doors and in stairwells, printed in stark black lettering: AS OF JANUARY 10, 2005, STUDENTS WILL BE REQUIRED TO LEAVE THE BUILDING AT THE END OF THE SCHOOL DAY, UNLESS PARTICIPATING IN A PRE-APPROVED AFTER-SCHOOL PROGRAM. DOCUMENTATION WILL BE REQUIRED IN ORDER TO STAY IN THE BUILDING.

It could be said that this is one of the sacrifices of the modern educational system, that freedoms are often curtailed in the interest of safety. But this is Murrow, and Murrow has never fit the mold. Murrow was always different. Murrow was a safe school, with freedom to roam and freedom to goof off. But this is the new reality at a school marred by overcrowding, and victimized by its own lack of power. There are no metal detectors, but security has been upgraded by the new principal, Anthony Lodico, and more deans have been hired to help with discipline problems (and to make sure those kids who are hanging out in the hallway aren't *supposed* to be in class), and students are required to swipe their ID cards when they show up in the morning.

Back when it was recognized as an elite school, back when Bruckner was at the height of his powers and Murrow was drawing nationwide attention for its system, it was easy enough to *encourage* kids who didn't fit with the system, who simply weren't mature enough to handle the freedom at Murrow, to transfer to other schools. There were places for them to go. "But now the kids can't move anymore," says Ron Weiss, the school's longtime assistant principal. "Opportunities have been thwarted. I can have a parent begging me to transfer their kid, but I have no place to send them."

This, in part, could be traced back to the president. It could be traced back to the president because his No Child Left Behind Act mandates the closing of underperforming schools. And in Brooklyn, if one of those schools is closed, well, where are those students sent? They're sent to a stable (and already overcrowded) institution like Murrow; because the trend in New York City under Mayor Michael Bloomberg is toward smaller, more specialized institutions, large schools like Murrow become reservoirs for overflow. All of this is part of the radical attempts at reform by Bloomberg, who abolished the 160-year-old Board of Education, took control of the schools himself, and hired a litigator named Joel Klein as chancellor. It was Klein who set in motion a small-schools initiative, starting nearly a hundred and fifty specialized schools while phasing out many larger, nonworking schools.

But what about the larger schools that still worked?

This was a problem that Klein hadn't foreseen: The initiative "foundered during his first term, when it set in motion a slew of 'unintended consequences,' the most visible of which was overcrowding of several large high schools," wrote John Heilemann in *New York* magazine.

In Murrow's case, for those first few years, it didn't matter if the transfers fit in with the system or not. Two years earlier, Murrow had been forced to take two hundred kids, most of whom were deflected there from closing schools. Around that same time, on September 30, 2003, according to police, a sixteen-year-old boy named Jose Diaz, who was not a student at Murrow, found his way inside the school. He was interrupted in the midst of a conversation with a female student by a freshman named Allen Bryant. Moments later, police said, Diaz stabbed Bryant in the back, and then he fled. "Murrow really is a safe school," a student named Anna wrote on Gothamist, a New York City Web log, on the day of the stabbing. "Things like that definetly [sic] don't happen everyday [sic]. But they do happen in general and it's just awful how easy it is to bring a weapon into school. The results are awful too."

So the problem is this: How does a school made great by its acceptance of personal freedom go about curtailing freedom? "Keep giving me No Child Left Behind kids, kids whose schools are closing, and put them in an environment like this," Ron Weiss says. "You'll watch this school go down the tubes."

You still won't witness many blatant acts of truancy at Murrow, unless you count the kids sneaking smokes in the parking lot across the street, or someone writing *Got Pot?* on a desk in Eliot Weiss's classroom. Most days after school, the bulk of the student body floods peacefully toward the subway turnstiles at Avenue M, and the first-floor hallways are clotted with disabled special-ed students. The easy solution to any serious problems, of course, would be to install metal detectors at the front entrance, but that would render Murrow into an altogether different type of school, a bastardized version of what it was born to be. How can a feeling of freedom prevail amid a lock-down?

This is not something the new principal would prefer to see happen. He insists that most of the kids haven't complained about the subtle changes he's made, that the courtyard—now off-limits to students—was a petri dish for bad (and borderline illegal) behavior. And he'd like to maintain Murrow's essence, despite all the outside pressures. If he had been brought in, after nearly two decades as a drama teacher and administrator at Port Richmond High School on Staten Island, to turn Murrow into, say, Midwood, then he wouldn't have taken the job in the first place. He'll admit it: The whole Murrow system scared the hell out of him when he first happened upon it, just as it had shaken Ron Weiss thirty years before. "Things had to be tightened up," Lodico says. "But the whole philosophy they built this school upon? I really believe it can still work."

♛

A week before the cities, Sal wanders into the chess club meeting, appearing lost and disoriented. He's still trying to catch up with all the school he missed, and he's hoping Eliot Weiss can speak to his teachers, perhaps afford him a temporary reprieve. "I have a lab I need to make up right now," Sal says, "or I'm going to flunk." That's fine, Mr. Weiss tells him, and then he shows him a copy of a *New York Times* article that appeared the same week, about players studying online databases of previously played games to determine each other's tendencies. Before the state championship and the national championship, Mr. Weiss tells him, when Murrow might actually have competition, they're going to study their opponents' tendencies.

It is a notion to which Sal does not react with enthusiasm. But then, that's been a trend lately. Ever since returning, Sal has felt lost and overwhelmed, and his demeanor has been erratic.

"I couldn't care less about him," Ilya had said a few days earlier. His description of Sal's behavior while in Washington borders on the unbelievable: that when he was interviewed by a local television crew in D.C. about their visit to the White House, the first thing he said was, "I didn't want to come here in the first place." That he spent much of the trip yearning to get back home, and that at one point they held a team meeting and discussed throwing Sal off the team, but Mr. Weiss convinced them to give him another chance. That Sal kept saying, "You *need* me." And it was true, they *did* need him in order to win, and maybe this was just Sal's way of posturing, his way of reasserting his worth during this time of crisis.

"I don't know what it was," Ilya says. "But he's going to have a fun time getting to Saratoga for the state championships. Because he's not riding in my car."

♛

"You know when the cities are?" Mr. Weiss says.

"Yes, yes, yes," Sal says. "I have the flyer at home."

"When are they?"

Sal gives him a puzzled look, as if he cannot quite determine the precise meaning of the question, as if he is shocked—shocked!—that someone would require confirmation of his knowledge of such facile information.

"January twenty-seventh and twenty-eighth?" he says.

"No," Mr. Weiss says.

"No, right. January twenty-eighth and twenty-ninth."

"It's only one day for high schools," Mr. Weiss says.

"Right," Sal says. "Right."

Silence.

"January thirtieth," Mr. Weiss says.

"Right, right, right," Sal says. He curls his upper lip, and then he edges out the door before Mr. Weiss can corner him about something else. He has to go. Wherever Sal is, there's always someplace else he could be. But then, he knows where he's needed. Even if he doesn't know exactly when.

PART TWO

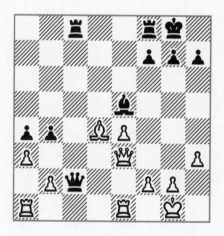

MIDDLE GAME

NINE

THE THIRTY-NINTH ANNUAL GREATER NEW YORK SCHOLASTIC TEAM AND INDIVIDUAL CHESS CHAMPIONSHIPS

Manhattan

Current USCF Ratings:

Sal Bercys	2419
Alex Lenderman	2358
Shawn Martinez	1920
Oscar Santana	1763
Willy Edgard	1681
Ilya Kotlyanskiy	1675
Dalphe Morantus	1586
Nile Smith	1572

A vertical village, where every vote of the citizens sends two thousand servants scurrying to satisfy their daily whims, is making history in the heart of New York. This town, which rises instead of spreads, reaches 43 stories toward the skies at Thirty-fourth Street and Eighth Avenue—The New Yorker, Manhattan's largest and tallest hotel. The New Yorker is a vertical city, for without stretching a point to make a phrase, it includes everything that any town has—and in many aspects, much more.

—From a 1938 brochure

In a hallway on the third floor of the New Yorker Hotel, amid the signs urging silence and order and propriety (SHHH! KIDS PLAYING CHESS!), the boys of Manhattan's exclusive academies, the boys of Dalton and Columbia Grammar and Preparatory School and Buckley and the Browning School, the progeny of some of the wealthiest families in America, are performing a timeless primary-school aria, which goes something like this:

PPPPHHHHMTTTTTT . . . PPPPHHHHMMMTTTTTT . . . PPPPHHHRRRTTTTTTTMMMPPPHHHTT . . .

Here is the paradoxical nature of the city chess championships and, for that matter, of virtually any chess tournament that happens to involve young children: At the merchandise tables, manned by members of the Rochester Chess Center, they sell dense manuals and intricate DVDs offering instruction in the Caro-Kann and the Grunfeld defenses, right next to boxes of Super Balls and Silly Putty and sputtering whoopee cushions that form the percussion instruments in a symphony of flatulence. Inside the closed doors of the Grand Ballroom and the Crystal Ballroom, to observe the absolute silence of several hundred first-graders is to bear witness to a low-grade miracle. And in the public areas, the shouting and drooling and weeping masses toss footballs and trip down the stairs and hurl uneaten bits of bagel at each other and mimic bathroom noises in abundance and behave in the way you'd expect first-graders to behave when they've been shuttered indoors on an otherwise fine weekend afternoon.

In order to accommodate all ages, the city championships are a full weekend event. The first day, Saturday, is given to the junior-high sections (ninth grade and under) and the primary sections (third grade and under); the elementary sections (sixth grade and under) and the high-school sections (twelfth grade and under) are held on Sunday (higher-rated players are welcome to "play up" into another section— for instance, a seventh-grader with an especially high ranking might try to play in the high-school section). And since many of the A-list private schools in New York have massive chess programs aimed at the lower grades, Saturday is largely their day. The best schools, the most prestigious schools, are set up in their own private team rooms (an expense of several hundred dollars that no public school could afford), and they are tutored by men like Bruce Pandolfini, who coaches at Browning, a $29,000-a-year, hundred-year-old academy on the Upper East Side, and Joel Benjamin, the former New York City and three-time U.S. champion, who teaches at Columbia Grammar and Prep, a $26,000-a-year, 240-year-old institution on the Upper West Side.

"If you have any problems during a game at all," another of the Columbia coaches is saying to a small army of children in electric-blue Columbia Knights T-shirts, "you shouldn't let it go and complain about it after the game. Don't let it get to you if they're doing something abnormal. Pay attention to your game. Do *not* get into an argument with your opponent; don't waste your energy."

And then he repeats it once more, in case they couldn't hear him above the din in the room, above a raging game of Monkey in the Middle taking place in the hallway of a hotel that once played host to senators and film stars and big-band legends: *"I don't want you arguing with your opponent."*

The New Yorker Hotel, a forty-story Art Deco skyscraper on the west side of Manhattan near Penn Station and Madison Square Garden, was erected for $22 million back in 1930. At the time, it was the largest hotel in the city and the second-largest hotel in the world. It was sparkling and state-of-the-art, with elevators that traveled at eight hundred feet a minute, radio speakers in each room, and a forty-two-chair barber shop purported to be the largest on earth. In those early days, the New Yorker hosted celebrities and luminaries like Spencer Tracy and Joan Crawford and Senator Huey Long. Nikola Tesla, the scientist and inventor, lived in room 3327 for the final ten years of his life. Benny Goodman, Glenn Miller, Tommy Dorsey, and all the giants of the Big Band Era played the Terrace Room in the forties and fifties, and the Brooklyn Dodgers used it as a headquarters during the 1941 World Series, which they lost to the New York Yankees.

But not long after Hilton purchased the hotel in 1953, its luster wore off, and people stopped coming, and in 1972, as the surrounding neighborhood decayed, the New Yorker was shut down. The French Polyclinic Hospital attempted to buy it and convert it into a hospital and medical school, but their plans fell through, and in 1976, the same year the Reverend Sun Myung Moon declared at a Yankee Stadium rally that "New York has become a jungle of immorality and depravity," his Unification Church bought the New Yorker for $5.5 million and renamed it the World Mission Center. It became church headquarters for the next eighteen years, and its members (many of them single missionaries) used it a residence, as a gathering place, as a meeting spot for men and women who consented to mass marriages performed across the street at Madison Square Garden, and as "the hub of church activities," according to one ex-Moonie.

Of course, Moon's attempt to recruit new members and make his church the world's "third central religion," behind Judaism and Christianity, didn't last long before it receded into the cultural woodwork. By 1984, Moon was serving a thirteen-month prison term for income tax evasion, and in 1994 he and his church decided to reopen the New Yorker as a one-thousand-room hotel. Five years later, the New Yorker, though still owned by Moon, became part of the Ramada hotel chain and a temporary refuge for another awkward religion, a gathering place for the oddballs who play competitive chess. For a brief period before its death in 2002, the Manhattan Chess Club was headquartered here, in Suite 1521. Today, the city championships are held in the New Yorker on a regular basis, along with fur sales and vintage jewelry bazaars and whatever else brings in revenue.

Much of the action on Saturday takes place in the Grand Ballroom, on the second floor, in the same massive space where Reverend Moon once delivered his speeches, watched over by his disciples from the balcony high above. The ballroom is still painted a stark shade of white, and garish French chandeliers refract pink sparks of light, and it's into this room that parents lead their children before each of the five rounds, grasping their hands, ushering them to the proper table, and reminding them to think before they move, reminding them to write down their moves, reminding them . . .

"PARENTS, WOULD YOU PLEASE LEAVE THE ROOM. PARENTS, COACHES, PLEASE LEAVE THE ROOM."

The opening anecdote of *Searching for Bobby Fischer* describes a scene at the 1984 National Elementary Chess Championship, in which a lone father began whispering moves to his son, prompting a number of parents to start whispering at each other, prompting their children (six, seven, and eight years old) to call for quiet, and finally prompting a pair of frustrated fathers to fall into a fistfight.

It is, of course, the youngest and most vulnerable competitors who tend to inspire such protectivist feelings in their parents, and it is the young ones who, for much of the past two decades, have been purposefully sequestered by tournament directors and officials. The hard part is not making a decision like this (although one can imagine the outcry if this happened in, say, a suburban youth soccer league). The hard part is getting the parents to leave the room once the tournament begins, and then keeping them out. This is largely the duty of a smallish woman inside the door, whose job is simply to keep it closed. "If you could," she says, once, twice, three times, "*please* move away from the door."

Once the parents are gone, once they've returned to their newspapers and their books and the endless game of waiting on the other side of the door, the silence comes rather quickly. The tables are set up in long rows, and when a tournament official gives the OK to start, there is only the clicking of time clocks and the clacking of pieces. Here is a boy standing over his board, surveying the position, and here are boys with baseball caps turned backward and angled sideways. They tap their pencils in their hands, and they cram erasers into their nostrils, and they scratch behind their ears. For five minutes, the games go on, a hundred at a time, and then the first one ends: A blond girl (one of the only females in the room) wearing a white turtleneck slides her queen toward the back rank, takes a pawn from her male opponent, and whispers "Checkmate." She raises her hand, and over comes a man named Harold Stenzel to verify the position. When it's finished, the boy attempts to fold up his pieces within the rolled-up foam-rubber board they've been playing with, but it crumples in his fingers and the pieces rain onto the ballroom's plush carpet with a series of dull thuds.

"You've got to fold it in four pieces," Stenzel whispers. "Like a crepe."

Stenzel has been officiating chess tournaments for more than two decades. This may or may not have something to do with the fact that he happens to resemble a roadie at a Journey concert. He has a blond mullet and a matching mustache, and his pants are pulled up high above his waist, and he's wearing a bright yellow T-shirt. He teaches chess at schools and in private lessons on Long Island, and to make ends meet and support his children he works as a piano tuner. He also claims to have "the highest level of tournament-directing credentials in the country." Exactly what this entails remains a mystery, but Stenzel has been at this, the business of directing chess tournaments, for much of his life, and considering it is not exactly a lucrative business, his dedication is weirdly admirable.

"You have to show a little more latitude with the little kids," Stenzel says. This is because they're often easily intimidated: One kid showed up this morning, saw the size of the crowd in the ballroom, and decided he didn't want to play. Also, young kids often don't know the rules, and even if they do, they tend to want to take advantage of them. For instance, if they make a bad move, they may attempt to make it back by "adjusting" a piece. In common tournament parlance, this is a compulsive gesture in which a player moves a certain piece to the center of its respective square in order to neaten the board. Among the younger kids, it takes on an added dimension: Pieces magically shift from square to square. This is often their best attempt at cheating, and most of the time, Harold Stenzel says, they're not very good at it.

Meanwhile, the woman manning the door is working to beat down the masses. After fifteen minutes, twenty minutes, thirty minutes, the parents begin lining up outside the doorway to the Grand Ballroom, as if waiting for their luggage to flop onto the carousel at the airport baggage claim. "It's awfully noisy in there for your kids," says the woman at the door. "Could you please keep it down?"

By force of sheer numbers, the private schools dominate most of the primary-school divisions on Saturday, and in the junior-high varsity division, the Collegiate School (Upper West Side, tuition $25,000), led by a former national primary-school champion named Sarkis Agaian, defeats I.S. 318 by two and a half points. And by the time the trophies are awarded on Saturday evening, the children of private schools, the sons and daughters of scions of industry, are wrestling on the floor and hurling projectiles of varied shapes and sizes and locking each other up in vicious half-nelsons.

"But did you notice," one public-school teacher says, "that it's mainly these private school kids who are running around like lunatics?"

♛

On Sunday morning, the day Murrow will defend its run of three consecutive city championships, the participants begin showing up at the New Yorker at a little past nine, an hour before the first round is scheduled to start. Teams are arriving from the suburban wilds of Long Island and New Jersey and Connecticut (while this is technically the "city championship," it is open to regional teams as well), and they're staking out their territory, engulfing the mezzanine on the second floor with massive piles of down jackets and rectangular carrying cases with the pliable foam boards rolled up inside like yoga mats.

Ilya and Willy are already here, in the third-floor Skittles Room, and they've commandeered a table by the time Mr. Weiss arrives, his wife and children in tow. There is no money in Weiss's budget for him to reserve his own team room; he wouldn't dare ask Rita to spring for such an extravagance.

Nothing at a chess tournament ever starts precisely on time, and so the first-round pairings don't go up until 10:15, on the bulletin board in the hallway near the elevators, while kids are still straggling through the revolving doors of the New Yorker from the subway. Shawn Martinez, Murrow's No. 3 board, still isn't here, and nobody knows where he is. This news is not entirely surprising, given Shawn's penchant for flaking out. He lives according to his own timetable. He does his own thing. "I was on the phone with him last night, and then he put me on hold for ten minutes," Oscar says. "I have no idea where he went."

"He did the same thing to me," Nile says.

Nile and Dalphe Morantus, Murrow's No. 7 and No. 8 boards, are playing in the junior-varsity section, which is downstairs in the Crystal Ballroom, while Murrow's top six are up on the third floor, in the Gramercy Park Conference Room. Or, at least, this is where they're supposed to be. Except somebody's sitting at Oscar's board and nobody can track down Shawn, and Willy and Ilya aren't here yet, either, and Sal's sitting at one of the front tables (reserved for the top players), near the window overlooking McDonald's, wondering where the hell everyone is.

They begin to straggle in one by one, Oscar in an oversized gray T-shirt and work boots and cuffed jeans, Willy in a Sean John T-shirt, carrying a Discman loaded with the latest CD by a rapper called The Game, Ilya in slacks and a pullover, Alex in a sweatshirt three sizes too large. Willy forgot to bring a pencil. And Shawn? Well, Shawn ain't here, Willy says. Shawn woke up late, and he's stuck on the train somewhere in lower Manhattan, and the first round will go on without him.

♛

Most American chess tournaments are contested using a format called the Swiss system. In the Swiss, every player competes in the same number of games; no one is eliminated. As players continue to win games, the level of competition gets progressively stronger. Those who lose in the early rounds drop toward the bottom, and no one is paired against another player more than once (in team competitions, teammates are paired only when it's absolutely necessary), and the color of the pieces each player draws usually alternates from round to round. In the first round, the top player in the upper half of the field is paired against the top player in the lower half, which means that the highest-rated contestants, like Sal and Alex, often have it easy for the first couple of rounds. This, of course, is the way it *should* work out, but even in chess, even in a game where ratings take on so much meaning, no one is immune to being surprised.

So there are thirty-five players in the high-school varsity section, and in the first round, Sal faces Michael Zletz of Hunter High School. Zletz's rating is 1713, and Sal's rating is 2419, which means Sal should hardly even have to think in order to win this game, that he can coast through these first couple of rounds and conserve his energy for later in the afternoon. The games at the city championship are relatively short; each player gets thirty minutes on his clock (as opposed to two hours per side at Supernationals), with a five-second delay each time a move is made and the button is depressed, a factor that can become crucial late in an endgame. (In "sudden-death" tournaments like these, if your opponent's time runs out, you win your game, although this is partly dependent on technology: The newer digital clocks allow for the time-delay feature, but since most tournament officials don't provide them, and since they cost a hundred dollars or more, some games are still played with analog clocks. In these cases, if you're down to your final two minutes but feel you could win the game if you had ample time, you can make an appeal to a tournament director to rule the game a draw based on "insufficient losing chances.")

In games like these, known as Game/30, the action tends to unfold quickly, and most of the heavy thinking comes in the early moments. So Sal decides to sacrifice his queen to gain an early advantage in position. In the hands of a lesser player, this would be a reckless decision, but in Sal's world, at Sal's level, such sacrifices—defined in *Pandolfini's Ultimate Guide to Chess* as "the voluntary offer of material for the purpose of gaining a greater or more useful advantage in either material, attack on the enemy king, or some other factor"—comprise the fundamental beauty of this game. An innovative sacrifice of a queen, of a piece worth nearly twice as much as a rook, and nine times as much as a single pawn, is what elevates chess to the quality of art. In skilled hands, a devastating queen sacrifice, like the one Sal has just made, or an early *gambit,* which usually involves giving up a pawn in the opening in order to gain position, can render an opponent impotent.

And so with just ten seconds remaining on his clock, with the position in Sal's favor, Zletz resigns.

Sal is not the highest-rated player in this tournament. That distinction belongs to Dmytro Kedyk, a Ukrainian boy who was recruited to Murrow by Eliot Weiss but instead chose to attend Environmental Studies, a small high school on the west side of Manhattan ("I think he realizes he made a mistake," Weiss says). Kedyk, whose rating is 2512, is already done by the time Sal finishes his game, and he's been watching this one, and when Zletz resigns, Kedyk gets up and starts reshuffling the pieces to shift the position back to what it once was, to demonstrate what might have happened. He's going too fast for anyone else to catch it, but it's clear that Zletz missed something, and when Sal sees it, he starts to giggle, and Dmytro starts to giggle with him, and they stumble out of the room caught up in paroxysms of laughter while a tournament official hushes them and shoos them away from the games that are still active.

"How did he not see it?"

See what?

"A stalemate," Sal says. "He had a stalemate and he missed it."

A stalemate is something a player of Sal's caliber should have foreseen; this is what happens when someone's king is not in check, but they cannot make a legal move without landing in check. Like the diagram at the top of page 129, for instance, if it were black's move.

The lure of a stalemate is often the last desperate gambit of an overmatched player; it is a way to turn what appears like a certain loss into a half-point draw. If Zletz had seen it, if he had forced Sal into that position and then called the tournament director over and declared

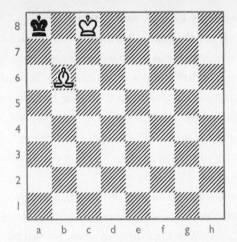

the game a draw, Sal's path to the city championship would have been severely crippled. A stalemate, and Sal would have shed ratings points, and both his reputation and Murrow's streak would have been at stake. And now that it's over, now that the threat has been averted, Sal cannot stop laughing, all the way down the hall and into the Skittles Room, where he recounts the story for Mr. Weiss, where he says, over and over again, to anyone who will listen, what a beautiful way that was to start his morning.

Back in the Gramercy Park Room, Willy, playing at a furious pace and drawing his opponent into sloppy mistakes, is about to pull off an improbable upset over a 2218 named Adam Maltese. Ilya is losing to Stuyvesant's No. 1 board, Josh Weinstein, a 2111 ("I'm not upset, losing to him," Ilya says), and Oscar, who's also playing fast and loose after engaging in a series of blitz games before the start of the tournament, manages to stave off one of the lowest-rated players in the section, Jacob Ehrlich, an 1172.

Downstairs, in the high-school novice section, the newbies are playing their first competitive games, and fighting against the clock, an impediment that renders the game into something else entirely. It's one thing to go against each other during chess club after school, but to be here in a ballroom, shrouded in silence, with an analog clock *tick, tick, tick*ing next to your elbow—that, Renwick says, is *pressure.* "The guy I was playing, his opening wasn't that good," Renwick says. "But then he brought out his queen and took over the board."

"I was playing well," Adalberto says. "I was up three pieces. I just didn't see the checkmate."

♛

Shortly before eleven, Shawn finally shows, bleary-eyed and mono-syllabic, wearing an oversized T-shirt and a Yankee cap turned backward on his head. He's blaming the train for his tardiness, and this excuse doesn't pacify Mr. Weiss, who wants to ensure that it doesn't happen again, not when it matters, not when they're on their way to the state tournament, or to the nationals. This tournament should be easy enough, even with the looming presence of teams from Stuyvesant and Brooklyn Tech, but it gets progressively more difficult from here. "I'll come to your house if I have to," Mr. Weiss says.

But then, it's hard to tell Shawn much of anything and make it stick. The kid's been an enigma since junior high school. He has a gift, this much is clear, and he's managed to discover it amid a life that has been fraught, like so many in the city, with disappointment. Ask Shawn about his family, and he'll tell you the bare minimum: His father died when he was two. How? *Heart attack.* He has three siblings, including an older brother who lives in Erie. What does he do in Erie? *He lives there.* Where does he work? *I dunno.* And that's pretty much it. End of story. What else is there to say? To tell you anything more would be to let his guard down, and this is one thing Shawn has learned never to do.

Out in the hallway, out near the board where the second-round pairings are about to be posted, Shawn finds Willy, who's still listening to The Game, and passing his headphones around to Nile and to Os-car. They're jawing about the rap business, about Kanye and Eminem and Cam'ron, and attempting to build a consensus on what's the real thing and what's record-industry fluff. "A lot of West Coast rappers are garbage," Shawn says. "It's easy to get a deal out there, you know?"

"Not really," Willy says. "If you look at it, there's not a lot of rappers from the West Coast."

Ilya has no idea what any of this means. He's standing around waiting for the pairings to be posted, and listening to a Russian pop song on his MP3 player. A few minutes earlier, Mr. Weiss and Sal and Ilya were talking about visiting Red Square in Moscow, and Sal was telling the story about how he tried to wear shorts into a church and how they wouldn't let him inside. Now Willy and Nile and Shawn are deconstructing the oratorical skills of Marshall Mathers, the cultural phenomenon known as Eminem, the white rapper from Detroit, the square peg of hip-hop. And in the midst of all this, a photographer from the one of the local newspapers, *The Bay Ridge Courier,* shows up to take a team picture, so they crowd into the frame together, all of these boys with so little in common except this one thing.

"Yo," Shawn is saying. "Eminem is *hot.* You hear that last song off the new album? That's *hot.*"

♛

All goes according to plan in Round Two: Those who are supposed to win (Sal, Alex, Shawn, Ilya) take care of business, and those who are paired against higher-rated players (Oscar, Willy) lose their games. Oscar, playing with white and facing Lenderman's old I.S. 228 middle-school teammate Alexander Pelekhaty, a 2238 who attends Bronx Science, tries to throw him off by playing the orangutan opening, and it nearly works. Pelekhaty, who has a blond brush cut and lively dark eyes, sits perfectly still and considers that lone ivory pawn on b4 for close to five minutes before responding by pushing a black pawn to c6. For a while, Oscar still looks good, and he's way ahead on time, but after a series of exchanges, he's down to only a king and pawn, and then he's left with just a king, and with thirty-four seconds on his clock, he resigns.

"I didn't play too bad, right?" Oscar says to Pelekhaty, on their way out of the room.

"You had me down there early."

"I think he sucks," says a boy named Boris, walking in the other direction.

"Nah," Pelekhaty says. "He played good."

"I had *time,* man," Oscar says. "I was *up.*"

♛

Four or five hours into a chess tournament, the room begins to take on an organic stench, redolent of an unkempt high-school locker room. One of the competitors has torn off his sweater and is wearing only a sleeveless undershirt, his armpits exposed to the world, and the smell is fast degenerating from overripe to horrifying.

Before Round Three, the tournament organizers discover that the pairings in the high-school varsity section have been sabotaged by a boy who came in during the first round and "just sat down wherever he wanted to sit." This, of course, not only violates the protocol called for IN CAPITAL LETTERS on every official tournament handout (ASK YOUR OP-PONENT HIS/HER NAME—*MAKE SURE* IT'S THE RIGHT PERSON!), it goes against every notion of common sense, a quality which has never been synonymous with genius.

So in the meantime, while the mess is sorted out, a few of the best youth chess players in New York City pass their time playing illicit card games, fraught with wagering and trash-talking. They have com-mandeered a patch of carpet in the Skittles Room, and they're sitting on the floor cross-legged playing Stupid, the convoluted Russian card game that involves exchanges and trickery. It is a game played not to lose: the twos, threes, fours, and fives are removed, reducing the deck to thirty-six, and each person is dealt six cards. Normally, it is played in groups of four, with two teams, and the game proceeds in a series of "attacks" and "defenses," of lay-downs and pickups revolving around a trump card of a particular suit. Eventually, the game winnows its way down to two players, and the last player with cards in his hand is the loser. In the end, luck gives way to strategy, just like chess.

Dollars are changing hands rather rapidly at this point: Oscar is winning, and Ilya is losing. In fact, Oscar is having a better day playing cards than he is playing chess, which has become a trend lately; he's been spending as much time on Web sites like Partypoker.com (where most of the time, he plays for fake cash, though on occasion he plays with his friend's account) as he has on the Internet Chess Club.

Downstairs, in the novice section, the newbies cannot find their bearings. Robert is checkmated early, and Adalberto's opponent again pushes his queen out early and destroys him. Of the four newbies, only Rex and Renwick have won a game, both of them defeating a boy from Paramus, New Jersey, who, like them, has not played enough to carry an official USCF rating. In the end, these are the only wins they get: Rex and Renwick also land a couple of draws, and Adalberto and Robert, facing each other in the final round, decide to take a draw so as not to finish with zero points.

"Just one bad move," Robert says. His forehead is pale and damp and his entire face contorts into a grimace and his voice becomes a bag of marbles, a near-indecipherable mumble born of frustration and fatigue. "I was playing well, and I made one bad move."

♛

After three rounds, after three relatively easy victories against lesser opponents, Sal's rating has skyrocketed from 2419 to . . . 2421. "I'm getting two points after three games," Sal says. "That's like, .67 points each. Wow, what a tournament!"

It doesn't get any harder for Sal in Round four; after a series of minor upsets (Kedyk, Pelekhaty, and Josh Weinstein, a 2111 who's Stuyvesant's top board, all lose), he faces a player rated six hundred points lower, Boris Senderovich of Brooklyn Tech, and wins once more, with hardly any effort. Stuyvesant's only hope at an upset was for Sal or Alex to falter in some way, and it doesn't happen. Alex beats his old teammate, Alexsandr Pelekhaty, and even though Oscar hangs a rook—just leaves it out there unprotected and able to be captured without gaining anything in return, perhaps the biggest blunder one can make—against Stuyvesant's Anna Ginzburg and loses, and even though Shawn loses to a player rated four hundred points lower, the team championship has essentially been decided. And the only question now is what will happen when Sal plays Alex.

It is inevitable at this point: Because Sal and Alex are the only two undefeateds remaining in the varsity section, they'll have to face each other. Neither of them seems particularly disturbed by this turn of events. It's happened before, and it will happen again, and as they've done before, they'll conspire to take a draw. If this were a tournament based on individual performance, and based on money prizes, a premeditated draw might be frowned upon (certain players do this often in order to maximize the amount of the purse they take home—for instance, they might agree to a draw and then split both the first- and second-place awards). But not here, not at a tournament that carries no real weight for players of their caliber, not at a tournament that means more to their coach than it does to them.

"Why play him?" Sal says. "What's the point, really?"

But then, today Sal has exposed another side of himself. Just a few minutes before this, he was scolding Shawn for his loss, a loss that means nothing in the grand scheme of things, but inexplicably seemed to get at Sal in a way little else had gotten to him in months. "Shawn, how dare you! To lose *again!*" Sal had said, and it came off like a joke, but there was a certain harshness to it, as if Sal couldn't stand to bear witness to such an obvious lack of focus.

So when Sal says he's fine with this, taking a draw with the one player he'd like to beat more than any of the other thirty-four in this room, it is difficult to believe him.

According to statute 14B6 of the *U.S. Chess Federation's Official Rules of Chess* (fifth edition), premature or prearranged draws are "unethical," and they are "unsporting," and in cases "of clear violations of the moral principles of the game, penalties should be imposed at the director's discretion." But this is such a vague prohibition that it essentially means nothing, and since it is often impossible to discern one's intentions, it becomes unenforceable. So players conspire: They do it so they can split a larger amount of prize money, they do it so they can achieve more prestigious titles, they do it to improve their ratings, and they do it because they simply don't have the will or the reason to truly compete against each other, statute 14B6 and its companion, number 20L (which declares illegal any attempt to "fix or throw games") be damned.

Perhaps in the case of Sal and Alex, it can be defended, since there is nothing to gain from their actually playing this game out, since it will mean nothing to the team's overall score (Murrow will get a total of one point, regardless of outcome) and it will mean nothing to their ratings (since they are nearly identical) and it will mean nothing monetarily (since there are no cash prizes). But if this is an ethical issue, shouldn't it matter in *every* case? At the moment, this is one of those great existential debates that rage among competitive chess players; but on this day, all the hand-wringing will not change anything.

In eighteen moves, and in less than three minutes, the city championship is decided. Sal starts by pushing a pawn to d4 and Alex responds with pawn to d5, and then they move their c-pawns and their knights and it's all one big charade, they're smiling through the whole thing, until Alex pushes his bishop to d6 and they declare this an intractable position, and they shake hands, and they agree to a draw. In the end, even though they've both finished with four and a half points out of five, by virtue of a more difficult slate of opponents, Alex will officially be declared the city champion, and will take home the larger trophy, which means nothing to either of them. A larger trophy is just something more to lug home on the subway or in the backseat of your father's car. A larger trophy can't replace the real reward of this tournament: The top players in each section get free entries for four months to the tournaments held at the Marshall Chess Club, where real competition can be found, and real money can be won. And it's the money, even the *opportunity* to make money—so rare and precious in this game—that matters, isn't it?

For a while, Sal and Alex disappear from the proceedings. In the Gramercy Park Room, Ilya refuses a draw from Boris Senderovich and beats him to finish with three and a half points, in a tie for sixth place, and Willy defeats Evan Rabin, a 1788 who goes to the Dwight School, a private academy on the Upper West Side, to finish in twelfth place with three points.

Back in the Skittles Room, as if driven by the emptiness of their premeditated draw, Sal and Alex have settled into a furious round of five-minute blitz games, slapping the clock so hard that the entire table rattles, moving their pieces so fast that it's virtually impossible to keep track of what belongs where.

"Shit," Alex says. He's giggling, and he's sitting on his knees, reaching his entire arm across the table to slide his queen to d8.

"Yes, that is shit," Sal says, and Alex giggles again.

"Shit!" Alex says. *"Shit!"*

"Should I play b-four?" Sal says. "Should I? I should."

"So what? You think I should resign?"

"Yeah. You should. Ooh, ooh, you missed *this*."

Back and forth it goes, until the clock is down to single digits, and they're slapping at it and moving without thinking and the pawns they've captured are rolling onto the floor. Soon they'll leave the pieces in disarray and get up and tiptoe back into the Gramercy Park room to check on their teammates, and a short time after that, they'll troop downstairs to the Grand Ballroom and accept their trophies, first place and second place, and then Mr. Weiss will rush out of the room with his family and a team trophy the size of a German shepherd, in order to catch the eight o'clock train from Penn Station back to Long Island. And Alex's father will drive him home to Ninth Avenue and Sal will take the subway back to his home on Avenue U, and they will continue to insist that two people could not possibly have less in common than they do. But for a moment, at least, all is even between them, and this is just a game.

"Check," Alex says.

"Whooooo!" Sal says. He moves out of check, pummels the clock, and throws a hand to his forehead, swooning like a bad actress. "Oh my *God*. I almost *died* there."

TEN

THE WOMEN IN THE ROOM

HER MOTHER MOVED TO ENGLAND TO BECOME A STAGE ACTRESS, AND wound up becoming a nurse instead. Her father was a doctor. They met in London, and they fell head over heels, so much so that on their first date, at the intermission of a play, she leaned into him and whispered, "I want to sleep with you and never see you again." Which didn't make much sense, not on a practical level, because they worked in the same office.

Whatever. They were young and impulsive and prone to silliness and impetuous behavior. Practicality was the last thing on their minds. After they'd been dating for a couple of months, they enlisted in the Salvation Army and went to Zambia as volunteers. One problem: The Salvation Army was a Christian organization, and so naturally frowned upon premarital cohabitation. They asked Elizabeth Vicary's mother and father to either produce a ring, or go home. So right then and there, in the middle of Africa, they decided to get married. And during a layover on the way home, swollen with the hormonal glow of the enviably youthful and pretty, they conceived their first child.

"My father was a doctor," Elizabeth says, "but they still believed if you were breast-feeding, you couldn't get pregnant." Hence, a year after her sister emerged on this earth as an unintended bounty of a hasty marriage, Elizabeth emerged upon this earth, and another year after that, she and her sister were both children of divorce.

Her father got engaged five more times before he settled down in London. Her mother went back to America, and Elizabeth went with her, wherever she decided to go. She was restless. She liked to shift jobs and locations approximately every eighteen months. They lived in Minnesota, and then they moved to North Carolina, where Elizabeth went to high school, and her mother got a job summarizing research papers, and eventually took work running trials for medical research. Her sister was a wayward soul, and Elizabeth became the closest thing to a voice of reason within an unhinged household.

It helped that she showed sparks of brilliance. When she was eleven, she learned how to play chess through a program at her junior high school, and her first rating was 1223, three hundred points higher than her instructor's. She stopped playing chess in high school, because, well, "that's what girls do—they stop playing in high school." She went to Duke for a year, couldn't put up with the preppiness of it, the packs of frat boys and bulimic girls, and she moved to New York and transferred to Columbia. She started out majoring in math, and then once she realized she didn't know what she wanted to do, she defaulted by majoring in English literature.

She'd played in her first major chess tournament in 1993, at the U.S. Open in Philadelphia. At the time, she was fresh out of high school, and it was her first real trip far from home. Her rating was up to about 1800, and in the first round, she faced a grandmaster named Alex Shabalov, who would later become a close friend. That tournament changed her attitude toward competitive chess; there were a ton of men and not very many women, and even fewer women who could actually play well enough to earn a measure of respect, and Lizzie, as the men started to call her—tall, impossibly thin, and pretty, with soft features and a delicate nose and long brown hair—was treated like a rock and roll queen.

Her first job out of Columbia was as a writer of encyclopedia articles for the Oxford University Press. She did it for eight months, and the series she worked on got published, and she was out of a job. She started dating a man whose mother was a hairdresser, and whose regular clients included a Jordanian princess who was in the market for a new personal assistant. The princess had enrolled as a student at Columbia, for reasons based more on aesthetics than education, and she needed someone to help with her homework and papers and type up her class notes so she could digest them more easily. The princess either didn't want to or didn't know how to do any of these things herself. Elizabeth became her surrogate. She made forty dollars an hour, running errands and taking care of all the mundane tasks that would otherwise serve to complicate the daily life of a princess. In one two-month period, the princess spent fifteen thousand dollars on dry cleaning. She owned more outfits than there were days of the year. She had a closetful of shoes that would have made Imelda Marcos blush. At one point, because she didn't need *everything,* she decided to sell a painting, which turned out to be a portrait. Of the princess herself. Painted by Pablo Picasso.

For two years, Elizabeth endured these things. She kind of enjoyed the job, to tell the truth, because it afforded her a measure of freedom in her own daily life. But in 1999, the princess graduated, and Elizabeth was on the market once again. That's when she applied to become a teacher at Chess-in-the-Schools. She had no teaching experience at all, but she was bright and personable and she knew the game and they hired her anyway, and assigned her to rotate between four different schools. One was a progressive elementary school in upper Manhattan, and another was I.S. 318, which happened to be in the neighborhood where she lived.

Intermediate School 318 is a squat rectangular building set on a city block between Walton and Lorimer Streets, in the southern quadrant of Williamsburg, a nebulous neighborhood on the outer edges of gentrified Brooklyn, an uneven pastiche of brownstones and auto repair shops and bodegas and warehouses, bisected horizontally by the elevated J/M/Z train and vertically by the G train. Two thirds of the students at 318 (which is officially named after Eugenio María de Hostos, a Puerto Rican educator and independence advocate) are Hispanic, and most of the rest are either black or Asian; fewer than ten percent are white. The Lindsay Park Houses, a cluster of red-brick towers on the opposite side of the elevated train tracks, are a federally subsidized middle-income co-op populated largely by Chinese immigrants, and the Marcy Houses, once regarded as one of the most dangerous projects in the city, are a few blocks to the south. Two decades earlier, long before much of Williamsburg became an outpost for young white hipsters looking for cheaper living space, a boy named Sean Carter, from the Marcy projects, attended I.S. 318, and later found fame as a rapper named Jay-Z.

Today, 318 is regarded as the best public middle school in the district, which also includes the neighborhood of Greenpoint, north of Williamsburg. That wasn't necessarily the case before Chess-in-the-Schools first brought its resources to 318 back in 1998. But the school's longtime principal, Alan Fierstein, much like Saul Bruckner at Murrow, was willing to take chances on experimental programs and, after attending a meeting with CIS officials, presumed that bringing chess to his school would be in keeping with the eclectic atmosphere he'd fostered. Under Fierstein, who spent thirty-seven years at the school and took over as principal in the late 1980s, 318 took on an innovative bent: It may be the only school in New York City that offers after-school programs in guitar and dance and photography and gymnastics and botany and Web design. (How many middle schools have their own *marching bands*?) "Other schools are focusing so hard on English and math test scores," says the current principal, Fortunato (Fred) Rubino, a genial man with spiky hair and a bushy mustache. "Our test scores are just fine."

That first year, a social studies teacher named John Galvin oversaw the chess program, along with a rotating series of CIS instructors, and it was a small notion, like every other after-school club, with no real direction and no grand aspirations. The next year, Elizabeth Vicary arrived, and Galvin continued to oversee it, and almost immediately, the scope of the program changed; everything changed, really. The change was forged out of convenience (it was simply easier for Elizabeth to spend more of her time here, so close to her apartment, than to travel to the other schools where she taught), but the change also came because Elizabeth met Oscar Santana.

She didn't know at the time that you weren't supposed to play favorites; that first day, she showed up at the school to teach and was so nervous that she somehow *lost* the first game she played, to one of her students. So she was still trying to live that down, above everything else, including the fact that she had no idea how to go about actually *teaching* anybody. And despite all of that, here was this boy welcoming her to school every afternoon, as if he couldn't wait to see her, as if a few simple chess lessons had illuminated his psyche in a way that no school subject could ever do. So she kept coming back to 318 because she wanted to see Oscar, and she gave him more attention than she gave anyone else. She tried to teach him to memorize certain lines of attack; it seemed like too much work, so he studied tactics instead.

Later that year, Chess-in-the-Schools helped to pay to send some of the kids from 318 to Tucson, Arizona, for the national championships. They competed in the under-750 section, and when her team took a lead in the early rounds, one of her colleagues at CIS told Elizabeth to snatch the score sheet off the wall and save it, that if nothing else, this would prove these kids had held on to first place in *something*, if only for a while. Elizabeth didn't bother taking the score sheet. She'd already done the calculations; they were going to win, and she knew it, and it didn't matter that Oscar (who, at that point, still considered his primary strategy the four-move checkmate) played a miserable tournament, because all the others played far above their heads, and when Elizabeth went over their games between rounds, she could hardly believe how much of what she'd taught had actually sunk in.

Alan Fierstein couldn't believe it either. Maybe this was beginner's luck, but it was also an inner-city administrator's dream, the sort of saccharin-sweet tale that no media outlet can resist, of the same sort that Maurice Ashley had once exploited in order to advance the lives of the children he coached in Harlem: POOR MINORITY CHILDREN MAKE

GOOD IN SPORT OF GENIUSES. Fierstein's little school had won a *national championship*, and it didn't matter that they'd done it in one of the lower-rated sections, and it didn't matter that, in certain haughty circles of tournament chess, a victory in a lower-rated section was hardly even considered a championship. Fierstein bragged to every newspaper reporter he could reach, and he called the Board of Education, and a picture appeared in one of the papers of Oscar playing chess against the schools chancellor (he checkmated him in twenty seconds). The school threw more money and more resources into chess; eventually, a grandmaster named Miron Sher was hired to help Elizabeth teach. Soon after that, Greg Shahade, a former national high-school champion from the Masterman School in Philadelphia, and his sister Jennifer, one of the top women's chess players in the country, started teaching at 318 as well.

The summer after Tucson, Elizabeth held a chess camp at the school, and Willy Edgard was one of the attendees. He had already applied to 318 once and been rejected because his grades weren't good enough. Elizabeth told Willy to apply again, and the second time around, Willy was accepted.

Elizabeth began finding chess players in all sorts of places after that. Nile Smith used to hide in the back of the room, shrouded in his down winter coat; one day, during a lesson with a grandmaster, he solved a puzzle, a checkmate in five moves, and Elizabeth declared him a genius, and in the eighth grade, buoyed by her proclamations, he found his rating jumping four hundred points in two months.

Another time, while one of her students was in the midst of a game, his friend, a heavyset sixth-grader whom Elizabeth recognized only vaguely, suggested a move to him that he said would guarantee checkmate. Elizabeth didn't believe him, so they played it out, and whether guided by luck or by intuition or by some higher understanding, the boy was right. Elizabeth wouldn't allow him to leave until he agreed to join the chess club. "You're amazing," she said. "You're a genius," she assured him, and it was as if Shawn Martinez, long ago dismissed as a hopeless case by his teachers, had been waiting his entire life for someone to tell him these things. Given the benefit of a single gesture of kindness, Shawn developed an obsession akin to Bobby Fischer's. He spent the next couple of years playing for almost twelve hours a day. He played online, he played out games against himself, he played at home, and he played at school. His attendance remained spotty; he even failed the chess class that 318 had instituted as part of its curriculum. Sometimes he'd hide out in Elizabeth's third-floor classroom and she would find him in there, with the lights out, squinting at the pages of some book on esoteric opening theory or pawn-king endgames. Elizabeth tried to trick him into learning, assigning him to write book reports and administering tests on the books she saw him reading. He failed those too. And yet when he played, it was clear that he'd read the books, and he'd not only understood the books, but had incorporated the theory into his game. He just didn't want to be told what to do. (Earlier this year, when Shawn had stopped by a CIS-sponsored tournament at 318 to say hi to Elizabeth, he was thrown out for refusing to take off his hat.)

Shawn's best friend was another stocky boy named Angel Lopez, who wore glasses and had a big, goofy grin, and the two of them went everywhere together. The teachers starting calling them Tweedledum and Tweedledee. Angel played chess, too, at about the same level as Shawn, and went with him to Murrow, then transferred out after a few months. By this time, championships at 318 had become the expectation, and Fierstein's vision of the program had expanded; every sixth-grade student who enters 318 is now required to take a ten-week chess class. Those who enjoy it can take it as an elective, and those who want to compete at the major tournaments are invited show up at the chess club after school. Elizabeth teaches exclusively at 318, showing up every day and handling a full load of classes while working part-time toward a graduate degree in teaching, and John Galvin, the social studies teacher, continues to oversee the team's trips and outings and its expense budget.

Galvin is a soft-spoken man with heavy-lidded eyes and a playful streak who, over time, has perfected the Zen-like art of herding several dozen restless junior-high schoolers through strange airports (318 regularly brings about forty children to each national tournament, far more than any other school). He was born and raised in New York, and lived in Staten Island and Brooklyn, and taught himself to play chess during college. He's still not particularly good at it (his rating is around 1200, lower than many of his students'), but he's developed a low-grade obsession: More than once, when he has visitors to his classroom at 318, he has to tear himself away from a game he's playing online.

Over the past seven years, 318 has become a citywide dynasty, a minor-league version of Murrow. On occasion, parents have moved into the neighborhood so their kids could play chess. Other kids, like Dalphe Morantus, who lives in Canarsie, have traveled halfway across the borough to study with Elizabeth. I.S. 318 pulls kids from feeder schools like P.S. 31, an elementary school in Greenpoint that is also sponsored by Chess-in-the-Schools. Galvin calls 318's program the "Yankees of chess" (he likens himself to a general manager, and Elizabeth to the manager). It's a claim that's been proven at the city championships and the state championships and the K-12 nationals, held each fall (in which teams are separated by grade; Murrow doesn't participate), and the more prestigious junior-high nationals in the spring (which, this year, will be part of the Supernationals). The travel budget alone for the chess program is more than fifty thousand dollars, and at this point, less than ten percent of that comes from Chess-in-the-Schools, which has grown increasingly more detached from 318 as the school has proved its own self-sufficiency in chess. The hope, says Galvin, is that eventually the program can survive on its own, without any assistance from CIS, which puts Vicary—still a CIS employee—in the midst of an awkward push-and-pull.

The problem is one of vision: The administration at 318 sees nothing wrong with breeding winners, striving for victory, and loading the trophy cases in the school's stairwell with a staggering amount of hardware. But CIS would like to think of itself as a purely altruistic organization, as a refuge for inner-city children, concerned more with long-term than with short-term results. Perhaps because of that, ever since that first championship, 318's accomplishments have gone almost unnoticed: CIS no longer bothers to issue press releases or contact the newspapers or the board of education when 318 wins another championship, and despite the fact that the school has an exponentially larger chess club than any other city school, the money they get from CIS, according to Galvin, has actually been cut by fifteen percent each of the past two years. Marley Kaplan, the president of CIS, seems almost embarrassed by what 318 has done, by the way it continues to monopolize the major championships. "Some teams become dynasties," she says. "But eventually that dynasty is going to die. We don't want dynasties. It's not really what we're looking for. Our program isn't really about chess; it's about what chess can do for kids. We aren't trying to create champions."

This theory makes no sense to John Galvin, and it makes no sense to Rubino, who took over when Fierstein retired five years earlier. They have trouble understanding why other schools are allocated an equal number of instructors' hours even though they bring six or eight or ten kids to each CIS Saturday-afternoon tournament, and 318 often brings four dozen. It's not a question of need at this point—the school has its own segment of its discretionary budget dedicated to chess (between sixty and seventy thousand dollars), and last year got a significant donation from an unnamed benefactor—but it's an issue of common sense. It's not about the winning for 318, either, Rubino insists ("Sooner or later," he says, "we'll lose"), but how can winning and opportunity be considered mutually exclusive?

Witness Shawn and Nile and Willy and Oscar and Dalphe Morantus, all of whom won championships at 318 and, because those championships gave them a reason to strive, slipped through a back door into Edward R. Murrow, one of the best high schools in Brooklyn, and a far better option than they might have had otherwise. "The real world of chess," Galvin says, "tends to be zero-sum. It's win or lose. Their mission—it tends to be more social."

The problem, as Galvin sees it, is the game doesn't work that way, and *life* doesn't work that way, and if anyone understands that, it's kids like Willy and Oscar, kids who never caught a break until they happened into a class taught by a woman who happened to find herself at the same time they did.

♛

She has a half decade of teaching experience these days, and Elizabeth Vicary appears to have discovered her life's calling. She still lives five minutes from I.S. 318, in a sparsely furnished fourth-floor walk-up apartment on Union Avenue, with a galley kitchen and one small bedroom and a chessboard set on a tray table in the center of the living room, near the computer. It is a no-frills building in a no-frills neighborhood, near a Walgreen's and a gas station, but this is her home. Most of the kids in the neighborhood are her current or former students. (Once, Oscar and his little brother came by to visit when she wasn't home, so they found a way to break into the front door of the building, and left her a note.) The kids call her Miss (as in "Hey, Miss, can I go to the bathroom?") and in return, she calls them geniuses and visionaries. Her classroom is a virtual laboratory, with a library of books on the back wall and a bank of computers near the window and the chessboards set out in a U-shaped pattern in the back of the room. There are aphorisms *(Being Wrong Is The First Step To Being Right, It's OK To Make A Mistake)* and principles and instructive series taped to the wall above the door and next to the coat closet and beside the bulletin board, handwritten on oversized pieces of newsprint, with titles like "The Four-Move Checkmate" and the "Notation of Pawns" and "Tactics" and "In the Opening."

On a bleary winter afternoon, Elizabeth is perched on a stool in front of thirty sixth-graders, wearing a leather skirt and a pair of knee-high brown leather boots and using the pieces on an oversized two-dimensional chessboard to expound on what she calls "threats." The children have arranged their squat wood-backed chairs into a semicircle at the front of the room, facing the blackboard and the caricatures above the blackboard of recent world chess champions.

"Threats in real life? Good or bad? Bad, right? Well, threats in chess are"—and here she elongates the word like taffy, enunciating each syllable in a dulcet voice that still carries traces of a British accent—*"ex-cell-ent."* She has a list of students' names in her lap, and every time she raises a question, a half-dozen arms shoot up into the air, and she either calls on someone (by name) or chooses someone at random from the attendance list (by name). If there is one trick she has learned over the years, it is to invoke names. This she does with alarming regularity.

Once, not too long ago, a student waltzed through the door of her classroom, Room 319, and declared it "the Fun Room." The fact that many of her kids take naturally to her subject, that they see as it more like a recess than another dreary class, serves to her advantage. "I didn't think I'd have the patience to teach," she says. But in here, she is in charge, and if anyone tries her patience, if anyone dares to mouth off or disobey orders or neglects to clean up their mess, they spend their time exiled in the hallway during the final segment of class, that precious time reserved for playing games. Often, in the midst of giving a lesson, she will halt in midsentence and fix a frigid stare upon the child (or children) who is trying her goodwill.

"Who's talking? Louis, is that you?"

And most of the time, because this is the Fun Room, because it is the one room in this school that feels nothing like *school,* a single well-placed threat will shut their mouths.

♛

Her best students have been the progeny of cabdrivers and hardware-store employees and laundry workers. Most of their parents remain distant and removed from Elizabeth's tutelage; they sign permission slips and they show up for car pools, and this is the extent of it, and it is nothing like what goes on at the private schools, where the mothers and fathers have been known to dictate the tenor of their children's activities. Often, as with Oscar's mother and father, they don't quite understand this sudden fixation with something they've always regarded as a game, a glorified version of checkers. Suddenly, they're bringing home permission slips to travel to Florida and Tennessee, and asking their parents, many of whom have never boarded a plane themselves, to sign for them.

It means something different to all of them. They can treat the game with grave urgency, as Shawn did, or they can consider it a social outlet. One of Elizabeth's current students, an eighth-grader who lives in the Lindsay Park Houses, says that his mother is so obsessed with him passing the test to get into Stuyvesant that she hardly lets him leave the house. So chess club is his one place for making friends. He doesn't much care about winning or losing, but his rating has jumped six hundred points in the past year. "I just want to be popular," he says. "I've never been popular before."

Marta, on the other hand, doesn't have this problem. Marta is both popular and remarkably mature for a seventh-grader; before she started playing chess, her average in math was a 94. Now it's gone up to a 99, and this never ceases to amaze her, how those two things seem to correlate, how she can go from her chess class to her math class and everything seems to make so much more sense, because chess class doesn't *feel* anything like math class.

Marta, whose parents are from Poland (and whose father still frets over all the traveling she does for chess), who lives in Greenpoint and commutes half an hour every morning just to get to 318, is already something of an aberration among her classmates. This is because she is a female in a culture subsumed by testosterone. And this is a reality that doesn't seem likely to change anytime soon.

♛

The third cycle of Murrow's unorthodox four-part school year begins in February, the week after the city championships, and by that time, the Thursday-afternoon chess club meetings have become a decidedly boyish affair. Most of the girls who showed up those first few weeks of school have vanished without explanation, and the few who remain are of the decidedly casual sort, like the striking sophomore and aspiring model who does not seem to belong here at all, yet continues to come, if only to engage in a series of barbed flirtations with Sal. (*Sal:* "All three things you say about me are wrong." *Girl:* "No they're not. You're sad, you're depraved, and you're a little boy.")

There is one exception, and her name is Nataliya. She is fourteen years old, petite and pale-skinned. She wears her chestnut hair tied back in a ponytail and often leaves her coat on while she plays. Nataliya was born in the Ukraine, and lives in Brighton Beach, and graduated from I.S. 228, the same diverse middle-school that Alex Lenderman attended. In the ninth grade, she wound up at Lincoln, the massive Coney Island high school. After hearing about Murrow, Nataliya transferred. And even though her father doesn't play chess, and no one else in her family plays chess, Nataliya decided to learn. She tried playing on the computer, but it wasn't the same thing, so she joined the chess club, and she started playing in the Right Move tournaments, and by the time of the city championships, her rating was a respectable 990.

One day at chess club, in a slow moment between games, Nataliya sat atop a desk, reading the final ten pages of *Catcher in the Rye.* None of the other girls in her class, she was saying, had a *clue* about Holden Caulfield. "Every time they start talking," Nataliya said, and then she rolled her eyes and mimed dropping her head to the desk. They think he's gay, because all he does in those first few pages is talk about boys, or they think he's mentally ill, or they think he's all of the above. "I don't think he's either one," she said. "I think it's something everybody goes through."

Nataliya was the only girl to play for Murrow at the city championships, in the high-school junior-varsity section. She spent the time between rounds writing in the pages of a journal she'd brought with her, surrounded by hyperactive young boys venting their competitive fury through card games and hip-hop music. She finished in thirty-sixth place out of fifty-nine entrants, with two points, and when it was over, her attendance at chess club meetings grew more sparse. And eventually, by the time the weather began to turn, by the time eight of her male classmates started making plans for the trip to the New York

State Chess Championships in Saratoga Springs, she would stop showing up altogether.

♛

Anna Khan was sixteen years old and the reigning women's chess
champion of Latvia when she enrolled at Murrow High School, the
latest pubescent prodigy to arrive in Brooklyn from a distant corner of
the crumbling Soviet empire. This was in 1993, ten years after Eliot
Weiss founded the school's chess club and a few months after it won
its first national championship. And for reasons entirely beyond Weiss's
control, Anna Khan was the first female ever to compete on his traveling team.

Anna Khan would lead Murrow to two more national championships, in 1993 and 1994. Eventually, after changing her name to
Anna Hahn, she won the U.S. Women's Championship in 2003 and
earned the title of WIM, which is the abbreviation used for a "Women's
International Master," a less stringent title than "International Master," and one that many of the best male players in the world deride as
a second-class designation. On a Web site that archives past games from
top players, the comments under Hahn's entry and photograph are a
catalog of puerilities ("Anna Hahn can mate me any day. Growl.") But
then, this is the way it has always been. Since the inception of competitive chess, the upper echelons of the game have reeked of sexism,
and women who dare intrude upon this sanctity are often treated with
as much subtlety as if they'd wandered into the back room at Scores.
"Guys aren't going to stand around and watch a guy's game because
he's a guy," Bruce Pandolfini says. "Maybe if he's Bobby Fischer, but
not for any other reason. But that's not why they stand around
women. And if they say it's for any other reason, they're lying."

Forty-five years earlier, when a U.S. women's champion named
Lisa Lane drew a sudden barrage of media attention (she was on the
cover of *Sports Illustrated,* and was profiled in *Newsweek* and *The New
York Times Magazine,* which described her as "comely" and "shapely"),
Fischer, an equal-opportunity bigot, dismissed her and her entire sex

with a barrage of insults. "They can't concentrate, they don't have stamina, and they aren't creative," he said of female chess players. "They're all fish." And that attitude didn't cease with Fischer: In 2002, Garry Kasparov told the *Times* of London that "chess is a mixture of sport, psychological warfare, science, and art," and that "when you look at all these components, man dominates. Every single component of chess belongs to the areas of male domination."

Of the top players in the world, only one, Hungarian Judit Polgar, is female, and fewer than ten of the world's 950 international grandmasters are women. Some efforts are being made to alter this: In recent years, Kasparov's own foundation has sponsored an all-girls national championship. But there remains a consensus among many of the best male players that this imbalance exists for a reason, that women are not *wired* for chess in the same way as men, that they are, by nature and through societal pressure, more social creatures, and that they would prefer to interact with others than be locked in a room by themselves, poring over esoteric middle-game theory. Which is why most of these girls, when they reach the age of twelve or thirteen, an age that Bruce Pandolfini calls "crucial" to one's development as a chess player, simply fade away. Which is why approximately ninety-seven percent of competitive chess players in the United States happen to be male.

Of the thirty-five participants in the high-school varsity section at the city championships, two were girls. One of them was Anna Ginzburg, who came up through the Chess-in-the-Schools program and landed one of those coveted spots at Stuyvesant High School. Ginzburg wears wire-rimmed glasses and has a tangle of thick brown hair and a penchant for feminine accessories, like her "Mrs. Affleck" tote bag. On the back of her Chronos digital clock, she's written her name in permanent marker, dotting the *I* with a flower and underlining the whole thing with a feminine flourish. When she was younger, she was painfully shy, but now she's gotten used to it, to being outnumbered and overlooked. At times, she is able to assimilate into this boys' world, beating them at cards and surprising them over the board and returning their banter when necessary. (Anna's rating is 1656, about the same as Oscar's, whom she defeated at cities after an overconfident Oscar hung a rook.) But the worst part, she says, is that when she travels to tournaments, she has so few people with whom she can share a hotel room. In that sense, she is very much on her own.

♛

Because there is such disparity in numbers, the women who break through in competitive chess, the women who can manage to thrive amid a sea of testosterone, tend to be unique and forceful personalities. Some, like Elizabeth Vicary, admit that they thrive on the attention (one Russian women's GM, Alexandra Kosteniuk, has posed for so many risqué photo shoots that she's been called "the Anna Kournikova of chess"). Many say they've never felt discriminated against, and that if anything, it's just the opposite: Men are so deferential, so cowed by their presence, that their brains often seize up and start melting when they play. Adults turn into randy adolescents. They make silly moves they would never make against other men, and when they are called on these things, they attribute their carelessness to the sex of their opponent: *Against a man, I would* never *make such a move.* "In most games, I am thinking about girls for fifty to seventy-five percent of the time, another fifteen percent goes to time management, and with what's left over I am calculating," grandmaster Alex Shabalov once admitted to Jennifer Shahade, the strongest female player ever to be born in this country.

Shahade is in her mid-twenties, with a shock of reddish-blond curls that she has, in the past, both dyed and disguised with a succession of wigs. She has a degree in comparative literature from NYU and a part-time job as a teacher at I.S. 318 and CIS, where, along with her brother and Elizabeth, she helped teach Nile and Willy and Shawn and Oscar and Dalphe. She also gives private lessons, participates in performance art, and has published a feminist manifesto called *Chess Bitch,* a memoir/history of women's chess in America (she appears on the cover wearing a come-hither expression and a bright pink wig).

Shahade grew up in Philadelphia. Her father and her older brother were both master-level players by the time she started taking chess seriously, while still a teenager at the Masterman High, a public school for gifted students (in 1996, Greg Shahade led Masterman to a national high-school championship). A few months later, her father, a burly man with a commanding presence, told her she would never be as good as he was; she went running out of the house. She began playing the game with absolute, naked aggression. "In retrospect I see my chess style was loaded with meaning—to be aggressive was to renounce any stereotype of my play based on my gender," she wrote in *Chess Bitch*. For practical reasons, she's toned down her style of play since then, but she remains almost pathologically competitive, an attribute that, Bruce Pandolfini would say, hampers her abilities as a teacher.

The Shahades and Elizabeth Vicary and their clique of friends imagine themselves as a new breed of chess player, more hipsters than nerds, more artists than actuaries. When the old stereotypes are reinforced, as when a television show called *Beauty and the Geek* puts up fliers at the Marshall Chess Club searching for a few misfits to fill the latter half of the title, this pisses off Jennifer Shahade. She's witnessed the next generation, and she's taught boys like Nile and Willy, who are anything but the traditional definition of a geek, and the way she figures it, the best thing she can do for the game is to bring it to places it's never been before. In 2003, she played an exhibition match at a downtown art gallery, and she wore a slinky black dress, black gloves, and a black flapper's wig. And her opponent, friend, and rival, who may turn out to be the most talented chess player ever to graduate from Edward R. Murrow High School, wore the same outfit, entirely in white.

♛

The circuitous route to America took Irina Krush and her family from the Ukraine through Austria and into Italy, and while they waited in limbo for their papers to arrive, with nothing else to do, Irina's father, an accountant, taught her how to play chess. This was in 1989; Irina was four and a half. When she was six, she won twenty dollars in a tournament at the Manhattan Chess Club, playing against men six and seven times her age. When she was twelve, she became a master. By the time she was fourteen, Irina's rating had risen above 2400, and Murrow's reputation as a home to exiled Eastern European chess talent had been firmly established. If you were a competitive chess player from Brooklyn, you just *knew,* the way Irina did, that this was where Anna Khan had gone, and this was where you belonged.

Maybe she could have taken the test and gotten into Stuyvesant, but what did she want with Stuyvesant? She had no desire to spend her formative years doing complex math homework and competing for college admissions. To tell the truth, she'd never much liked math. This might have been due to her eyesight, which started to degenerate somewhere around the third grade; in the five years it took her to get over her pride and admit that she couldn't see the equations on the chalkboard, any passion she had for numbers died.

And what did she want with numbers, anyhow? The reason her eyesight had deteriorated must have had something to do with all the reading she did in poorly lit rooms. She loved to read; she still does. If only she could have been a writer, or even a dancer—but for reasons she couldn't explain (maybe because she was an accountant's daughter), chess became her mode of self-expression. This has always been the way she's viewed the game, not as a clash of egos, not as some grand metaphor for war, not like Fischer and Kasparov have characterized it, as an opportunity to emasculate another human being. The best games, like that time in Buenos Aires when she sacrificed her knight and then her rook (and still managed to win), form like pearls do, over time, over a series of moves, which is why she does her best work in games with longer time control, games that unfold in four or five glorious hours. Oh, she knows there's an inescapable logic at work here, and she doesn't deny it, and she can respect that sort of thinking as well. But this is not the essence of chess. The essence of chess is all wrapped up in beauty. Even if you lose. And maybe this is a feminine perspective, but hell, she's known plenty of men who can appreciate the beauty of the game as much as she can. Otherwise, why would they spend all those hours studying by themselves? Otherwise, what would be the point?

That's how it worked for Irina too: As soon as she stopped working exclusively with teachers (first her father, until she was nine, and then a professional coach) and started working alone more often, around age twelve, that's when she fell in love with the game. Just *thinking* about a move made her happy. By thirteen, that love had grown, and by fourteen, by the time she wound up at Murrow, it had consumed her, to the point where the traditional subjects she studied in school just couldn't measure up.

Irina wanted freedom and understanding from a high school. She wanted room to roam, permission to play chess tournaments in Europe and take her assignments with her. She wanted a program tailored to her needs, and this is what Murrow and its flexible system could offer. "She didn't give a damn about school, and her father didn't give a damn," says Saul Bruckner, the former principal. "So I made up a special program, and I convinced her to stay."

Even Bruckner, who didn't play chess, who knew nothing about the game, understood that Irina Krush was a once-in-a-generation talent, a fact that became clear when she won the U.S. women's championship at the age of fourteen. "Coaching Irina is like coaching Wayne Gretzky," Eliot Weiss told *The New York Times* in 1999, when Irina was fifteen. "How do you coach Wayne Gretzky?"

The simple answer was that you didn't. In fact, Mr. Weiss hardly saw Irina, except when she accompanied her team to tournaments; his job was to smooth things over with her teachers when she was absent, to legitimize this pursuit of hers. Her high school years are such a blur that she can't remember much of what she did while she was there. By the end of her sophomore year, in 1999, she had finished virtually all of her class requirements. Her junior year, she came to school in the morning, took an American history class, and went home and studied. Her senior year, as far as she can remember, she didn't go to school at all, except when it came time to graduate. A Web site called Smartchess.com sponsored her travel and her lessons. When she was fifteen, she won acclaim for her innovative thoughts as an advisor in a chess match Garry Kasparov played against "the world" on Microsoft's Web site, in which visitors to the site voted on the moves to play against him. One of Krush's suggestions was so novel that even Kasparov didn't see it coming. She had her own instructional videos, known as "Krushing Attacks," which were sold on Smartchess.com. She studied the game for five or six hours a day, sometimes more. She had no real friends at Murrow because she was a ghost, a vague concept of a student, perhaps the most extreme example yet of the freedom Saul Bruckner was willing to grant to those who had earned his trust.

And how else was she supposed to compete with those young Russian masters, the ones who were either home-schooled or didn't go to school at all? She always finished her work, and she always went to class when she was supposed to. So why go through the motions of *getting an education,* when all she wanted to do with her life, at this moment in time, was to play chess?

By then, Murrow needed Irina Krush much more than Irina needed Murrow. These were lean years for Weiss's team, which was suddenly bereft of highly rated talent. They had finished fortieth at the nationals in Los Angeles in 1998, and with Irina elsewhere, they placed twenty-third in Sioux Falls in 1999. But in 2000, Irina's junior year, they arrived at the nationals in Charlotte after winning both the city championship and the state championship for the first time since 1994. Eliot Weiss brought seventeen kids with him that year, which was Rita's first year as the team's silent partner.

Here is what Irina remembers about that trip: The weather was nice. Charlotte was a pretty town. And at some point, she lost a game.

How she lost that game, she can't remember; that might have been the time she tried an e4 opening instead of d4, just fooling around with something new, and by the time she tried to dig herself out of trouble, extending the length of the game, it was too late. It didn't seem like much of a big deal at that point, but then the final round ended, and the results were tabulated, and Murrow had lost. By half a point. The Masterman School, the Shahades' alma mater, finished first. Afterward, Irina left her bag in the hotel, which was adjacent to the airport, and she went running off the plane at the last minute to retrieve it. When she didn't come back, Mr. Weiss got off to find her, and the plane left without them, with the rest of Mr. Weiss's family on board. They had to wait another six hours and take a connecting flight through Greensboro, and they arrived in New York exhausted and deflated.

So Irina figured she owed it to Mr. Weiss to play at the Supernationals in Kansas City in her senior year, in 2001. These tournaments meant nothing to her, really, in the midst of her quest for more exclusive titles (International Master, grandmaster) and more money to help pay for college, but it was the least she could do to repay her coach's kindness. Among the five thousand players at that Supernationals, Krush, at 2445, was the highest-rated, and she won her first three games with ease, until history repeated itself in an eerie way: She lost to a boy from Georgia named Richard Francisco, with a rating almost four hundred points below hers. And Murrow lost the team title to Hunter College High, another public school for the gifted (this one on Manhattan's Upper East Side), by half a point.

These losses hurt Mr. Weiss much more than they hurt Irina, of course. And it's not like either of them still sulk about it much. But for all of this talk of beauty trumping victory, for all this talk of scholastic tournaments meaning so little to elite players, Irina Krush remembers the losses. Even if, four years later, nearing her graduation from NYU, she can't remember the details of these trips, even if she can't remember a damn thing about her senior year, even if she can't even remember what *city* she traveled to for Supernationals in 2001. Of course, there were other players who lost in Kansas City, some in the final round with the pressure on, but Irina wasn't like them. Maybe it had something to do with her background, with that vestigial regard for Russian culture she carried within long after she became an American girl. This game, it meant more to her to than most people could ever know.

ELEVEN

TIRESOME DAYS AND
SLEEPLESS NIGHTS

HERE COMES OSCAR SANTANA AT THE END OF THE SCHOOL DAY, shambling through the halls in a red patent-leather jacket spangled with corporate racing logos, and here comes Sal Bercys, fresh out of gym class, wearing track pants and a fleece sweatshirt and looking like he's got Sisyphus's boulder crammed into that gargantuan backpack of his. They meet at a crossroads on the fourth floor, just as the last band of the day lets out, as their classmates swirl and duck and chatter all around them. Oscar fishes a deck of cards from the pocket of that shiny Technicolor coat, and then, as if driven by a subconscious urge, he begins to shuffle. "Me and my cards," he says. In these hallways, in this new era at Murrow High School, Oscar's deck is considered contraband material, but he and his friends have found ways to get around these draconian regulations. Mostly, they do this by hiding in the back of the lunchroom during their free periods and falling into marathon sessions of Stupid and Texas Hold 'Em. At times these sessions are so long that they neglect their next class, and this is one more reason why Oscar's chances of graduating this spring are looking more and more bleak. He's trying, though. He really is. And his flow of pocket money, well, that's never been better.

"Who is this guy, anyway?" Sal says, through clenched teeth.

This guy he's referring to is Lev Khariton, a chess teacher, chess writer, and all-around chess gadfly who's been invited to lecture this afternoon, Thursday, February 17, nine days before the start of the state championships in Saratoga Springs. And, for the first and only time all year, Mr. Weiss has declared attendance at chess club mandatory, for both the newbies and the traveling team, which does not sit well with Sal. "Sal has a very busy life," Oscar says, his tone deadpan and nasal, his eyes trained on the cards.

Sal ignores the joke entirely.

"This guy isn't even a *grand*master," he says. "He isn't even an IM. He's just a 2200. What are we going to do with this guy, anyway?"

"I think we're playing a simul."

"Uh-uh," Sal says. He's spinning in place now, his Diesel jacket flapping up above his waist, backpack twisting around his shoulders. "I'm not playing in any simul with this guy. No way. If he wants to lecture, fine, but I'm not playing any simul."

"You can beat him," Oscar says.

"I don't care," Sal says. "Maybe if we bet ten dollars a game, then I'd play him. What is this guy, a million years old, anyway?"

Oscar shrugs. "Is it just us?" he says, meaning the traveling team, the top eight.

"I think it's everybody."

"You mean I gotta sit there with all those clowns I ain't never seen in my life?"

"Remember when they took that team photo, and they said it was the chess team?" Sal says.

"I think Mr. Weiss just grabbed some of those people out of the hallway."

"I know. I think he posed a bunch of dummies."

Here come Willy and Nile now, joining the summit, and here comes one of those faceless newbies, Adalberto, his hair gelled and teased into spikes, unsure whether to join them or not. *"You,"* Sal says, and Adalberto stops dead, and his eyes widen, and he braces himself.

"No new players on the team have pride, except for you," Sal says.

Adalberto tries to take this coolly, but he can't help it. He nods, and then the whole charade breaks open and Adalberto is grinning, big and silly and proud. He keeps on walking toward Mr. Weiss's class-room, past the flyers posted on the hallway walls *(Senior Prom, Senior Trip, pay your dues now!!!)*, past the display of angst-ridden pencil drawings from the senior art classes, utterly mystified that the top chess player at Murrow High School, one of the best high-school chess players in this *country,* even knows who he is.

♛

It was hard to tell at the time, but Sal's comments to Adalberto could have been taken as a hint that Sal was changing, that behind the grand pronouncements, a certain humility had emerged. His failure last No-vember in Crete at the World Youth tournament had led Sal to ques-tion his entire view of himself, his attitude toward the game, and his views of those around him. That tournament was *horrible,* Sal kept on saying. Just horrible. So he had gone to the U.S. Championships with fewer expectations and less self-assuredness, and he'd had what he would describe later on as "the best tournament of my life." After that, he'd told himself there was no room for overconfidence.

Oh, he was still *confident:* He knew when he could win, when he *should* win, and he wasn't about to deny that he had certain abilities that others didn't. He still liked to tease and to mock, because that was his way, and he still didn't think it was worth debasing himself by playing against a clearly inferior opponent, someone like Lev Khari-ton. On the outside, he was still very much Sal. But he had found out something about himself that some teenaged boys never do. He had found out that he had limits.

♛

So this is the scene that greets Lev Khariton: Shawn sits in the back of the room, tossing a small rubber ball to himself, and Nile is wearing a Miami University basketball jersey that appears to have swallowed his entire torso, and Sal is sitting three rows back, flirting with the aspiring model once again (this time, she's showing him her portfolio, and Sal is rolling his eyes), and Willy and Oscar have once again fallen into an interminable argument (about hotel accommodations in Saratoga, specifically regarding the unlucky soul who will be forced to share a bed with big ol' Shawn), and Dalphe is measuring the time until he has to leave for the Thursday Chess-in-the-Schools session, and Ilya turns around and whispers, "I doubt this guy even knows what he's up against." Somewhere in the midst of this, a birthday card for Rita's eightieth is going around, and Mr. Weiss is urging everyone to sign it, even the newbies who have never *heard* of Rita, who aren't sure if Rita is another teacher, or Mr. Weiss's mother, or what. "If it wasn't for her, we might not be here," Mr. Weiss says. And then, a muttered punch line: "Well, we'd be *here,* anyway. But not anywhere else."

When they've settled into their seats, gathered before this small man with a nimbus of gray hair clinging to his scalp for dear life, Lev Khariton begins to lecture in a voice thick with Russian inflection. He's all hard consonants and elongated vowels, and he uses the word *yes* as a bridge, the way teenage girls fall back on *like.* He's wearing blue jeans and sneakers with velcro clasps, and he squints at his audience through a pair of foggy polyurethane lenses. "So," he says. "I don't exactly know your level, yes? I came to know you from the newspaper. I don't recall which one."

"We were in all of them, yeah," says Mr. Weiss. "We have all levels here. We have twelve hundreds and fifteen hundreds and two thousands and above."

Rex and Renwick and Adalberto and Robert, sitting on the far side of the room, exchange blank stares. Twelve hundred? Fifteen hundred? Yeah. *Right.* Try nothing, zero, nada, and zilch. Maybe pride counts for something with Sal, but not with the opponents who embarrassed them at the city championships. They come to this game so late; no doubt, they're starting to think maybe they've come *too* late. Even getting to twelve hundred is starting to look like an impossible dream.

"In New York, there are many tournaments," Lev Khariton is saying. "I meet a boy who is seven years old, and he plays in tournaments every weekend. But let me say, chess is also a science. In a sense, you can always improve, you can always learn, with all this computer science. But I show you an endgame, yes? This is from some years ago, from a tournament. I was in terrible time trouble, yes, and I still found a way to draw this game, yes?"

Through all of this, Sal's face is frozen in a metallic and vaguely sinister grin. Eventually, he lays his head flat on his desk, and when that position grows tiresome, he pulls a penny from his pocket and bats it around on his desk. Halfway through Khariton's lecture, Mr. Weiss can sense the boredom among his top players. He pulls them out into the hallway and goes over the arrangement for the trip to states: Meet up at school next Friday; half of them will ride with Ilya's father and the other half with Alex's father. When he's finished, most everyone scatters, except for Ilya, who sticks around to play in the simul against Khariton before he succumbs to the dreariness of his afternoon at the bank.

It is clear from the way he considers the board, the way he props himself up on one leg to peer over the entire board as the middle game progresses, that Ilya is determined to win this game. Khariton is a good five hundred rating points above him, but this is a simul, which means Khariton will be playing seven other opponents at the same time, which means Ilya has the benefit of a singular focus. And Ilya is always foisting little challenges on himself like this. He is not afraid of losing; he is afraid of not living up to expectations, and when he does meet his expectations, he raises them ever higher. Often, his performance is not so bad at all, but if it does not live up to Ilya's standards, or if he's made an obvious blunder, he will not hesitate to denigrate himself.

Khariton, playing black, opens the game with the King's Indian, a complex series of moves that frees up a knight and bishop on the side of the board in order to attack white's center. On his way out the door, Sal notices this and says, "Ilya, you're playing against my favorite opening, you know that?"

"Everybody plays the King's Indian," Ilya says.

"Yeah," Sal says. And then, as if he can't resist a barb, he says, "But I'm special at it."

Ilya puts up an extended fight; he is the last surviving player in the simul, long after the newbies have all been vanquished. But he is not quite strong enough; he is not *special* like Sal, and the fact that he is more well-rounded than Sal, that he plays an instrument and works a part-time job and does well in his classes and has abiding interests beyond the game, means little to him at moments like this.

"That boy, he reacts well, yes," Khariton says after Ilya leaves. "But he just couldn't get things together."

♕

A week later, Lev Khariton stands on a busy corner on the Upper East Side, where he has just finished giving a private lesson. This is how he makes his living, as a full-time chess teacher. When he left Murrow that day (he had simply cold-called Mr. Weiss and asked to come in and lecture), he said he'd like to start visiting regularly. Then he asked, "Is there any way you could remunerate me?" To which Mr. Weiss replied that he'd have to check with the administration.

Khariton also teaches twice a week at the Ramaz School, a Jewish yeshiva on the Upper East Side, and all of this produces just enough money for him to squeeze out a living, to support his wife and pay the rent for their apartment on Ocean Parkway. But then, it is hard for him to imagine doing anything else; his whole life has been defined by the game. In the time and place where he was born, in a nation that regarded chess as a pillar of its system of government, that was not such a fantastic notion.

In the wake of the Russian revolution, in 1917, "came the idea of the game as a *socialist* sport," wrote authors David Edmonds and John Eidinow, in *Bobby Fischer Goes to War.* "Chess in particular could help educate the proletariat and sharpen the minds of the workers, offering an ideologically sound activity after the rigors of a hard day's toil in the factory or on the collective farm." With that in mind, the All-Union Chess Section was created, under the auspices of a thick-necked Bolshevik named Nikolai Krylenko, and experts were hired by the state to spread the gospel of the game. Between 1923 and 1928, the number of chess players in Leningrad alone leapt from a thousand to 140,000. (The American Frank Marshall, on his return home from a chess tournament in Moscow in 1925, recounted traffic snarls caused by the hundreds of people hoping to gain entrance.) By 1951, the number of registered chess players in Russia had swelled to more than a million. The game had seeped into every aspect of the culture; at lunchtime, the stories went, factories all over Russia descended into deep silence while workers sat over their chessboards.

Lev Khariton's brother was fifteen years older and graduated from an institute in Moscow in 1952, with the nation in the last throes of Stalinism. Because the Khariton family was Jewish, Lev's brother couldn't get a job, and so he and his Jewish friends would come to the family's downtown apartment and play chess all day long. They played blitz, and Lev, who was seven, would join in, and he would lose over and over again. For six months, he would lose, and then he would cry. Lose and cry, lose and cry. "Then the day came when I started winning, yes?" he says.

He won again and again, until the winning actually started to get boring. So he asked his father to take him to a chess club, and they went to their district's House of Pioneers, a cultural clubhouse situated in a nineteenth-century mansion where the neighborhood's young children could study photography and dancing and singing, and where, in one musty back room, twenty-five or thirty boys would sit and play chess. There was no ratings system back then, so the boys were separated into five simple categories. Within a couple of years, Khariton had advanced from a fifth-category to a third-category player, and by the age of thirteen he was a first-category player. He was sent off to the nation's central chess club, where he took group lessons with a coach and theoretician named Alexander Kostantinopolsky. Eventually, Khariton played for the championship of Moscow, went to university, studied English literature, and became a translator for the chess federation in Moscow in the era leading up to the Fischer-Spassky match of 1972.

By then, his first teacher at the House of Pioneers, Yuri Brasilsky, had become an editor of chess literature in Moscow. In August of

1971, while Khariton was on vacation in Estonia, Brasilsky sent him a four-word telegram: LEV WE'LL TRANSLATE FISCHER. And this is what they did, in less than a month, at the urging of the government, who, given the inevitability of a clash between the Russian champion and Fischer, had decreed an urgent need for a translation of Fischer's *My 60 Memorable Games.* The book was published in April of the next year, in time for the Fischer-Spassky match, and sales were brisk. Fischer had grown up studying the Russian masters; now the Russians were studying Fischer. "Overnight, I became very famous," Khariton says. "Everybody knows me for translating this book, yes?"

There is a certain irony to the fact that Khariton recounts all of this while he sits at a top-floor table in a multistory McDonald's on Third Avenue in Manhattan, just about as far on the other side of the Cold War divide as one could get. Khariton's jacket is zipped tight over a sweater and a button-down shirt, and every so often when he gets especially excited, a small piece of french fry, a potato projectile, shoots between the gaps in his crooked front teeth.

These days, even without the same level of government support that Khariton once had, gifted young chess players still emerge on a regular basis from the former Soviet Union. Of course, by the time they come of age, they wind up scattered around the world, like Sal and Alex and Ilya, like Irina Krush and Anna Hahn. They emigrate to Europe and America, in search of more fruitful lives, just like Khariton did (he spent time in Paris and Israel before moving to New York in 1999). And here in America the opportunities are greater, and the fast food is tastier, and the distractions are plentiful, and the notion of chess as a serious sport simply doesn't exist. Maybe Garry Kasparov has done well for himself, Khariton admits, but alas, he's not exactly Schwarzenegger. Here in America, a man like Lev Khariton, a man who gained fame in his native country simply for translating a book filled with chess games, has to plead for work. Here in America, the students Lev Khariton does have don't treat the game with the same reverence he did when he was young. They consider it a *game,* an entertainment. "Russians study chess very seriously," Khariton says. "We had to work,

because chess is not enough to give you a living. But you had to ana-
lyze, yes? It is not like I just came and improvised. Here, there is no
professional approach to chess. In this country, if you can be a teller in
a bank and make more than you could as a chess player, why should
you bother yourself with tiresome days and sleepless nights, yes?"

This very fact is what has always astounded Lev Khariton about
Bobby Fischer. He saw Fischer in person once, when he came to visit
Moscow in the summer of 1958 and played at the city's Central Chess
Club. Fischer was fifteen; Khariton was thirteen. (In 1992, when Fischer emerged from isolation for a lackluster rematch with Spassky, he
declared the Russian translation of *My 60 Memorable Games* an illegal
act because he received no royalties.) But Khariton had this support
system, the chess clubs and the instructors and the government infrastructure devised to produce champions and validate the entire system. Fischer had few people to turn to, and fewer places to go. With
the exception of certain acquaintances, he was very much alone in
Brooklyn.

So Fischer was a miracle, and Khariton doubts very much that a
miracle like this could occur more than once. It requires something
more than devotion, something more than commitment; it requires
love. And this love cannot be forced. And this love must be coupled
with other attributes, such as stamina ("You mustn't break down") and
the ability to withstand defeat, which means the ability to overcome
self-doubt. A few years ago, when Khariton interviewed Boris Spassky,
he asked if Spassky had ever feared an opponent. To which Spassky
replied that he feared only himself. "You should be totally devoted to
the game," Khariton says. "At one point, if you have a winning game
and you lose it, you should come home and not be able to sleep at
night, yes?"

One of Khariton's best students is a boy of grade-school age
who lives on the Upper East Side and attends a private school in
Manhattan. This boy, T, despite being American, has the love, no
question. He can spend five or six hours staring at a chessboard and
never lose his focus. But what does that mean? His parents, they ask

Khariton sometimes if their son has what it takes to become a grand-master or a world champion, and Khariton tells them he cannot answer this question. "Even the Lord cannot answer this question," he tells them.

This is another problem: The parents must understand what it takes as well. They must understand what chess *means*. They must regard it as a professional pursuit, just as Lev Khariton did when he was a boy. At a recent tournament, T's parents came to watch, and T had a winning position, and he made a horrible blunder and was checkmated in a single move. He fell into a fit of hysterical crying. And his mother, his dear American mother, pulled him to her breast and she whispered to him, over and over again, "It's just a game."

Just a game? And to think, Khariton says: It will only get harder for T, as he grows older, as temptations beyond chess emerge, as this country reveals itself as a place that sees no value in subsidizing talented young chess players, any more than it sees reason to subsidize Scrabble or mah-jongg or backgammon.

"This boy, in his heart, already he thinks it's something serious, yes?" Lev Khariton says. He is almost shouting now. "If the people around him think it's a game, it's very difficult to make progress, yes? You have to suffer a little bit. If someone is crying, it's *good*. Yes?"

Twelve

The 2005 New York State Scholastic Championships

Saratoga Springs, New York

USCF Ratings:

Sal Bercys	2453
Alex Lenderman	2436
Shawn Martinez	1897
Ilya Kotlyanskiy	1756
Oscar Santana	1752
Willy Edgard	1694
Nile Smith	1610
Dalphe Morantus	1586

Almost home now, and he's riding this one out high above the board, with a foot on the floor and the opposite knee on the cushion of his chair, like Washington crossing the Delaware. His head is sagging toward his left shoulder, and his eyes are darting back and forth, between the seconds on the clock (38, 37, 36 . . .) and the position of his pieces *(What did I miss? Where is the trap?).* That's his queen poised in the center, and he pushes his king to the d2 square, a time-killing move, and he punches the clock and there it goes again, down under thirty, down under twenty, come *on* already *(Don't fuck this one up, do not fuck this one up).* Saturday, 6:34 P.M., inside the Grand Ballroom of the Prime Hotel and

Conference Center in Saratoga Springs, and Ilya Kotlyanskiy is this close
(10, 9, 8 . . .) to pulling off the upset of the day (. . . 7, 6, 5, 4 . . .)—
hell, the upset of his *life*—over Josh Weinstein, Stuyvesant's No. 1 board,
rated 2111, the all-city soccer player, the future Ivy Leaguer, the handsome fellow who just kicked off the bathroom slippers he was wearing
and yanked the hood of his black Princeton sweatshirt (3 . . . 2 . . .) over
his ears. Even Sal is watching, and Sal is grinning, and Sal has just turned
around and let loose with a look that says "Can you believe this?" *Snap,*
goes the clock, as Weinstein flails at a piece and punches it with a single
second remaining on his side, but it's too late. Ilya makes another delay-
ing move, and when it *(snap!)* comes back to Weinstein, he has only the
standard five-second delay between moves to ponder a desperate flourish before his clock starts running again, one, two, three, four, *five,* and
then that last 0:01 runs off and Ilya stands up from his crouch, head still
pinned to his neck, and Sal slaps his back and Weinstein shakes his hand
and it's over. He's done it! The perfect day of chess! Three wins, no
losses, no draws! And he's beaten Stuyvesant's top board!

He clears the pieces with as much calm as he can muster, sweeping
them into his blue vinyl carrying case. Then he gets up and goes to
pour himself a drink of water from a silver pitcher in the hallway, and
his hands are shaking so badly he can hardly do it without spilling.
Last night he shared a bed with his father and woke up with a stiff
neck; he's been popping Motrin just to get through the day. His father
(who had served as one of the designated drivers, along with Alex's father, since Mr. Weiss and his family met up with the team in Saratoga
after spending the previous week skiing upstate) is upstairs in their
room on the third floor, passing the time while his son plays chess.
And for the first time in months, Ilya cannot wait to get back to him.
"I'm going to go up and tell my dad now," he says. And then, to himself, he says, "No one believed I could win it."

♛

Before all of this, before Ilya's father got lost on the wrong freeway
and wound up taking six hours to make what should have been a

three-and-a-half-hour trip, before eight city boys converged in this quaint little hamlet thirty miles north of Albany and twenty miles south of the Adirondack Mountains, Ilya had been abandoned by his teammates. This was a couple of weeks earlier, out in the concrete-and-strip-mall wilderness of New Jersey. It was not an intentional snub, but it was something Ilya had gotten used to by now; so often in this dynamic, he was the odd man out. He wasn't a member of the Russian elites, like Sal and Alex, and he wasn't part of the Chess-in-the-Schools clique, and so what was he? He was their captain, and yet sometimes he hardly even felt like their friend.

Every February a series of team tournaments are held, known as the U.S. Amateur team events. There is one in the South, one in the Midwest, one in the West, and one in the East, which is held at a Hilton in a middle-of-nowhere industrial park in Parsippany. Each team at the U.S. Amateur has four players, and the cumulative team results determine the winners. Because there are no cash prizes (only plaques and digital game clocks, which go to the winners in each section), and because it is one of the few chess tournaments of the year in which every man is not fending for himself, the pressure is more diffuse and the atmosphere is more congenial. Each team comes up with its own name, which cannot be obscene, but can certainly delve into the risqué (Rock Out With Your Rook Out) or the topical (Wepawns of Mass Destruction) or the nerd-fantastic (Hippogriffs), and the teams with the best chess-related name and the best chess-related "costumes or gimmick" win back their entry fees.

The team that named itself Fock Lenderman wasn't looking to win anything, except perhaps a small measure of revenge. They were out to embarrass Alex, who had withdrawn from their roster at the last minute when he realized he didn't want to lose any ratings points over a tournament that was essentially meaningless. It was becoming increasingly clear, as his rating improved, that this was the way Alex and his father wanted to handle his burgeoning chess career. Their concern was for the bottom line, for what the games could provide them (in terms of both money and ratings points), and if that pissed off certain people, if it left them scrambling to find a fourth board at the last minute, well then, so be it. Let them have their fun. Alex and his father would spend their weekend at home.

But Ilya had been looking forward to this, to a weekend away from his mother and father, to a couple of days in an overcrowded hotel room in New Jersey with nothing to do but lie around and watch bad television and eat junk food and play chess. He was supposed to form a team with Willy and Oscar and Shawn, but then, because CIS had paid for some of its students to play in this tournament, it saddled their team with another member, an Elizabeth Vicary protégé now at Brooklyn Tech (they called their team the I.S. 318 All-Stars). And it was too late for Ilya to join up with his other non-Murrow friends, who had already formed their own foursome (which was plaintively dubbed Size Doesn't Matter). Maybe he could have gone there just to hang out and play blitz, but this wasn't Ilya's way. That would have been a waste of time, and Ilya didn't waste time, and besides, the state championship was looming and the SATs were coming up in early May and the preparation for that alone (he was taking a Kaplan course, which he had paid for himself with the money he made working at Washington Mutual) was about to swallow him whole. So perhaps it was better this way; he'd come to states with a fresh outlook, with his brain uncluttered by potential openings and novel strategies, and maybe he could surprise the hell out of all those people who didn't believe what he was capable of doing.

♛

It does not take them long to figure out that this place is not exactly Brooklyn. The site of the state championship revolves from an upstate location to a downstate location each year, and this year it's upstate, in Saratoga Springs, whose downtown business district consists primarily of one main street, known as Broadway. But this Broadway, well, it's not exactly Broadway. The Prime Hotel and Conference Center stands at the far end of town, near a liberal-arts college called Skidmore, near the bars where Dylan got his start and Don McLean is said to have written "American Pie." Before it became known for its bohemian culture and its horse races, held in front of capacity crowds each August, Saratoga Springs was a resort town, replete with spas and mineral springs. It was founded a few miles north of the site where the Battle of Saratoga turned the American revolution in favor of the colonies. Even now, the town feels like a placid retreat: the buildings on and off Broadway, down narrow side streets that dead-end within a couple of blocks, are small and quaint, and chain stores coexist with used book-stores and coffee shops, and nearly everyone you see on the street is white.

None of this really matters to the Murrow boys, of course—the history, the geography, the world outside of the hotel. As long as they can get some kind of fast food, pizza, Subway, McDonald's, and as long as there are chess sets and a deck of cards, they can subsist in this environment for as long as necessary. They can fend for themselves. Friday night they order from the local Domino's and Oscar works his magic, somehow managing to sweet-talk the deliveryman ("Brooklyn-style," Sal says) into reducing the price of the pies by ten dollars. And when they are finished eating, they play cards. And they keep on playing well past the "curfew" Mr. Weiss has established, so that the next morning it is not hard to discern those impulsive souls who stayed up half the night. Even Dalphe Morantus, the innocent little freshman, who has done all he can to not get sucked into this vortex of dubious behavior, was jumped by his roommates at four in the morning for no apparent reason. And now they are all paying the price.

Just take a look at Oscar, who's wearing a rumpled red bowling shirt and taking life-sustaining hits from a bottle of Mountain Dew. Or Shawn, he of the lead-weighted eyelids and the drooping skull, or Willy, staring at a brick wall in a hypnotic daze. Oscar and Shawn shared a bed last night, the two biggest boys on Murrow's roster wrestling over the blankets, and now Oscar is accusing Shawn of cheating at a game neither of them has actually played before, this thing called *Plunder* Chess, whose inventors have strategically placed sets throughout the hotel accompanied by hyperbolic press materials, in order to market their novelty. *"Imagine what would happen in a game of chess, if your chess-men could acquire additional moving capabilities as they played? What if your queen could move as a queen or a knight and your pawn could move as a pawn or a bishop? How about escaping check by letting your king move as a rook? Well . . . imagine no more."*

To be honest, these notions do not excite Oscar very much. It is almost eleven in the morning, time for the start of Round One, and Oscar would be quite happy to imagine crawling back into bed for a few more hours, thank you very much. The only good news is that the competition this year is almost nonexistent: Of the thirteen highest-rated players in the high-school section, eight are from Murrow. If they can stay awake, they should be able to win. Only their rivals at Stuyvesant, at one of the best public high schools in America, could think of keeping up with them. And with Sal and Alex as Murrow's top boards, even that seems like a long shot.

"It's gonna be like a fricking head-to-head matchup," Oscar says to one of the boys from Stuyvesant, Daniel Rohde, rated 1674, a skinny boy in a Peyton Manning football jersey whose father is a grandmaster and whose mother, Sophia, a scholastic chess teacher, is an official at this very tournament. And at this very moment, Sophia Rohde is con-sidering the first-round pairings board she has just posted, loaded with names from Murrow, and she is muttering, "Poor little Stuyvesant."

♛

It is hard to take this lament seriously, given the circumstances. In few aspects of life do the boys from Murrow have the edge over anyone, let alone a flock of kids from a high school whose student body's av-erage SAT score is somewhere around 1400, and whose number one board and team captain seems destined to wind up as a congressman. Josh Weinstein, in addition to being an all-city soccer player, is also a club hockey player, and he joined the track team for the hell of it this spring, and on top of that he runs a popular school-related Web site. He has a winsome smile and mussed brown hair and the self-assured presence of a boy who has never wanted much for anything. He grew up on the Upper East Side, the son of an art dealer and a fashion designer, and he attended private schools all his life before gaining admission to Stuyvesant. In the fall, he will start his freshman year at Princeton, where he will major in public policy, with the goal of becoming a politician, in addition to being the fourth board on the Princeton chess team. He has played the game on and off since taking kindergarten classes at the Dalton School, mainly because he was one of the only kids in his class to stay awake during chess instruction with the school's renowned teacher, Svetozar Jovanovic. One year at Dalton, his team won a national championship. They were honored at an assembly, and their classmates and teachers afforded them the requisite applause. "After that," he says, "nobody really gave a shit. People liked it if we won, but if we didn't, nobody really cared."

He made some good friends at Dalton, but the whole insular private-school vibe wasn't really his thing. Some of his friends were pushed so hard by their parents that they quit playing chess. But Weinstein always found a way to motivate himself. When he was in the eighth grade, he wrote an essay about Woodrow Wilson and decided he didn't want to go to college anywhere else except Princeton. Once he gained admission to Stuyvesant by scoring in the top couple of percent on a citywide entrance exam (the same exam used to determine admissions to Brooklyn Tech and Bronx Science; top scorers get their first choice among those schools), Princeton became a concrete possibility.

There are three thousand students and a hundred different clubs at Stuyvesant, not to mention the several dozen social strata present at any large high school, let alone one with such underlying competitive pressures. Josh Weinstein is one of those rare teenagers who is able to move among them. After soccer season ended in the fall, he transitioned straight into chess club, which meets on Monday afternoons in a classroom on the eighth floor of a building so close to the World Trade Center that it was used as a base of rescue and recovery operations in the aftermath of September 11. Ever since the old advisor, William Arluck, retired a few years back, the students at Stuyvesant have essentially been running the chess club on their own; this year, Weinstein's father is footing the bill for their trips to the state and national tournaments, with the expectation that the school will reimburse him for the expenses. This is part of the reason they see themselves as underdogs here. They have no Eliot Weiss to organize them, and they have no Rita to bankroll them, and they have no Sal, and they have no Alex. They have the advantage in so many aspects of life, except this one, and maybe this is fair play, or maybe, as some of their opponents have claimed, it's hellaciously unfair, but it certainly puts a boy like Josh Weinstein in a position to which he is not accustomed.

The first-round pairings might as well be a joke; Shawn's got a 995, a cherubic kid chomping on a stick of gum whose rating is half of his own, and Sal's got a 1700 (for Christ's sake, he could beat a 1700 if he were *still* sleeping). There is nothing even resembling a challenge here, except the one issued by the tournament director, Steve Immitt, a disheveled man with a stooped walk who issues the same unheeded decree at every scholastic tournament he's ever officiated. "There are going to be times when you're going to want to cheer your teammates on," he says. "We can't really have that. We're not going to allow it. We ask that you check your board quickly and get out of the tournament site."

The good news for Murrow, at least in this round, is that there is nothing worth hanging around to watch in the Grand Ballroom, yet another bland and windowless cavern, this one with maroon patterned carpets and mirrored walls. Some of their opponents are so inexperienced they don't even have ratings; they come from upstate schools with fledgling programs. "My goodness, what's an Edward R. Murrow?" says one of their parents, upon scanning the pairings.

These are longer games than what they faced at the city championships, sixty minutes per side instead of thirty, but against such weak opponents, who needs the extra time? The pace of a chess game can be contagious. Sometimes you're better off moving fast, forcing the pace, throwing off the timing of a less-experienced opponent and leading him into a trap.

Down the hall, Sal and Alex have been sequestered in Seattle Slew, a small conference room named after the 1977 Kentucky Derby winner and adorned with oil portraits of thoroughbreds. It's set up in the manner of a professional tournament, with three rows of chairs facing the top four tables: two from the high-school section, two from the junior-high section. These chairs are ostensibly for spectators ("They're trying to be like nationals or something," Willy says), and despite a story planted on page three of *The Saratogian,* the local paper—"Some of the country's best scholastic players will compete, including 15-year-old Salvijus Bercys (former junior champion in Lithuania) and Alex Lenderman, 15, the No. 1 and No. 2 players, respectively, in the United States"—for most of the next two days, the spectators are comprised almost entirely of the following people: Mr. Weiss, Elizabeth Vicary, Alex's father, and John Galvin, the teacher at I.S. 318 whose students are playing at the top two junior-high tables. The doors to Seattle Slew are left open and nobody seems bothered by the tinny stream of elevator music trickling into the room like the sound track to a root canal; accompanied by Seals & Crofts, Alex sacrifices his queen, which leads to an easy victory over an opponent who never saw the checkmate coming. Murrow finishes round one with eight wins, and zero losses. They are on their way once more.

♛

This is not the best day to be Josh Weinstein. He's been fighting off some kind of bug all morning long; now he's sucking on saltines and drinking Gatorade and trying to bring himself back against Willy Edgard, Murrow's, what, No. 6 board? This shouldn't be happening, but, hell, this is what happens when you actually start caring about chess. Sophomore and junior year, for the first time in his life, Weinstein didn't put much effort at all into his chess, just kept at it so he could put it on the résumé he sent to Princeton. So senior year, he starts to find that love again, figures he should give chess one last full go before he graduates, and what happens? He starts playing worse, and he starts second-guessing every move he makes.

And now he's down to nine seconds on his clock against Willy. And each time he captures a piece, he sweeps it onto the floor with an angry flourish, so there are black pawns and bishops and knights littering the carpet at his feet. It doesn't look good for Weinstein, but there is good news: Willy is running on empty himself. The lack of sleep has begun to catch up to him, and he's playing defensively, trying to milk a victory by speeding up his own pace. He knows he shouldn't get caught up in a blitz game against an opponent like Weinstein, but this is Willy, and he can't help himself. Weinstein is able to conjure each move within the five-second delay before the numbers on his clock dribble any further. He starts picking off Willy's pawns. Willy offers a draw; Weinstein refuses. And by the time he pins Willy's king, he still has those nine seconds to spare.

And what is going on with Oscar, at the other end of this long row of tables next to the mirrored wall? Well, Oscar's dog-tired, too, which explains why he just drew with a 1200. Hard enough playing three games of chess in one day, let alone playing three games of chess in one day on three or four hours of sleep. And despite all of this, nobody seems particularly concerned that the team score, the cumulative results of each team's top four boards, now goes like this: Murrow 8, Stuyvesant 7.

♛

It is impossible to escape the tyranny of the ratings system in chess. It is a measure of one's intelligence, one's self-worth, one's identity, and one's importance within the societal hierarchy. Your rating is the cumulative statistical evaluation of every tournament game you have ever played, and because of that it is considered a foolproof system, one that has been evaluated and reevaluated by professors and statisticians with a fanaticism for the game and too much extra time on their hands. Part of its beauty is that it can determine precisely the odds of, say, a 1700 like Ilya beating a 2100 like Weinstein: somewhere around eight percent. But none of these numbers take into account the human element, mental fatigue, physical ailments, the tendency of the mind to wander or to freeze up when faced with added pressures like a running clock or a captive audience. "It's a game of little differences," says Bruce Pandolfini, the famed chess coach. "Working slightly harder. Focusing slightly more. Perhaps looking a half-move further ahead, or sleeping a little bit more so you're in better shape, or eating better. Those things *do* matter."

Often, these things work against a boy like Ilya, so self-aware, so high-strung. But as afternoon slips into evening, and Ilya goes back downstairs to check the pairings and sees that he's facing Weinstein, he figures, for once in his life, that he has nothing to lose. He had said that he wasn't ready to eat before the second round, that food only made him fatigued, but Ilya had already met his goal by Saturday afternoon, to win two of his three games each day, so he figures he can relax his restrictions. In midafternoon, long before he becomes aware he will face Josh Weinstein, Ilya feasts. On his way toward the elevator, while trying to balance a cup of soup atop a sandwich and maintain a grip on the soda in his other hand, he says, "I figure my third game will either be easy or hard. So I'm breaking the fast."

And because Weinstein is tired out and sick and still pissed off about his near loss to Willy, the numbers start to mean less and less. For those couple of hours, Ilya is free: no worrying about his job or his classes or the SATs or where he might get into college or what he might study once he gets there or how he might possibly live up to the expectations he's built for himself.

Weinstein, playing white, opens by pushing a pawn to e4, and Ilya responds by meeting that pawn at e5, and the game progresses, Weinstein playing a variation on the Vienna opening. (See the first diagram on the following page.)

Ilya *hates* the Vienna; never plays it himself. But he was ready for this; he knew what was coming. He'd played Weinstein at the city championships, and he was black then, too, and with his third move, instead of taking a pawn, he'd moved out his bishop to the c4 square. This was a *book* play—it makes the most sense, according to common

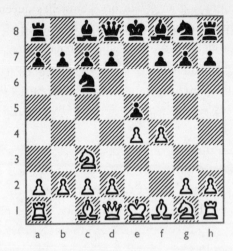

theory—but in this case, with this opening, Weinstein knew the book on the Vienna a *hell* of a lot better than Ilya did. (Before they'd started the game, Weinstein had even said something to him about that last game, about bc4 and what a futile move it was, anticipating that Ilya might try it again.) So he was better off taking the pawn, throwing him off. What did he have to lose?

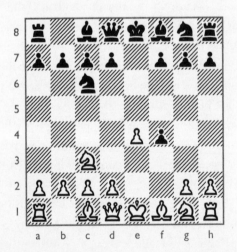

With his sixth move, Ilya takes a knight with his bishop and briefly puts Weinstein into check, giving up his bishop to gain an advantage in position, mounting an attack on Weinstein's queen's side. It goes back and forth from there, the castling, the trading of pieces—"I had many problems in development and counterattacking," Ilya would say later. "The only thing that saved me was that I surprised him by taking that pawn early on"—until Ilya begins advancing his pawn on the queen's side, the game sliding toward a draw. And then, suddenly, he sees it—knight takes pawn on c4:

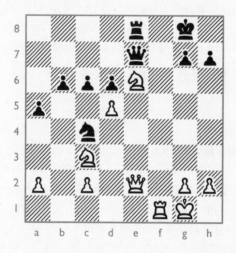

Twenty-five moves per side to this point, and Ilya has the distinct advantage. In chess notation, an exclamation point signifies a good move, and two exclamation points signify a very good move. This move, Ilya labels with three exclamation points (!!!). It is bold, it is shrewd, and it is debilitating. Weinstein can capture Ilya's knight with his queen, but then Ilya is up a pawn heading into the endgame, and more than that, he has a distinct advantage in position: Eventually, he will queen one of his pawns, which means that eventually he will win. Instead, Weinstein plays a safe move, and Ilya takes another pawn, and then it is only a matter of time, a matter of playing it out until the end and bleeding those final seconds off the clock.

That night, after Ilya's miracle, after Murrow wins seven of its eight third-round games to take a two-and-a-half-point lead over Stuyvesant (11.5 to 9), Mr. Weiss orders pizza again, and they eat it downstairs in the common area of the hotel, and even Ilya's father, the weekend's designated driver, a man so small and so quiet that he can sit in one place for hours and go virtually unnoticed, leaves the sanctuary of his hotel room to join them. Ilya's father doesn't play chess, even though his own father was once a master in the Soviet Union; all he knows is that his son either plays well or plays poorly, based upon his demeanor. But he has such grand expectations for Ilya, his only surviving child, the first member of the family to grow up in this country, free of religious bias and economic destitution. How can Ilya, such a bright and promising young talent, not succeed in *everything* he does?

"All right," Mr. Weiss says. "In bed by midnight tonight, right?"

♛

The fifth round, on Sunday afternoon, is where the whole thing unravels. All those years of training, all that instruction, all the effort by Mr. Weiss to bring a team like this together, and it doesn't mean a damn thing if you're too tired to think straight. They could make it for only so long on such little sleep, on a harried Vegas itinerary of play all day and play all night. The good news for Oscar is that he's turned fifteen dollars into seventy-six by playing Hold 'Em; the bad news is that he has three games of chess to play yet, on virtually no sleep. Somehow, fueled by the bagels Mr. Weiss buys for them on Sunday morning, they win six of eight matches in Round Four, although Ilya, despite being way up on time, breaks his winning streak against a 1900, and an exhausted Willy gives up a draw to a 1200.

And then, at 12:20 P.M., the pairings go up for the fifth round, with this at the top:

Sal Bercys v. Alex Lenderman (FORCED!*!*)

That word, and the trail of punctuation that follows it— FORCED!*!*—are meant to assuage them both, to help them realize that despite the fact they are teammates, and this match will almost certainly cost their team a half of a point regardless of the outcome (they'll get a total of one point out of it, instead of the two Sal and Alex could pick up if they were playing separate opponents), the tournament organizers had no choice, since Sal and Alex are the only two undefeated players remaining in this tournament. FORCED!*!* How much good did that word do either of them? None. Absolutely none. And nobody hates being forced into this more than Sal and Alex, who would have to perpetuate the charade of competition once more before accepting another draw. For the first time since they'd started playing on the same team, with the help of his "victory" at the city championships, Alex's USCF rating (2436) has nearly caught up to Sal's (2453). It's a sign of how the status quo seems to be changing, how Sal has discovered his limits after his experiences last fall, how Alex is growing ever more protective of his rating, and how the irreconcilable differences between the two of them seem to grow week by week. There is nothing Sal would like to do more right now than play this one out, but because Mr. Weiss is his teacher and Mr. Lenderman is his ride, he can't do it.

That the winner of this tournament would qualify for the Denker Tournament of Champions in Phoenix, a scholastic event pitting the best players in each state against each other, means nothing to them, either, and neither does the fact that the winner of the Denker could win a college scholarship to the University of Texas in Dallas.

"What's the weather in Arizona?" Sal says.

"It's hot there, but it's air-conditioned," says Harold Stenzel, the ubiquitous and mullet-haired Long Island chess official, who happens to be working the Seattle Slew Room this morning.

"How hot?"

"It's like a hundred and eight during the day."

"Do they have sun-conditioning too?"

"The best time to go out is early in the morning," Stenzel says. "When the sun's coming up."

Sal rolls his eyes. As *if*.

"What's the point of going there?" Alex rasps. "So I can go to Dallas College? I'm not going to go there."

"Well," Stenzel says, looking at Sal, "*you* already won the scholarship two years ago, when you won the U.S. Juniors."

"I'd say I'm not going there either," Sal says. "It's too far."

"Well," Stenzel says, "Dallas is a little bit cooler than Arizona."

"Yeah," Alex says. And now he turns to his father. "But you still have to go far away from your parents for four years."

"You might change your mind by the time you're a senior."

"Maybe," Sal says. "But I'm a sophomore. A stupid, stupid, sophomore."

♛

The draw takes approximately one minute to play out, and when it's over, Sal and Alex retreat back to the hotel hallway to play blitz, to attempt to settle their ongoing power struggle once more. At the same time, events in the Grand Ballroom are unraveling quickly and catastrophically. The pairings have fallen into place for Stuyvesant, affording them three head-to-head matchups against Murrow: Shawn versus Justin Li (1470); Nile versus Eugene Belilovsky (1759); and Ilya versus his friend, Anna Ginzburg (1585).

The disaster commences with Oscar, who plays the Orangutan, the b4 opening, against Gregory Kimmel, the 1900 who ruined Ilya's streak. Then he decides to sacrifice his queen, as he says afterward, "for no apparent reason." Down he goes. Nearby, Willy is leaning forward in his chair, the back legs dangling in midair, trying to find a way to milk a draw, down a queen and a bishop against an Indian boy who seems far too little to be playing in this section. And Ilya is trying to force Anna out on time, since she has only eleven seconds on her clock and he has sixteen minutes and everybody knows Anna struggles with time trouble, but he's down a knight and she's in better position. She's taking deep breaths and sipping from a foot-tall can of some kind of energy drink and her Nikes are bobbing up and down. And Ilya's back to worrying about where he'll finish, about whether those three wins yesterday might land him in the top five, whether a top-five finish might be worth mentioning in his application essay to Georgetown or MIT or NYU, whether he's ready for the SAT, whether his father will still speak to him if he loses to Anna, a girl he *knows* he should be able to beat. He had a premonition the afternoon before, that if he somehow managed to beat Weinstein, the gods of chess would punish him with a bad day on Sunday, and now the prophecy is fulfilling itself.

Shortly after Ilya resigns, Shawn does the same, the victim of a sneak attack from Justin Li, Stuyvesant's fourth board. Then an overmatched Nile does the same against Belilovsky, so now Stuyvesant's picked up at least three points in this round alone.

"I can't see anything," Willy says on his way out of the room.

"You drunk?" Shawn says.

"Naw," Willy says. "I'm tired. You guys kept me up all night. Why would I be drunk?"

"You said you can't see nothing. I thought you was drunk."

"What the hell's going on?" Sal says. "How are we losing to Stuyvesant?"

"Hey, Willy," says a passerby, one of his friends from Chess-in-the-Schools. "How did you lose to that little midget?"

"Huh?" Willy says. He's standing near the pairings board, listening to a Cam'ron CD and zoning out.

"How'd you lose to that little dude?"

"I'm hungry," he says, "and I can't see anything."

♛

Not that Dalphe isn't hungry too. He's starving, actually. For such a little boy, one who's often mistaken for a sixth-grader instead of a high-school freshman, Dalphe can put away the calories. But he's trying not to think about the sandwiches for sale in the lobby, or the meal Mr. Weiss promised he'd buy them that afternoon. He's trying to finish off this game against an 1884, a kid rated three hundred points higher than he is, and while he doesn't realize it, he just might save Murrow's weekend in the process.

At a young age, Dalphe Morantus was something of a prodigy. His mother, a Haitian immigrant who works in the administrative offices of a Queens hospital, sent him to P.S. 233 in their Canarsie neighborhood, where he learned the game from a Chess-in-the-Schools instructor named Eric Hutchins. When he was in the fourth grade, he beat a Russian women's grandmaster in a simultaneous exhibition at Borough Hall in Brooklyn. He went to his first nationals with Chess-in-the-Schools that same year, in 2000, and he tied for first place in the K-6 under-900 section, cementing his place as one of the program's great young successes; there is a an enlarged photo of Dalphe, a close-up of those great big eyes and that round expressive face, on the wall near the entry to the CIS offices. He applied to I.S. 318 for junior high (even though it's halfway across Brooklyn from Canarsie, a working-class neighborhood at the end of the L subway line) so he could continue playing chess, but then he got lazy when he got there and found other interests, like hip-hop dancing classes. By the time he got to Murrow (Mr. Weiss had first made contact with him in the sixth grade), with a rating somewhere around 1500, his enthusiasm for the game had begun to wane. At Murrow, he had no one who could teach him. He had no Ms. Vicary, he had no Mr. Hutchins, and he certainly couldn't afford to pay for private lessons.

But the week before this tournament he'd gone to see Mr. Hutchins at the CIS offices, and Mr. Hutchins had taught him an opening he'd never seen before, a variation on the Vienna, and his opponent fell into the trap Mr. Hutchins had explained.

With his sixth move, Dalphe pushes a pawn from d2 to d4, and now he's attacking one of black's pawns and opening up the center of the board, and while his teammates are shriveling up all around him, Dalphe is on the offensive. His win (over an 1800!) is the only one of the round for Murrow, and he emerges from the Grand Ballroom with a dazed grin and Sal rubs his head and Oscar hugs him and Willy shakes his hand, and they all realize that their littlest member, who had enough sense to get a solid night's sleep in a different hotel room last night, has just bailed their asses out.

"You've got to be joking," says Daniel Rohde, running a finger over the previous round's results, the yellow Xerox tacked to a bulletin board detailing Murrow's carnage: Draw, Loss, Loss, Loss, Loss, Loss, Loss, Win. "We're up by half a point on you guys."

"No," Willy says. "*We're* up half a point."

Rohde rubs Dalphe's head. "I forgot about this little joker," he says.

"I beat an eighteen hundred," Dalphe says.

"Is that such a great thing?" Rohde says. "Because I don't think so."

♛

The team scores now read like this: Murrow 16.5 (Bercys 4.5, Lenderman 4.5, Morantus 4, Santana 3.5), Stuyvesant 16 (Weinstein 4, Li 4, Belilovsky 4, Ginzburg 4).

"I'm really furious at everyone who lost to Stuyvesant," Sal is saying.

What this means is that Sal must win in the final round, and Alex must win as well. But even if that happens, Stuyvesant could *still* win. So Oscar has to win too, and if he doesn't, and Dalphe loses as well, and Stuyvesant's players win four games, the upset is theirs. What *all of this* means, of course, is that the pairings will determine everything. In the meantime, they wait in a hotel lobby in a strange town with little money and nothing to eat, with Mr. Weiss far off in another wing of the hotel watching his children play in the lower-rated sections, oblivious for the moment to all of these harrowing scenarios.

"I need to win," Willy says.

"Everyone needs to win," Sal says.

"I need to play Anna Ginzburg," Dalphe says. If he can beat anyone on Stuyvesant, he figures he can beat her. "But I want food."

"Mr. Weiss said he'd buy us Chinese food," Sal says.

"I don't care what food. I just want some kind of food."

"Where *is* Mr. Weiss?" Willy says.

"If I play Lenderman," Josh Weinstein says, working his way into the conversation, "I'm going to bust out the new shit."

"What new shit?"

"You'll see," Weinstein says. "The new shit."

"I can't play Justin Li," Dalphe says. Li's only a 1400, but he's been on a roll this week, upsetting Shawn and winning four of five games and leading people to wonder whether he might be far better than what his rating indicates. "I can't beat Justin Li."

"Hey," Sal says. "Be *optimist*."

"If I had some food in my stomach, I could think more positively."

"We can blame the tournament director for this," Willy says. "For making you and Alex play each other."

♛

As it turns out, Dalphe will not have to play Justin Li. *Oscar* will have to play Justin Li. The pairings go up at 3:14 in the afternoon, and they look like this:

> Sal versus Gregory Kimmel (1906)
>
> Alex versus Josh Weinstein, Stuyvesant (2111)
>
> Oscar versus Justin Li, Stuyvesant (1471)
>
> Dalphe versus Eugene Belilovsky, Stuyvesant (1759)
>
> Ilya versus Riyath Mallahi (1411)
>
> Nile versus Brett Cimorelli (unrated)
>
> Willy versus Aditya Doddpameni (1214)
>
> Shawn versus Courtney Kaplan (1500)

By now Mr. Weiss has returned to appraise the situation; it's the first four matches that truly matter, and Mr. Weiss has informed Oscar that if ever there was a must-win in his chess career, this is it. Oscar has never really heard anything like this before; he's always gotten by on charm and instinct, and he doesn't have any idea how to defuse his anxiety except to keep on doing what he's accomplished with such success all weekend: He places a wager. He makes a bet with Eugene

Belilovsky, Stuyvesant's No. 3 board (and Dalphe's opponent)—not on his own game, but on the match between Lenderman and Weinstein. If Alex wins, he gets another two dollars and fifty cents. It is a bet made of wishful thinking, of course, because if Alex defeats Weinstein, a certain amount of the pressure is off. But if Alex loses, then Oscar simply cannot lose.

The chess clocks in the Grand Ballroom are set off at precisely 3:30 in the afternoon. Oscar, playing with white, opens with the Orangutan, pawn to b4. Li answers by moving his knight to f6. He has seen Oscar play the Orangutan before. He does not seem taken aback at all. He has the momentum here.

In the Seattle Slew Room, Weinstein has unveiled the new shit against Lenderman. The match is a study in physical contrasts, the robust young jock against the gawky little boy with the head for numbers. Weinstein had been studying a new opening called the Budapest, but openings have always been his weak point; his openings were full of tricks and tactics, and against Lenderman, that wasn't going to work. He's not playing it properly, anyway, and he's down on time, and this is what's always hacked him off about playing someone like Lenderman: He just waits for you to make a mistake. Now that he's made one, there may be no way out.

And then there is Sal, up against Gregory Kimmel, the 1900 with the anachronistic Prince Valiant haircut who's already beaten Oscar, Ilya, and Dalphe. And yet this is the one game Mr. Weiss isn't concerned with at all. Sal does not look anxious. Sal does not *get* anxious; Sal gets pissed off, like he is right now at his teammates for shirking their duties, and then Sal wants to *crush* someone. Figuratively speaking, of course. Most of the time, Sal beats you by playing positional chess, by reserving his aggression for the proper moments, by turning the slightest edge into an insurmountable advantage, by slowly demoralizing his opponents. Sometimes, this can take a good long time. An hour and a half into the game, the pieces are even, the position is even, but Mr. Weiss has no real doubt that Sal will find a way to win. It's Oscar and the others who worry him. He wants to see them *do* this, to prove they can win under pressure. If not for their school, then for themselves.

But Oscar is down on time, and it doesn't look good, and Dalphe, down a bishop and a pawn, has just resigned, and Ilya's curse has perpetuated itself and he's lost once more, to go from 3–0 one day to 0–3 the next. Oscar had a beautiful position early in the game, he would say later, but he made a couple of missteps. Now his clock is down to six seconds, which is when, driven by desperation and outrage and his own jitters, he makes one last massive and inexplicable gamble, sacrificing his queen in an attempt to . . . well, he can't explain why he does these things sometimes. Except in that cluttered mind of his, Oscar figures the only way to dig his way out of an inextricable mess like this one is to do something entirely illogical.

Five minutes later, he resigns.

♛

Good thing for Oscar that Weinstein has completely bombed with the new shit. When he resigns, the score is Murrow 19 (Sal 5.5, Alex 5.5, Shawn 4.0, Nile 4.0), Stuyvesant 18 (Weinstein 4, Belilovsky 5, Li 5, Ginzburg 4), and the last hope for an upset resides within the head of Anna Ginzburg, who's in the process of drowning against a 2032 named Robert Cousins. A draw isn't good enough; somehow, she has to pull out a win.

"There's no way she's going to win it," Willy says, after undertaking a scouting mission to the Grand Ballroom to check on her progress. "It's down to bishop and pawn versus bishop and rook."

"Alex won," says Sal, who has already won with ease. "That means we'll win."

"All right," says Willy, "so then we won."

"But Anna has to lose."

"Anna lost! Anna lost, yes! Anna lost!"

The cries come from Dalphe, rushing out of the doors of the Grand Ballroom at 5:28 in the afternoon. And with that, the team from Edward R. Murrow High School—tired, hungry, and mostly broke—finally, absolutely secures its sixth consecutive New York State High School Chess Championship. And the immediate reaction is one of utter relief.

"Now," Sal says, the words spilling drolly from his lips, "we can shake hands."

♛

It has been decreed that the victory celebration will take place at a restaurant called the China Wok on Broadway, which comes as a great relief to the starving masses. Dalphe, dazed and approaching delirium, is ecstatic at the mere mention of it.

On the way back up to their rooms in the elevator, Mr. Weiss asks Ilya if his father is coming with them.

"No," Ilya says.

"Why not?"

"He just—he doesn't feel like it."

"How come?"

Ilya says, in a mumble, "Because he's not happy with the way I played."

"Why? You played well."

"Not well enough for him."

"Well," Mr. Weiss says, "what does he expect?"

Ilya doesn't respond, because he cannot respond, because if he tries to talk, he's going to break down right here in a crowded elevator, among his teammates, among complete strangers. He stares at the numbers as they count up to three and the elevator lurches to a stop. The doors open, and Ilya bolts toward his room at the end of the hall, where, for the past two nights, he's shared a bed with the only man on this earth who could possibly expect more from Ilya than what Ilya expects from himself.

"The Russians, they take it more seriously," says Willy. "It's, like, not just a game to them. Winning means more to them."

"I guess that's why Lenderman's dad goes everywhere with him," Oscar says.

"It's funny, though," Mr. Weiss says, "because that can be a mixed blessing."

♛

Alone in his hotel room, searching in vain for a wireless connection on his laptop computer, Ilya fights back the urge to break down again. He finished twenty-second in the high-school section, and the top twenty places at this tournament received a trophy, which means Ilya is the only member of his team who will go home without one. (Willy took the twentieth-place trophy after taking the twelfth and final trophy in the varsity section at cities, and bragged afterward, "I got last place at cities, and now I got last place at states.") And all that happened the day before has been washed away by Ilya's failure on Sunday.

His father is not there at the moment, but Ilya can feel his presence. In a minute, Mr. Weiss will knock on his door, and he'll have to face him as well. He knows they want the best for him. He knows they're looking out for him, and what he wants is to give those people, and his school, and even Rita, a woman he hardly knows, all that they deserve in return. They paid for him to come here, and he gives them a halfhearted performance? This is what he cannot stand.

There was nothing else anyone could say to Ilya at that moment to console him. This feeling of failure was one he'd have to overcome largely on his own. Mr. Weiss did his best to take Ilya's mind off it later, over egg rolls and sweet-and-sour chicken. When Ilya said he'd never been to Ben and Jerry's, never even *heard* of Ben and Jerry's, Mr. Weiss promised to take him there sometime soon. But he wanted to do something else, something more, because this was his captain, his best student, the one member of this team he could count on. So when a reporter from the *Bay News* showed up in his classroom a few days later, he saw his chance. Maybe if Ilya's father could see it in print—maybe if Ilya himself saw it—he could change their minds.

. . . Team captain Ilya Kotlyanskiy, 16, a junior at the school, also came away with a "monumental" win on the first day of the competition, Weiss said.

Kotlyanskiy defeated Josh Weinstein of Stuyvesant, a master level player [sic] rated more than 400 points higher than himself.

"He went into the game and I didn't think he had a chance," Weiss said. "He looked for the win and he found it, and that's a very difficult thing," the coach added.

Kotlyanskiy faced Weinstein in the city championships, and lost. This time around, he said, the Bensonhurst resident . . . learned from past mistakes. . . .

"I didn't have too much to lose, I can only gain from it," Kotlyanskiy said.

*The Murrow team (from left to right): Eliot Weiss, Oscar Santana,
Shawn Martinez, Sal Bercys, Ilya Kotlyanskiy, Nile Smith,
Alex Lenderman, Dalphe Morantus, Willy Edgard*

THIRTEEN

IT'S IMPOSSIBLE TO CHANGE
YOUR DESTINY

THE ORIGINS OF CHESS ONLINE DATE BACK TO THE MID-1980S, TO THE dark ages of UNIX and 2,400-baud modems and primitive ASCII-designed boards, with lowercase *p*s serving as pawns and uppercase *R*s standing in for rooks. This was before Netscape, before AOL, before Bill Gates became supreme ruler of the civilized world, before anyone save for a few prophets on the lunatic fringe had much of a vision of what the Internet would come to be. It was then that a genial man named Marty Grund discovered that he could dial up with his modem and play chess against his brother, and this was a miracle in itself, a radical advance over the age-old option of chess by correspondence. Or at least it was, until the day Grund got his phone bill.

Not long after that, General Electric began a pay service called GEnie; the initial price for a 1,200-bit-per-second connection, on the evenings and weekends, was five dollars per hour. From there, Grund and a small community of fanatics migrated to a gaming site run by *USA Today,* and then, in the early 1990s, they ran across a new interactive service known as the ImagiNation Network, which claimed to be "changing the way the world makes friends." For about one hundred and twenty dollars a month, you could log on to the network and play an unlimited amount of chess (or checkers, or backgammon, or bridge, or hearts).

And then came the first stirrings of the modern World Wide Web, which eventually led Grund to a site started by a couple of graduate students at Carnegie Mellon University in Pittsburgh. In 1992, Danny Sleator, a computer-science professor at the school, came across the site and eventually took it over. Two years after that, with traffic to the site growing, Sleator didn't know what to do; he thought about giving it away, but his friends convinced him otherwise, and eventually, along with three others (including Marty Grund, who had volunteered to do tech support), he turned it into a commercial site. The site became known as the Internet Chess Club, and sold forty memberships in its first month. At that point, most people couldn't grasp the concept of paying for anything on the Internet. "We were the evil capitalists," Grund says. "We had to explain it to the naysayers. And most of those naysayers wound up becoming members."

Since then, the ICC has become one of the most popular chess sites on the web, rivaled only by another server called Playchess.com. The company has fifteen full-time employees and several hundred volunteers, some of whom serve as the site's administrators. A yearly membership on ICC costs forty-nine dollars, with a fifty-percent discount for students. One hundred thirty thousand games are played on its servers each day by thirty thousand members; among them are simuls and exhibitions from grandmasters and International Masters, not to mention speed games and bughouse games and one-minute bullet games and odd variations like Fischer random, a novelty devised by Bobby Fischer in which the back row of pieces is set in random order at the start of each game. Most of the top players at Murrow have an account and a "handle" (or nickname) on ICC: Alex is Manest and Sal is Super13 and Nile is Peaceful Knight and Shawn is Quick Pawn. In a sense, ICC is their second home. In March, in the weeks leading up to Supernationals, this is their primary method of preparation. They have neither the time nor the inclination to slog through chess books, so instead they come back from school, they log on, they instant-message each other, they play games against friends, and they play games against strangers, amassing practical experience, tinkering with tactics on their own, and establishing their cyberpersonalities. When you "finger" their profiles on the site, you can find both information about their ratings in previous games and aphorisms or snippets of IM discussions they've added underneath. (Alex: "I like to make friends. Chess unites people over the world, so let's have fun." Sal: "It's impossible to change your destiny.")

Few things seem more suited to the Internet than chess, which explains why it was one of the first successful manifestations of online communication. Now a top-level chess player like Sal or Alex can find virtually everything he needs online: Databases, statistical analyses, gossip, instruction, inspiration, and several thousand potential opponents of both the automated and human variety. Since Kasparov's celebrated loss to IBM's Deep Blue computer in 1997, the automation of chess and the power of the computer have grown exponentially, and all of this information has changed the game in radical ways. Virtually every grandmaster does the bulk of his preparation on the computer now, if only because computers can study the possibilities in ways that humans never can. Certain openings and lines of attack can be studied for hours at a time with the aid of a computer, and every single variation can be accounted for, and counterattacks can be memorized. The element of surprise has been virtually eliminated, and because of this, the number of draws among top players has risen considerably. Once you know whom you're playing in the next round of an event, you can study exactly the openings they've played in past games. Imagine a National Football League in which playbooks are readily available on the Web. For serious players, then, the Internet has become a Pandora's box, and the line between *preparing* and *cheating* is often quite thin. There are stories of men who wear earpieces during games, then have friends look over the position, log on to computer databases, and relay the proper move to them. There are stories of grandmasters hiding in bathroom stalls and doing analysis on handheld computers, or getting text messages on cell phones.

But it's not just the cheating that looms as a concern. There's also the fact that chess is already a pursuit regarded as the territory of the antisocial, and the fragmentation of the Internet only worsens these perceptions. "Chess is a particularly enclosed, self-referential activity," wrote columnist Charles Krauthammer in *Time* magazine. "It's not just that it lacks the fresh air of sport, but that it lacks connection to the real world outside—a tether to reality enjoyed by the monomaniacal students of other things, say volcanic ash or the mating habits of the tsetse fly." Bad enough when chess players were loners who rarely left their rooms; now they're also techie geeks who can't break from the solace of their laptops. And while it is a beautiful thing for a boy in Brooklyn to be able to play against his friend in Moscow, it cannot serve as a substitute for the real thing, for the experience of facing a *human* opponent in a *physical* space, over an *actual* board. "I don't like playing on the Internet as much," says Jennifer Shahade, the Women's International Master who teaches at I.S. 318. "It's a little mind-numbing. I mean, it's good for the kids to do ICC, if maybe they have two weeks without any chess opponents. But if they're missing an opportunity to play with their peers, then it's not so good."

At times, Marty Grund has had parents call him and ask to have their children banned from the site until they can pass their classes. He's had members call him up and ask to be banned themselves. The last thing he'd like to accomplish through the ICC is destroy the notion of face-to-face, over-the-board chess. But in many parts of the country, those opportunities hardly exist anymore. Even in New York, only one major club, the Marshall, remains in operation, with a few small chess schools scattered throughout the boroughs.

The Marshall Chess Club occupies the first two floors of a town house on West Tenth Street in Greenwich Village. Founded by a grandmaster named Frank Marshall in 1915, the club has subsisted in its current location, in what has become one of the priciest neighborhoods in Manhattan since 1931. There are tournaments at Marshall most nights of the week, held in a back room on the first floor, behind a curtain with a sign reminding participants to turn off their cell phones. Upstairs is a ballroom with vaulted ceilings and ornate details and photos of grandmasters on the walls and banquettes adorned with chess sets. Membership for residents of New York and the surrounding areas is

$325 a year ($160 for International Masters), not including tournament fees, which is why the kids who yearn to play here, kids like Sal and Alex, so covet the free tournament entry certificates they can earn by finishing among the top placers at the city championships. The Marshall maintains its status because of the caliber of player it attracts. Since the highest level of chess talent is concentrated in New York, it is regularly populated by GMs and IMs, by men like Gata Kamsky and Leonid Yudasin. But despite all of that, despite the sense of community it offers, it is not nearly as cheap or convenient as the computer in one's own bedroom.

On ICC, a young chess player can practice against hyperintelligent computer opponents and he can play speed chess and he can keep up a constant dialogue with his friends, all at the same time. The site becomes a social network, like Friendster or My Space. At one point, in the midst of Sal and Alex's constant bickering, Sal says, "I'm not sure how he pissed me off, I just know that he pissed me off. And he censored me, then we had supposedly become friends again, and then— what did he do then?—we had another fight and he censored me *again*. I can't message him on ICC or talk to him. So I sent him a message and said if you censor me, don't ever expect me to talk to you. But he kept on censoring me and then messaging me and then censoring me again so I can't message him back. That *really* pissed me off, and then I censored him forever. But I think I did uncensor him. . . ."

So a server like ICC affords its members both a sense of community and a cloak of anonymity, allowing a grandmaster like Kasparov to play speed chess against a seventh-grader from Massapequa, if he felt so inclined. In 2001, a British grandmaster, Nigel Short, insisted he had been playing games on ICC against an anonymous player he was "ninety-nine percent sure" was Bobby Fischer. Marty Grund and the officials who run the ICC weren't convinced of Short's claims, but the speculation didn't bother them at all. This is the Internet, after all. The possibilities are infinite.

In late March, two weeks before the Supernationals, Bobby Fischer, sixty-two years old, detained in Japan the previous July for trying to leave the country with a revoked U.S. passport, is granted Icelandic citizenship. Fischer is still a wanted man in America, after breaking international sanctions by playing his 1992 rematch against Spassky in Yugoslavia. "Mr. Fischer is a fugitive from justice," a State Department spokesman tells one newspaper.

Fischer emerges from exile looking haggard and weary. His beard is untrimmed and he wears a baseball cap pulled low over his face, and even now, as a man who has been granted amnesty from his past misdeeds by a people he has no direct connection with, he cannot stave off the worst parts of his nature. At his first press conference in Iceland, he tells ESPN reporter Jeremy Schaap that his father, the late Dick Schaap, is a "typical Jewish snake."

There's something pathetic about the way the whole thing unfolds, and those who care about the image of the game seem to recognize it right away. "Maybe if we could get some top players to show some porn to kids we'd really strike it rich in the PR department," writes one chess blogger. Here is the preeminent figure in their sport, rescued by a few people in Iceland who still revered him for what he had accomplished thirty years before, and how does he thank them? He comes off like a troglodytic neo-Nazi sympathizer on national television. "It's quite sad," says Bruce Pandolfini. "Fischer should have died young, perhaps. He should have stayed invisible."

Before he found a niche as a chess celebrity, Pandolfini worked as an errand boy at the Marshall Chess Club. He'd show up at nine in the morning, long before the club opened. One day he arrived and there was Fischer, upstairs in the corner near the window, studying the notation of a series of games from the nineteenth century, full of antiquated attacks and tactics that had long been left behind by most modern players. "Why are you looking at those, Bobby?" Pandolfini asked. "They seem interesting," Fischer replied, and a few years later, at the U.S. championships, he employed a bishop's gambit from one of those games to crush his opponent.

"We've lost thousands of Fischer productions, artistic creations that would have enriched the chess world so much," Pandolfini says. "That's a tragedy, if you're a chess lover. If Fischer had stayed in the public eye"—and not lost his mind—"chess would be all over the place right now. Everyone in America knowing the moves and rules of chess? That would have been done already."

♛

The truth is, Sal doesn't care much about what Fischer might have done since '72. He doesn't give a damn about Fischer's anti-Semitism and his crazy proclamations and his contempt for the American government. For Sal, it's not about what Fischer has become, or even whether chess led him to that point. It's about what he used to be. When Sal was eleven years old and still living in Vilnius, there were two players whose games he used to study. One was Alexander Alekhine, the Moscow-born world champion who died in 1946. The other was Fischer. He'd play out their games beyond the openings and try to see if he could guess their moves, and in this way he taught himself.

It takes a prolonged effort to get Sal to open up like this about his past. He always has an excuse not to get into it. He doesn't have the time or the patience for such reminiscences. He's always got something better to do, even if it just means he'd rather go home after school and take a nap. It's almost as if Sal would prefer to be shrouded in mystery; it makes him more interesting that way, doesn't it? This is the aura that surrounds the so-called genius, isn't it? This is the mythology. A Cuban grandmaster named José Raúl Capablanca insisted that he *never* studied, and his legend became that much greater. It was as if his talents were simply endowed.

Sal would never declare himself a genius. A *stupid* genius, maybe, but nothing more than that. Sal is just . . . well, he's *Sal*. There are certain people he doesn't trust, and other people he thinks are too ridiculous to bother with. And if you think he's bad, well, his younger sister, Brigita, she's even worse. She's a tennis player, and she was doing fine, until recently, when she called her instructor stupid. "She has no respect for, like, older people," Sal says. "At least I don't call them stupid."

Honestly, though, Sal's learned quite a lot about himself these past few months. In these last few weeks before nationals, his life has finally begun to settle down. It was never his intention to make anyone angry, but he got back from that *horrible* world junior tournament he played in Greece last fall, and then he had to go straight to California and play in the U.S. Championships, and then he had to go to Washington when all he wanted was to go home and log on to ICC and catch up on his homework and maybe get some extra sleep. "That was the worst stretch of my life," he says one spring day at the Marshall Chess Club, where he's just come from the orthodontist, who tightened his braces, making his teeth hurt like hell. After all those trips, he failed a history class because he was hardly ever there. His average dropped from a 91 to an 88, which is still quite good for a boy who doesn't seem to care much about getting into a top college. By the time they went to see George Bush, and spend a few days in Washington—well, it was nice to be there, but Sal really *didn't* want to be there.

Sal and his sister and his mother and father once lived in a big apartment in Vilnius, the capital of Lithuania; they live in a much smaller one now, on Avenue U in Bensonhurst. Here are some other basic facts about Sal's existence: His father works as a financial trader in Manhattan. His mother is a nurse. Neither of them speaks particularly good English, according to Sal, but they make a living, and they support their children's avocations. He has always been good at math, and his dad (whose name is Raimundas, which means "King of the World") taught him certain equations before he sent Sal to school, and on his first day, when his teacher asked him to add two plus three, Sal came up with *four,* and when he came home and told his dad, his dad said, "You know it's *five*! I've told you that a hundred times!" And Sal still doesn't know why he got it wrong; all he knows is that two plus three equals four got stuck in his head for a long time after that. "It's not something that I would do," he says. "Such a simple mistake."

When he was seven and still living in Vilnius, Sal went to visit his aunt for the hundredth time (*bo*-ring) and her son had a chessboard on top of his wardrobe. Sal asked what it was, and his aunt showed him, and like the main character in Nabokov's novel *The Defense*, a terminally obsessed young man named Luzhin, it was "as if someone had thrown a switch, and in the darkness only one thing remained brilliantly lit, a newborn wonder, a dazzling islet on which his whole life was destined to be concentrated."

When he was eight, Sal's parents hired his first chess coach. And then . . . well, then nothing. He was talented, yes, and he knew it, and his teachers knew it, and his parents knew it. But he would go to the major youth tournaments and finish third, or finish fourth, or finish fifth. This was no good for Sal. Maybe for some other kids, but not for Sal. It wasn't just the losing that bothered him; it was that he *knew* he was better than the kids he was losing to, and yet he still kept losing. Two plus three equals four. He was tired of doing all this studying and not getting anything to come of it. He was thinking maybe he'd just quit. And then came the country's national junior championships, in 2002, the year before he came to America. That's when something changed.

The previous year at this same tournament, Sal was in second place through the eighth round. In the ninth and final round, he was paired against one of the weakest players in the field. All he had to do was win. And what happens? Time trouble. A draw. He takes third place. *Horrible.*

What exactly it was that changed, or how it changed, Sal has no idea. Here's how he tries to explain it: "Let's just say that they were wolves, and I was like a new wolf. . . ." No. That's no good. How about: "Let's just say I was like a country kid who comes to the city. From the small environment of chess, I came to the big tournaments. They were used to that environment so they knew the pressure. But I was *better* than them. I lost so many stupid games because I was, like, I don't know, down on time. Time was a really big problem. And then the last year . . . I beat my main rival from the past, and I knew he was not my main opponent in that particular tournament, because there was someone stronger—but he was the one who tied with me for first place."

So Sal went on to play in the junior championship of the Soviet Union, and to play in the world junior championships, and around that time his parents decided to make the move to America. They came to America in May of 2003 and in June, in the Bronx, Sal won the U.S. Junior Championship. He was a bored teenage boy in a strange new land, but his confidence over the board was unshakable. That first summer in America, he played chess and he played chess some more; the computer was his only outlet. At one point, he was so bored he decided to read the Bible. Then he read it again. And then he read it once more. Three times? The Bible? "Seriously," he says. "No joke. I was *that* bored."

He went to Murrow because he'd heard of the chess team (why else?), and Mr. Weiss helped to get him admitted. Freshman year, he was still getting a grasp of English (his mother and father still have trouble with the language after nearly two years in America), but he had chess to carry him. This was his thing, and he did it better than anyone else, even Lenderman. *Especially* Lenderman. Sal was cocky, but he's always been cocky. That's his way. That's just Sal. He's easily misunderstood. "When I insult someone, I half-joke," he says. " 'You suck!' I say, and then they laugh. That's not—that's like half-sarcasm, half-friendship. I'm not a mean person. They're my friends, and they're still my friends."

In late March, two weeks before the Supernationals, Alex Lenderman finishes with six points out of a possible nine at a tournament held at Foxwoods Casino in Connecticut, earning $803 and, more important, the second of the three "norms" (a designation awarded by tournament directors, based upon a convoluted combination of victories over top opponents and ratings points) he needs to gain the title of International Master. Sal finishes with five points and no norms and a certain amount of resignation. For the first time, he opens up to Ilya, telling him all about Foxwoods, all about his complex feelings toward Lenderman. Ilya was so taken aback by this confession that he didn't know what to think. But this was the new Sal; he had come to witness his own vulnerability. In the back of his mind, he knew Lenderman would realize the same thing eventually.

Everything had come so easily the year before. Sal was on a roll, and despite a draw in the final round he still finished third at the nationals in Dallas, and Murrow dominated at the high-school section, finishing a full point and a half ahead of both the University School in Fort Lauderdale and Stuyvesant. Sal thought he could do anything. He was odd and engaging and he came into each and every tournament absolutely certain that he could beat anyone he faced, and at some point, he did what many of the best chess players before him have done: He crossed a line from self-assurance to overconfidence. And overconfidence, Sal is now convinced, is the one thing that will kill you.

Not long ago, a Canadian grandmaster flew to Russia on the same plane as the best young chess player in America. They were headed to a tournament together but they were seated in different rows, and when they got off the plane the Canadian glanced at the boy's wrist and complimented him on his watch. Then the Canadian said that the man next to him had been wearing the same one. The boy said, "Oh? And how did he look?" *How did he look?* Normal, the Canadian said. Fashionable. He mentioned that the man was also wearing Prada sunglasses. And the boy replied, "Well, that man must be rich. Because only rich people would own a watch like this."

That boy, Hikaru Nakamura, who makes Sal appear reticent by comparison, will not lower himself to play against his lesser-rated peers at the Supernationals. Why would he bother, really? Even before he won the national championship the previous December at age seventeen, even before he became the youngest winner of that tournament since Bobby Fischer himself, Nakamura has been groomed for something bigger than high-school chess: A master at age ten, a grandmaster at age fifteen, Nakamura is the brightest hope for American chess in more than three decades.

So instead of wasting his time by playing at Supernationals, Naka-mura will give a guest lecture, and he will hang around and watch games, and he will play a few blitz matches on the side, thereby assuring all those who weren't already aware of it that he is better than they are. All of this winning has made Nakamura a curiosity, a fascination, and a talent of the kind this country hasn't produced since Fischer himself. That he lives by his ego and yearns to crush his opponents and exact revenge upon them, that he refuses to accept draws and often makes enemies—well, that's just something most people have gotten used to by now. It's a commonly assumed persona that existed long before Fischer came along to personify its every twist and quirk. It's the terrain of the *idiosyncratic genius*. "A lot of the Russian players are also kind of crazy," says Irina Krush. "If you're involved in an academic endeavor, there's something appealing about building yourself up to be so weird and so unreachable, you know? It's like Einstein: You want to differentiate yourself. You want to become a legend, so you make up something like how you don't remember where your own house is, you have to ask someone on the street. And you take on a life larger than yourself. It's easy to do if you're doing something difficult. If you're a garbage collector, it's not so easy to mystify yourself.

"That's not to say chess players aren't naturally eccentric," she says. "But chess makes them weirder as they go along."

♛

"Mr. Fischer is a very popular person today," says Miron Sher. "He is a citizen of Iceland."

Sher is a grandmaster and a former coach of the Russian national team, a generously apportioned and soft-spoken man with unkempt gray hair who teaches the Thursday afternoon alumni sessions at the Chess-in-the-Schools offices in Manhattan. This is a busy session, the last one before the Supernationals, and Nile and Willy and Dalphe are all there along with nine or ten others, and in a small conference room facing West Thirty-sixth Street, Sher expounds about something known as the Carlsbad structure, only to segue into a reminiscence of the time an opponent used the French Defense to defeat Fischer, and then into a discussion of time control at nationals. "Do not play quickly at the beginning of the game," he says. "It's very important to have a good position. Don't play for time. Two hours per side, it's a serious game. And you have to play open and slowly."

Anna Ginzburg asks about avoiding time trouble in the middle game, and Sher tells her that maybe she shouldn't get up to use the bathroom during her game, that maybe she's better off staying seated instead of getting up and wandering off to check out other boards between moves.

"I'm using my clock, I ain't using nobody else's clock," Willy says. " 'Cause they be cheating down there."

The lesson goes past six in the evening, and just as things are breaking up, Oscar walks in the front door of the Chess-in-the-Schools loft. He's glassy-eyed and disoriented, and he insists it's because he's been up studying all night, because Mr. Weiss threatened to not take him to nationals unless he can find a way to catch up on the schoolwork he's been ignoring for months now. All of that neglect has started to catch up with Oscar, and even Sarah Pitari, the academic advisor for Chess-in-the-Schools, has essentially given up on the notion of Oscar graduating this spring. But Oscar insists that he's really *trying* this time, that he's going to class and he's being diligent but he's getting a new mattress for his bed and he's been sleeping on a futon in the meantime and his hip is killing him.

He doesn't want to miss nationals, because this will be his last one, and the reality of it all is starting to set in, that he has to do something with his life once school is over. All those things his father told him, those little speeches that sounded as if they'd been lifted from a movie, about school being a one-way ticket out of the ghetto life, about how in this country, if you're poor, your education is your passport out of poverty? Now, Oscar is starting to see there's something to it. He can do this. He's smart, he's curious, he's personable, and if nothing else, he's enterprising. "At times," Oscar's father says, "I don't think high school is hard enough for him. He doesn't get that interest or challenge from it. Like sometimes, he'll stay up all night and read books. Personally, I think if he were in college, he wouldn't have any problems."

♛

Reality has begun to set in for Willy as well. He's in trouble because he failed a history class, and it looks like he's going to have to come back to Murrow and take it in the fall before he can graduate, and everyone around him is blaming this whole No Child Left Behind Act for all the ills of the educational system and of students like Willy. This was, of course, George Bush's policy. But part of the reason Willy failed the class is because he missed a test while he was in Washington. Visiting George Bush. (Oh, Willy! The *irony*!) But Willy, too, says he's tired of making excuses. Then again, he's also tired of school, and he's tired of Sarah at Chess-in-the-Schools always riding him about coming to SAT prep classes when all he wants to focus on right now is edging closer to graduation. He's been going there every day for four years and now he misses a few weeks and Sarah won't stop riding him—what does she *want* from him?

So he's going to night school two days a week in Prospect Heights to try to make up for all the ground he's lost, but that history class looks like it's going to keep him around for at least another semester. Then maybe in the spring he can take the test and get his GED. All that talk of Paris, of studying music production—it's all on hold. Right now, on a Sunday morning on the Upper West Side, at the last Right Move tournament before nationals, Willy's not sure what he wants to do. "I shouldn't have failed the class in the first place," he says.

He looks tired. He's done with his game early and he's standing outside the glass doors to the cafeteria and looking in on his friends, waiting for them to finish, and he's thinking about nationals. He's thinking that this will be his last one ever, and he wants to take it seriously, wants to improve on his previous performances, like a couple of years ago when, with time running out, he thought he had a dead draw in one game, thought he had "insufficient losing chances" (a subjective rule in which a player who is short on time but in an advantageous position can attempt to claim a draw), and the tournament director came over to look at the board and wouldn't give it to him, for reasons Willy couldn't quite understand within the moment. But this year, no excuses. This year, no messing around. This year, he'll be prepared, and he'll be in bed by *eight* o'clock every night.

"Well, all right," he says. "Probably I'm exaggerating with the eight o'clock thing. But midnight. Definitely midnight."

PART THREE

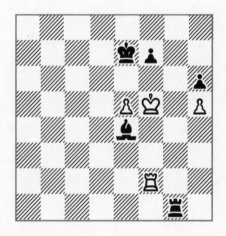

ENDGAME

FOURTEEN

SUPERNATIONALS III

Nashville, Tennessee

USCF Ratings:

Sal Bercys	2453
Alex Lenderman	2436
Shawn Martinez	1897
Ilya Kotlyanskiy	1756
Oscar Santana	1752
Willy Edgard	1694
Nile Smith	1610
Dalphe Morantus	1586

The Gaylord Opryland Resort and Convention Center, on the outskirts of Nashville, Tennessee, is a paean to American excess, a self-contained biosphere of overpriced gift shops and "authentic" Irish pubs ("Best Irish Food in Nashvegas!") and steakhouses and sports bars and saloons and swimming pools. It claims to be the largest hotel in the continental United States without a casino connected to it, and this means that it is an easy place to lose yourself, both in a physical and an existential manner. The biosphere is composed of a dense and convoluted web of catacombs and elevators leading to guest rooms and convention ballrooms and conference centers and hair salons and florists and a Kinko's copy center and a post office. In fact, there is no reason to leave the hotel to sustain one's existence, not even for fresh air, because at its center is a massive windowed atrium that does its best to mimic the feel of the outside world without ever actually leading you anywhere near the outside world. Why bother with fresh air when you can ride a fiberglass flatboat along a narrow river, winding beneath the carpeted footbridges and amid the antebellum architecture reminiscent of a cheap period movie, floating past the Chick-fil-A outlet and the Godiva Chocolatier and around a small forest's worth of banana trees and ficuses and miniature orange trees and ginger bushes, all imported directly from Florida?

During the three days of competition at the Supernationals III Chess Championships (Tagline: "Battle of the Minds"), most of the participants never left the building. In that sense, the Opryland is the perfect location for the nation's largest chess tournament, both literally and metaphorically: It is a world contained unto itself. Except having it all in one place apparently does not come cheap. On his first night in the hotel, groggy and parched, Ilya sees a bottle of water sitting next to the coffeemaker in the bathroom. What he doesn't see until the next morning, a Thursday, is that this bottle of water he drank in three or four long gulps will cost him two dollars and ninety-five cents.

Mr. Weiss has warned them in advance about the prices, but what could they do, really, as prisoners trapped within the biosphere? Dalphe's mother tried; she went to the grocery store and bought her son a pound of turkey and a loaf of potato bread and put it all in a cooler, hoping that would tide him over for much of the week, but even Dalphe seems skeptical about this plan. Oscar's scheme for survival is somewhat less conservative: He's brought with him a single twenty-dollar bill, figuring that as long as the card games went his way, he could survive four full days in this alternate universe of four-dollar Cokes and eight-dollar baked potatoes that makes even New York prices seem reasonable.

A hotel of this size and complexity cannot possess merely a single lobby, so Mr. Weiss has to specify what lobby the team will meet in on Thursday morning, on their first full day in Tennessee. By eight-thirty, they are all gathered on a trio of couches in the Cascades Lobby, near a piano and a snack bar and a rental-car station and some sort of garish statue ringed by snow-white pillars, and Mr. Weiss is informing them of the excursion he has planned for them this morning, one day before the tournament begins. It involves a twelve-person Econoline van and a two-hour drive to a small town in the middle of nowhere called Whitwell, where some students at a middle school have taken the extraordinary step of building a Holocaust memorial by placing eleven million paper clips, each representing one person killed by the Nazis, into a German railcar once used to transport Jews. Their efforts had been chronicled in a documentary film called *Paper Clips,* and Mr. Weiss had screened the movie for his kids and set up a tour of the railcar and a meeting with the teachers who had been profiled in the film. From there, they'll load back into the van and drive east to Dayton to visit the Rhea County Courthouse, the site of the Scopes Monkey Trial.

That virtually all eight boys would rather play speed chess and Texas Hold 'Em and subsist in the biosphere all day long does not matter to Mr. Weiss. Most of the time, his approach is laissez-faire: Curfew is supposed to be at eleven this week, but already enforcement has been lax, which is fine with Oscar. ("In order to win, we need our freedom," he says. "We need to play cards. We *need* to stay up later.") Yet just this once, now that they've come this far, he's going to show them *something* they can't see in Brooklyn. "Where we're going is Appalachia," he is saying. "It's not Nashville. Nashville is a city. Nashville is multicultural. But down there, you're not just representing your school, and you're not just representing New York City. You're representing your race."

They sit on a cluster of plush sofas within this artificial world, the eight members of the Murrow chess team, and Weiss's wife and two children: They are black, and they are Hispanic, and they are Jewish, and they are . . . Sal, who is none of above, although it might be argued that Sal is an altogether unique species. "I think you're the only one they might like down there," Mr. Weiss says to him.

"I'm not Protestant," Sal says.

♛

The van careens southward on Interstate 24, past Smyrna and Murfreesboro and Gossburg and Beechgrove and Hoodoo, through a torrential rainstorm, past the Jack Daniel Distillery and the Busy Corner Truck Stop and a Wal-Mart and billboards for Big Daddy's Outdoors and Davy Crockett's Roadhouse, just shy of the northern border of Alabama, before it reverses course, heading north onto State Route 28, past a trailer park and a roadhouse saloon and then . . . well, where did Whitwell *go,* exactly? How did they miss it? Was that the *whole* town? So back goes the van one more time, this time making a right onto Spring Street, and a right onto Main Street, and here they are, at Whitwell Middle School, a low-slung building located across the street from three separate churches, in the middle of—in the middle of *nothing.* No security guards at the front door. No bodegas at the end of the block. And Mr. Weiss expects them to actually get out of this van? Right here? "They're gonna get a police escort to walk us around," Shawn says.

"Shut up," Willy says. "You're gonna get us in more trouble."

It is only a short walk from the van to the railcar, which is fenced off and propped up at the edge of the parking lot, with a wooden ramp leading up to its entrance. It is as odd to see something like this here as it is to find someone like Shawn or Willy standing inside it; none of it computes, but that's the whole point, isn't it? To somehow bridge the gap in experience? In the front hall of Whitwell Middle School, there is a sign that says ALL RACES, ALL CREEDS, SAME DREAMS, SAME NEEDS, and then there are photos of the student body, which is ninety-eight percent WASP (Shawn and Oscar and Willy and Nile examine the pictures, searching for the other two percent). But ever since the documentary was released by Miramax a few months earlier, the railcar has become a magnet for school groups and tourists, drawing visitors from

Florida and Michigan and Canada and from a Manhattan yeshiva, drawing Jews and minorities and people of color, attracting as many as seven hundred visitors in a single month. "You'd be amazed at what happens to children when you just let them go," says one of the teachers at Whitwell, Sandra Roberts, which is the same sentiment that, two decades ago, led to the founding of Murrow High School.

The students at Whitwell have been trained to serve as docents, and Murrow's guides are a pink-cheeked girl and a towheaded boy with strategically placed freckles who looks like a refugee from the set of a Christian television program, and when the girl answers her cell phone, Shawn can hardly believe that the technology extends this far, that they've even heard of such things out here in the wilderness. ("I wonder if these kids cut class too," Oscar says.)

"What's your name?" Mr. Weiss says to the boy.

"Tee-mah," he says.

"Tee-mah?"

"No. *Tee*-mah."

Mr. Weiss shakes his head.

"Timmy," says the other tour guide.

"Oh," Mr. Weiss says. "*Tim*-my."

It is a small space inside the car, so they proceed through in groups, and they do their duty, walking through the small exhibit, examining the piles and piles and piles of paper clips. Oscar picks one up. Willy says, "He's trying to steal a paper clip."

"No I'm not," Oscar says. His classmates slide right through, but Oscar stands there for some time, contemplating the sheer mass of the paper clips, stowed in barrels and boxes and in glassed displays. This is the side of Oscar that he doesn't reveal in front of his friends. This is the sensitive Oscar, the boy who stays up all night reading books, the eldest son who dotes on his younger brother and sister, the boy who has suffered with his own kind of pain for years now, and would like to do something *good* with his life. Like that time last summer when he volunteered with mentally disabled children at a chess camp upstate. Hardest thing he'd ever done, but there was something to it, something that made it worthwhile. That's how it must have felt for these kids to do this.

"Imagine if all these were people," he says. "Ridiculous."

♛

The man standing before them says his name is David, but this David is like no man they have ever seen before. This David is a freaking *Goliath*. He is built like a whiskey barrel, and he is wearing a pair of Dickies overalls and a floppy-brimmed hat. Perhaps what is most noticeable about this David is that he does not have a face. Instead, David has a beard, a gnarly white thicket, an independent organism that long ago swallowed and digested his facial features. Where the hair ceases to grow, somewhere within the cavernous fault lines of David's neck, a small cluster of moles have sprouted. It is not easy to tell what's going on with David, whether he's the real-life incarnation of a Tennessee stereotype, or whether he's playing up the redneck persona for the purposes of serving as a proper tour guide at this particular venue, the Jack Daniel's™ whiskey distillery. David speaks often of life down here in the "holler," this place where the men are men and the liquor flows freely. "Is this guy's accent for real?" Ilya says while trying to decipher this strange new language, and when he's told that yes, it probably is, he nods. "All right," he says. "Because the only American accent I've ever heard is a Brooklyn accent."

"This guy," Nile whispers. "He looks like somebody from a video game."

How they have wound up in this place is strictly a tale of entertainment trumping edification. It is a long way in the opposite direction to get to Dayton, the site of the Scopes Monkey Trial, and nobody beyond Mr. Weiss wanted to bother with such esoteric history lessons, and they saw the billboards for the Jack Daniel Distillery on the side of the road, and they figured, why not? How often do you get to see something like this? So they exited off Interstate 24, stopped for lunch at a McDonald's, and drove on past Tullahoma and into Lynchburg, careening straight ahead until the air began to reek of boiled potatoes, and this was when they knew they'd arrived. They parked the van in a gravel driveway hidden amid a grove of trees, exited silently, and waited in the lobby for the tour to start, while Dalphe muttered, "I just want to go back to the hotel, man. There ain't no way in *hell* I'd live out here." And right then, David appeared before them, like a character in a low-budget horror film. Now David is leading them through the process of how whiskey is made, dark eyes rolling around in his head like marbles, and Sal can't even begin to figure out what the hell he's talking about, what's a *holler,* anyhow?

"How much money you think they make here?" Shawn says.

"Millions," Oscar says. "Now you know where to buy your stocks. It's all in whiskey."

David leads them through the fermentation building, past the wide-open stills, where the mash resembles churning bile and the smell of cider is suffocating ("I'm getting dizzy," Sal says) and finally into the barrelhouse, where David lifts the lids on the vats so everyone, even the underaged, can catch a whiff of the substance that they won't be drinking *for a while.* Too late, Oscar mutters. He's tried it already, just a taste, he insists, and then he doesn't say any more about it. It's not like you can live in Bed-Stuy and never come across a bottle of whiskey, after all; it's not like they don't have friends, cousins, aunts, uncles, who drink this stuff on a regular basis. At a nonscholastic team tournament once, both of Sal's teammates got drunk the night before the last day of the event and blew their chances at any sort of prize, and Sal, who doesn't drink and can't imagine why anyone would bother with something so silly, is still furious about it.

They all get their whiffs: Dalphe exhales deeply before breathing in, and Nile inhales *twice,* and Dalphe starts to giggle and can't stop. Before he can help it, he's got tears in his eyes, and this whole odd experiment has gone haywire by now, with the youngest member of the nation's best chess team drunk on fumes while being led around by a gnome in a Tennessee holler. How's *that* for an experiment in diversity? "I feel *mad* lightheaded," Dalphe says. "I think I'm gonna invest in some Jack Daniel's stock."

"What he means," Oscar says, "is that he's going to stock up on some Jack Daniel's."

♛

There is a replica NASCAR racer in the lobby where the tour lets out, and Willy and Oscar and Shawn and Nile are toying with the window guard, when the whole thing comes crashing down to the floor. And everyone does what they've been taught to do in Brooklyn when trouble pops up; they scatter. They get the hell away. All except for Willy, who seems to recognize that he's not in Brooklyn anymore, that he might as well be in another country, where people of his kind are not always completely understood. Even Nile, whom Willy has grown closer and closer to in these past few months, whom Willy has taken to calling *my son,* has abandoned him. "That's how black people get caught," Willy says. "They always run away."

The van passes a Kroger's supermarket on the way home, and so they make one last stop. The boys wander from one spacious aisle to the next, savoring the elbow room in a supermarket so huge that it wouldn't fit anywhere in Brooklyn, and sweeping junk food into their carts: sugared soda, Twinkies, Gatorade, provisions for sustaining energy throughout three days of non-stop chess. "These can't be that cheap," Oscar says. He's trying to conserve the money he has, and he's squinting at a box of cookie-dough-flavored Pop Tarts, list price $1.75. "I know what's gonna happen. I'm gonna get to the register and they're gonna charge me twice that. They're gonna rip me off."

Off he goes to the magazine aisle, where he picks up one of those hard-core gun-lovers' titles and starts paging through it. He can't get enough of this stuff. He's never owned a gun in his life—he's never even fired one, and hopes he never has to—but he could read about them, about how they work, the mechanisms, the firing pins, the clips, the way all this machinery comes together, for hours on end. So he calls Shawn over to show him one of the centerfolds in *Guns & Ammo,* and there they are at the end of an odd and inexplicable day, just two more Hispanic chess-playing teenagers from Brooklyn standing in the aisles of a Tennessee supermarket, ogling the AK-47s.

♛

By Friday morning, the Opryland biosphere is fully transformed. Chess games are breaking out in hallways and on sofas, on snack-bar counters and underneath banana trees and near the banks of the biosphere's artificial river. Small children are running with rooks in both hands, screaming and chasing each other, accelerating from zero to one hundred, from the contemplation of complex lines and attacks to the mass chaos of hide-and-go-seek, within seconds. A sports bar called Rusty's is advertising a week-long under-twenty-one party ("Root Beer Floats!").

Inside Presidential Ballroom C, vendors have set up displays: Generation Chess, the Rochester Chess Center, Tim Tobiason Chess Supplies. Excalibur Electronics is selling something called Glass Chess, in which the pieces are translucent and light up the board with each move. There are two fifty-foot-long tables crowded with books: *Secrets of Pawnless Endings, Taimanov's Selected Games, Secrets of Opening Surprises, Secrets of Chess Intuition, Think Like a Grandmaster, The Seven Deadly Chess Sins, Easy Guide to the Sicilian Schweringen, The Complete Sveshnikov Sicilian, Challenging the Sicilian With 2.a3!?* There are all three volumes of Mikhail Botvinnik's best games. There is a display from a company called My Chess Photos, which has come up with the sly marketing idea of photographing every child at this week's tournament, with the hope of selling their parents on a photograph of their son or daughter looking contemplative and serious. There are Supernationals T-shirts and Supernationals "trophies" with the word PARTICIPANT printed in a boldfaced sans-serif font on the base and there is a chess set modeled after *Spartacus* and there is a bumper sticker that says HONK IF YOU UNDERSTAND EN PASSANT.

This is the third incarnation of Supernationals, which brings together the elementary, junior-high, and high-school championships at a single site. As of this morning, there are 5,290 participants registered at this year's tournament, eclipsing the numbers at the 2001 Supernationals in Kansas City by more than six hundred, making this the largest rated chess tournament ever contested. "And I'm scared to death," says Diane Reese, the tournament organizer. She also announces, during a pretournament coaches and parents' meeting, that the Opryland has *run out of tables,* and that, as far as she can tell, there are no more long rectangular tables remaining in the entire city of Nashville. Then Reese makes the mistake of taking questions, and a man in a yellow T-shirt stands up and begins ranting about the fact that he hasn't yet received a program booklet and that he can't find the rules online and he's been to *ten* national tournaments before this one and he can't understand why it could be so difficult to distribute programs beforehand. And Reese is trying to explain how their numbers went up by four hundred just between last night and this morning, and they figured moving tables and chairs took precedence, and then the chief tournament director, a man named Robert Singletary, takes over the microphone. Shortly after he begins speaking, attempting to allay the concerns of the man in the yellow T-shirt, the fire alarm goes off, its merciful whine ending the session.

Because this is an *event,* because this is the *Super*nationals, a quadrennial occurrence of such massive proportions, it could not get under way without a proper opening ceremony (or "opening celebration," as it is called in the program, when they are finally distributed). It takes place in the Delta Ballroom, yet another massive space within the biosphere, capable of holding several hundred spectators carrying handheld video cameras, a marching band from a local high school playing John Philip Sousa songs, the mayor of Nashville, several honorary grandmasters (Anatoly Karpov, Jennifer Shahade, Hikaru Nakamura, and Maurice Ashley among them), and the nearly five dozen members of the Trophies Plus All-America Team, the best players in the country ages eight to eighteen, who are serenaded by the band and presented with red, white, and blue windbreakers. As the highest-rated players in their age group, Alex and Sal have both been selected; Alex is here, loping toward the stage, back hunched, lips pursed, to pick up his free jacket. Sal is not here, because Sal does not have the energy or the motivation, one hour before his first game, to attempt to search for the Delta Ballroom. So much easier just to stay in the room and lie around and play cards than to brave the interminable halls of the biosphere, and who needs that silly jacket, anyway? That's Lenderman's style. Let *him* have it.

♔

At ten minutes to one, the crowds streaming downstairs toward the competition rooms are so knotted and thick that it is becoming hard to breathe. For some reason, the tournament organizers have chosen not to open the doors, leaving five thousand competitors and their immediate families trapped outside, brushing up against each other in a swollen and overheated hallway, with nothing to do except read the backs of each other's T-shirts: *Bodkin Chess Team, Pasadena, Maryland: 2005 State Champs!* "If we don't clear these aisles," someone shouts, a frazzled tournament director, one would assume, "we're never going to get these pairings put up." Since no one can actually *move,* this announcement accomplishes very little, and twenty minutes later, after the doors to something called the Ryman Exhibit Hall have finally opened, the pairings still haven't been posted.

The Ryman Exhibit Hall, where the high-school sections have been set up, is of the size and complexion of an empty airplane hangar, with high ceilings and long tables demarcated by support beams in each aisle. The floor is hard concrete, and the air is cold and stale and smells musty and strange, like a basement that's been flooded one too many times, and the air-conditioning vents hum loudly enough to drown out the inevitable murmuring and whispering that occurs when placing a thousand high-school students in a single room. It is a slightly different scene in the airplane hangar next door, where the elementary- and junior-high-school-age students have been paired, where Elizabeth

Vicary and John Galvin have chaperoned nearly four dozen students from I.S. 318 in hopes of winning yet another national championship. Over there, a line of police tape has been erected at waist height, and, where that isn't possible, on the floor. *Do not step across this line.* And already there are parents poised with their feet on the very edges of that boundary, squinting and shading their eyes and peering off into the mass of numbered boards, trying to maintain some sort of distant and peripheral contact.

In the high-school area, the atmosphere is more welcoming, at least for the moment: The competitors are mingling in the aisles, and the Murrow boys are trickling into the room, and Dalphe has a fat pair of headphones placed over his ears, and he's swaying to the beat, trying to blast out his nerves. He listens only when he's tense, and then he puts the music down and plays without it. Maybe if he has the time he can hit the swimming pool between rounds to take the edge off.

Here comes Sal, whistling a little ditty to himself. He insists he's not nervous at all, except that he doesn't much like playing on the No. 1 board, which is situated atop a riser in the front of the room. He'd prefer not to be on display like that, if he can help it.

Ten more minutes. Still no pairings. Sal and Alex are jumping up and down now, and Alex's pieces, ensconced in the same withering Spanish department-store bag, are chuffing and rattling, and there is nothing to do but gossip and wander and stare at their surroundings. At 1:36, there is an announcement: Due to a computer error, all the players in the high-school under-1500-rated section, whose pairings had gone up earlier, are sitting at the wrong boards. A groan, and then, one minute later, the open section pairings are finally posted, and thanks to a late entry by a thick-necked boy from Armenia with a provisional USCF rating over 2500, Sal is spared having to play on the stage, and on display.

♛

Past two o'clock now, a good hour after the first of the seven rounds was supposed to start, and the masses are still finding their boards and settling into their seats. And the room is beginning to come together, and the room is a *sight,* man, just your average day at Bizarro High School, all these smart-ass intellectuals and hipsters and geniuses and wannabe geniuses and misfits and preppies and born-agains thrown together inside an airplane hangar. Here is a Goth wearing a trench-coat and purple lipstick. Here is a boy in a Slayer T-shirt with a gusher of corkscrewed copper hair like Maradona, the Argentinian soccer star, used to sport back in the day. Here is a boy in a Harvard T-shirt with long dark bangs drooping into his eyes, and here is a boy in Priest Holmes's Kansas City Chiefs jersey (because Priest Holmes is one of the few professional athletes who have admitted publicly to playing chess), and here is a bearded dude in a Chicago Bears jersey and a Sam Spade fedora. Here is a hyperactive young man with a ponytail and dark sunglasses who seems to think he's made it to the final table at the World Series of Poker, and here is a boy on crutches, and here is a boy wearing a Burger King crown, and here is a boy with a Lincoln-esque beard carrying a stuffed sheep with a studded collar (are those *diamonds?*) under his arm. Here are T-shirt slogans ad nauseam: *Will Party for Food, Nintendo Rehabilitation Clinic, Only Jesus Can Save You,* and others so crude and sexual and overtly hostile to women that they might cause a stir, if only there were enough females in this room to complete a quorum. As it is, there are hardly any, and even fewer among the top boards, although Anna Ginzburg has distinguished herself by donning a beret with her name printed on the front.

Finally, at ten minutes past two, the tournament director for the K-12 section arrives at the front of the room. She is a small, middle-aged woman with close-cropped rust-colored hair, and she is wearing a sport coat and a pair of jeans, and seventy minutes after the ap-pointed time, in a fit of misguided enthusiasm, she delivers this awk-ward proclamation: *"Let's get ready to rumble!"* And off they go, to the sound of hundreds of clocks being punched all at once. Oscar pushes a pawn to b4, Alex sacrifices a pawn early on to gain an advantage later, and Sal takes it slow and steady. Due to sheer overwhelming size, the field has been split into four groups based upon ratings, so that in the first round the top players are paired against those in the twenty-fifth percentile, the twenty-sixth percentile against the fiftieth percentile, and so on. Because of that, Sal and Alex have it easy; they're both facing 1800s. And Alex's father, who accompanies him everywhere, who has come with him all the way to Tennessee, stands in a nearby corner like a sentry, a pair of royal-blue New York Knicks sweatpants riding up toward the bulge of his considerable midsection. Sal is up and pacing between moves, peering over the other boards, checking in on his teammates; he looks restless, nonchalant, almost bored at times. He has not brought his own set of pieces, nor his own clock, nor his own scorebook. He says, "I barely have to think here" at this tournament, in comparison to what he might have seen in Greece or in San Diego or even at Foxwoods a couple of weeks ago, and this is Sal's ego talking, of course, because he still has one, he still knows he's *good*. Back and forth he goes, pacing along the aisles, tugging on the sleeves of his blue T-shirt, kibitzing with tournament officials and with Alex's father and with anyone who'll bother to listen to him, all of which begins to infuriate the copper-haired woman in charge, who is here to enforce silence and order.

Meanwhile, Ilya, who's never quite sure *what* he is from day to day, starts off strong, beating Benjamin Francis from Georgia, rated 1991, by sacrificing his queen. The guy never saw it coming, Ilya says, and this is exactly the way he wanted to play, like he did that first day at states, fast and free, the precise opposite of the rest of his regimented life.

It takes nearly three hours for Alex to finish off this blond kid from North Carolina, Matthew Green, and when he gets up, his father sighs and unfolds his arms. "Not an easy one," he says.

♛

Times like these are when chess ventures into the realm of the physi-cal, with seven long extended games, two hours on the clock for each side, packed into the course of three days. After a while, the synapses become stretched and the eyes become fatigued and it becomes hard to concentrate and even harder to plan ahead, to anticipate moves, to avoid making the type of blunder that leads to a lost game. At the highest levels of chess, no one would think of scheduling more than one game in a day. But this is the United States, and no one makes a living playing chess, and so tournaments are crammed into long weekends and after a certain amount of time the brain begins to melt, and you do your best to keep up, living off a sugar rush and a caffeine buzz and a catnap here and there. You try to conserve your energy against lesser opponents so you can expend it in the games that matter. But that doesn't always happen. And then you find you're exhausted. "You start to think, 'I can't play this game,' " says Irina Krush, who competed in this tournament in 2001. "You feel like you can't play, so why should you torture yourself?"

There are different theories and methods for combating this fatigue, depending upon the individual. "The key thing you can do before a game is silence your brain," says Maurice Ashley, at a lecture between rounds. "Sit, relax, turn the TV off, get into a nice, clear space. It's a bit like meditation."

Of course, these are teenagers, and mostly teenaged boys, which means their idea of a *nice, clear space* involves something much less spiritual than that. It involves pizza, poker, and innocuous daytime television talk shows. For Dalphe, after a win in Round One against Ahmet Erciyas, a 1460 from Minnesota, relaxation entails several trips to the biosphere's all-you-can-eat buffet. (So much for the turkey-and-potato-bread method instigated by his mother.) And now this little boy, barely five feet tall, is clenching his stomach and trying to keep it all from making a return visit before the start of the second round, at seven in the evening. Not to mention he's playing up in rating this round, a 1586 facing an 1817.

But Dalphe is not needed at this point. He is not among Murrow's top-four-rated boards, and the top four are all that matter when it comes to the actual score. With Sal, Alex, and Shawn as the clear top three, one of the others has to score well enough to put Murrow over the top. It doesn't look like that's going to be Oscar, after he blunders into a draw against Jonathan Bowerman, a 1413 from Florida; the kid opens with a pawn to d5, and Oscar *knows* how to respond to this, *knows* he should play pawn to b5, but it's just *instinct,* that force he's always fighting, that kills him again, and he plays his knight to f6 and can't quite recover from there. Two games, and he's got a total of half a point, but really, Oscar's having other successes: He's up from twenty bucks to a hundred and ten bucks in liquid funds; when this week started, he had a single bill in his wallet, and now he can hardly keep the thing shut.

So who's left? Ilya? He can't seem to keep his energy going, and he loses to Chris Claassen, a 1663 from Kansas, in Round Two. Nile? A draw in the first round negated his efforts, and he's rated only around 1500, which is asking a lot. Same for Dalphe. This leaves Willy, the quixotic one, the boy who is absolutely certain he could have scored four points at nationals last year if that kid hadn't puked right next to him and thrown off his mojo in the last round, the boy who gets distracted by funny faces, the boy who can never quite seem to find himself when it matters. But Willy's playing Christopher Williams, a 2049 from Massachusetts, in Round Two. What could Willy possibly do against a 2000?

For once, Willy gets lucky. Willy happens to be playing a 2000 who allegedly lost his first-round game to a boy he hates, and because of that, this particular 2000 has allegedly ceased caring, and has figured he might as well take a dive in this game as well. So he plays fast, and shifts all his pieces to the queen's side of the board, and Willy, playing an opening called the closed Sicilian (a 2000 should know how to counter this), attacks from the king's side, and before you know it, in under an hour, the game's over. Two games, and Willy has two points. "To me," Willy says, "I think he wanted to lose."

A couple of hours later, Alex queens one of his two remaining pawns and finishes off Matthew Fouts, a 1950 from Indiana, and three minutes afterward, as if he were just waiting for the proper moment, Sal beats Jeremy Volkmann, a 1968 from Missouri. When Shawn, playing over his head against a 2099 (Erik Santarius, Wisconsin), pulls out a victory forty-five minutes after that ("An *out*standing attack," Sal declares upon examining the board), the first day's tally is as strong as it could get: Sal, Alex, Willy, and Shawn all have two points, giving Murrow eight points, two more than any other high-school team in the field. So maybe, Mr. Weiss is thinking, this will be just like last year. Maybe there's simply no one in America who can keep up with them.

♛

There is too much to do here in the biosphere, too many games, too many distractions, too much real estate to cover, and even facing the longest Saturday of the year, Shawn and Oscar cannot resist. They blow off curfew and they play cards and they stumble into the room sometime past one in the morning, and when they wake up seven hours later and rush into the elevator, flit past the artificial river, swing behind the Chick-fil-A, bound down the stairs, and burst into the airplane hangar in time for the start of Round Three, they are bleary-eyed and unstable, and the only solace for Shawn is that he's facing weak competition. He offers up his queen, and his opponent, Marc Reichardt, a 1200 from Wisconsin, clenches his forehead and considers and looks away and then he looks at Shawn, this boy who is built like a nightclub bouncer, whose face is squinched like a sponge under an all-black Yankees cap, whose eyelids are trembling amid a desperate battle to maintain consciousness, and he refuses the sacrifice.

But it doesn't matter, because Shawn is not going to lose here. He has played so much chess in the past few years that in a game like this, against a weak opponent, he can operate almost entirely without consideration. All those games of speed chess he plays online force him to make split-second decisions, so that when he has time to think it can be like when a baseball player in the on-deck circle warms up by swinging two bats, and when he gets to the plate, his lone bat seems that much lighter. It can also backfire, of course, when he moves without thinking things through completely, but in this case, the next play just *comes* to him. So he wins easily, and when it's over he goes upstairs to the team room provided for the students and alumni of the Chess-in-the-Schools program, and Sarah Pitari is there, the academic advisor, the woman who's been trying so damned hard to get these kids to realize what they're facing in the future, when school and chess are no longer their buffers. She's tried to set up a meeting with Mr. Weiss, but he doesn't really have much regard for CIS in the first place, for the bureaucracy of the CIS system, and so nothing has come of it. It's not like he's oblivious to Shawn's plight; he's been on the phone almost every week with Shawn's stepmother, trying to explain to her that he's simply not showing up at class. He even thought about leaving him behind when they came here, but he didn't want to crush the kid's spirit.

Sarah Pitari is a small woman with long dark hair and a serious countenance, and while she watches Shawn play a game of blitz she chides him for his sporadic attendance at the academic sessions she's been running for CIS alumni. And Shawn gives her that face he reserves for situations when he either doesn't understand what they're talking about or doesn't *want* to understand what they're talking about, the one where his eyebrows dart straight upward and his pupils roll back into his head and his forehead compresses and you start to think maybe it's your fault, maybe you've just addressed him in Mandarin by mistake.

"What's *sporadic*?" Shawn says.

So Sarah defines sporadic. It is a word that could aptly describe Shawn Martinez's entire academic existence, after all, so he might as well know what it means. "And what's your attendance going to be like next year?" Sarah says.

"Uh, *un*sporadic?"

♛

By lunchtime that Saturday, the situation remains comfortable. Sal and Alex have both won again against inferior opponents, and the only one who is truly struggling is Ilya, who is at 1756 coming in but drops a game in the morning session to Russell Scott, a 1373 from Virginia, after touching a piece he didn't really want to move (at most tournaments, the "touch-move" rule is in effect, meaning once you've grasped a piece, you have no choice but to play it). This drops Ilya into one of his temporary states of depression, but he doesn't have much time to snap out of it, because the fourth round starts at two, and the matchups are not all that great. Of Murrow's four undefeated players, Sal and Alex are both facing opponents rated over 2000 (there are about thirty players with ratings above 2000 in the varsity section), good enough to at least keep up with them and force them into difficult situations, and Shawn is facing a 2092 (Eric Rodriguez, Florida) and Willy is facing Jouaquin Banawa, a kid from Los Angeles who, at 2446, is one of the highest-rated players in the entire tournament.

This is where Murrow's depth comes into play: If Willy loses and starts to struggle in subsequent rounds, it's important for the others to keep up, so they can potentially take his place among the top four. Mr. Weiss has tried to help Willy out, logging on to the Web and looking up past games of his opponent, trying to discern what opening he might unveil, but Willy goes in fighting the voices in his head, the ones that keep telling him that he's not good enough to beat a master-level player, that he can't possibly do this. This kid is rated higher than Lenderman, after all, and Willy can't beat Lenderman, and he fingers the gold chain he wears around his neck, the one with the studded *W* attached to it, and it feels like its grip is tightening with every move he makes.

♛

For eighteen minutes, at board number 202, Alex Lenderman faces an empty chair and a running clock. Where is Landon Brownell? What could he be doing? Was he afraid, as Sal had joked a few minutes earlier? Was he sick? Was he asleep? Was he lost somewhere within the catacombs of the biosphere? There is nothing for Alex to do but sit there and watch the clock and watch the games going on all around him. When Brownell finally does show and settles into his seat after offering his hand to Alex for a limp pregame handshake, he does not hesitate. He pushes a pawn straight ahead, formulating an opening that seems too perfectly calibrated to be spur-of-the-moment.

It's clear now: Landon Brownell, a rangy kid with glasses and a

2007 rating, from a high school called Catalina Foothills in Arizona, has been *preparing*. He's been studying Lenderman's games online with his coach Robby Adamson, a 2400-rated player and a former junior-high national champion, and they've discovered Lenderman's weakness: When playing with black, he really knows only one opening; he knows it extremely well, knows every intricacy of it, but he is incapable of adjusting his method. ("He never varies, *ever*," Adamson would later say.) So Brownell opens by pushing a pawn to e4, and Lenderman counters with a pawn to e5, and his strategy, known as the Two Knights Defense, plays out, with Lenderman taking Brownell's pawn on the d4 square on his third move:

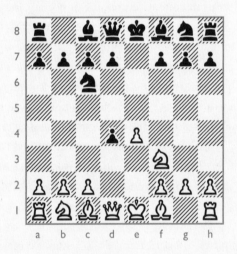

This is not good at all for Alex. He knows that Brownell has him figured, and Brownell *knows* he knows, and Alex is playing defense. His hands are folded over his cheeks, enveloping his face, and he's sinking deeper into his chair as his teammates begin to sink with him. Brownell makes a small mistake with his ninth move, losing track of the line Adamson had been teaching him up in the room. But then, with the pressure and the circumstances bearing down on him and his father pacing up and down the aisle, Alex takes a chance: With his twelfth move, he plays his knight to the c4 square, and with his thirteenth move, he shifts it again, to take one of Brownell's pawns on e5. This goes against the book and against every logical unfolding of the defense Alex is playing.

Now it's too late. He's made a mistake, and he knows it, and he can't disguise his consternation, which only compounds things. When you're playing at this level, and you sabotage yourself like this, your only hope is that your opponent doesn't notice, that he doesn't see the path to an easy victory, twenty or twenty-five moves ahead.

While all of this unfolds, Oscar loses to Marcus Williams, a 1513 from Michigan (afterward, he goes in search of payoffs from last night's bets), and Shawn loses, and Willy hangs in for more than three hours against the kid from L.A., but then concedes. Nile loses, playing five hundred points up. Of the bottom six on Murrow's roster, only Ilya (against Marjorie Heinemann, a 1391 from Minnesota) and Dalphe (against Chris Bechis, an 1827 from Pennsylvania) manage victories, Dalphe by sacrificing a bishop on the c2 square to facilitate an attack from both sides, a move he figured out by playing speed chess with Shawn.

And Alex is sinking deeper and deeper. "White gradually develops a kingside attack and brings the point home in an elegant, almost effortless manner," writes Alex Betaneli, annotating the game several months later, in an issue of *Chess Life* magazine.

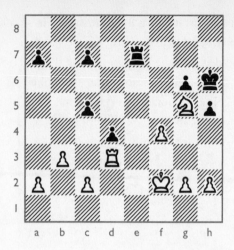

Alex's father is scanning the board and shaking his head and sighing. "It's a losing game. There's no way to win." Alex knows this now too, and he's shaking his head, and Brownell is squirming in his seat because he knows he's almost there, he's going to beat a kid who's on the verge of becoming an International Master, so how is he supposed to sit still? And all of this movement infuriates Alex's father, who is already upset, who cannot believe the lack of *respect* here. "He stands up, he's laying on the table," he says. "It's unbelievable."

At ten minutes after four, Alex resigns. Off he goes with his father in tow, the two of them stewing and chattering in hushed Russian. And with that, the whole tenor of the 2005 Supernationals has changed, because suddenly there is a threat to Murrow, a grave and serious one at that, and it comes from Landon Brownell's own school, Catalina Foothills in Tucson, which has fielded five players rated over 1800 this week, most of them trained by Robby Adamson himself. And now it has stood in the face of the beast, just as Adamson assured them they could do. He had told them this before they even got on the plane to come here. He had said, *Don't bother getting on this plane if you don't think we can win a national championship.* And while Catalina lacks a one-two punch like Sal and Alex, it has another weapon: It has depth that Murrow cannot match. "Lenderman played a bad line," Adamson says later. "On his part, that's a huge mistake. He should have played his normal stuff instead of trying to confuse Landon."

Just like it did at the state championships, the situation deteriorates fast for Murrow, their entire foundation crumbling in a single catastrophic round. Ninety minutes after declaring, "I think you can mark me for a win in about an hour," in the midst of a convoluted series of exchanges with a boy from Texas (Deepyaman Datta, 2058), Sal has no choice but to accept a draw. The team score now reads like this: Catalina Foothills 13, Murrow 12.5.

"OK," Sal says. "I'm thinking this is our worst round ever."

And on this, the longest Saturday of the year, there is still one more round to go.

♛

This cannot be good for anyone, this container of cream cheese splayed open and congealing right there on the dresser, next to the television set, where, in the bowels of the Delta Wing, a college hockey game is playing on low volume. But then, no one is paying much attention to the proliferation of rancid dairy products, or to the hockey game, or to the do-rags and towels and backpacks lying on the floor, or to the empty pizza boxes left on the cot that's been set up next to the window. There is a card game going on (a four-person round of Stupid involving Oscar, Shawn, Sal, and Willy), and there is a blitz game going on between Nile and Ilya when Alex comes in from the room down the hall he's sharing with his father and says, "I'm sorry." It is a general apology, and it is tinged with self-pity, and when someone asks Alex why he's apologizing, he says, "I don't know any openings. I'm just a thirty-minute player." Then he says, "I hope no one else prepares for my opening. I'm not bad, but I'm not twenty-four-hundred strength."

This burst of sincerity is enough to halt the card game for a moment. "Alex," Oscar says, "we have to talk. Just because you lost the game doesn't mean you're not twenty-four-hundred strength."

Sal says nothing.

It's 6:37, twenty-three minutes until the start of Round Five, and Alex wants to get downstairs early, wants to get back to business, but no one is willing to go with him and sit in that dreary and overly air-conditioned airplane hangar a moment longer than they have to. Ilya has finished playing and is taking a catnap now, lying back on the bed in a supremely uncomfortable position, his feet planted firmly on the floor. And Oscar can't find his shoe. He's lost his shoe. *Guys, guys, this isn't funny, where's my shoe?* But nobody has Oscar's shoe, and even if they do, they're not telling. He sweeps up the bedspread and peers underneath it, and he lifts up the pizza boxes, and he pushes the cream cheese aside—ecch!—and peeks behind the dresser and pokes his head underneath the television set. Still no shoe. How can he play chess with one shoe? "Guys, where's my shoe?" he says. It's ten minutes to seven and everyone else is on their way downstairs and Oscar is starting to think that maybe he'll have to hop all the way down there. "Maybe Dalphe *ate* your shoe," Sal says. "He ate everything else." They're all watching the last few minutes of this college hockey game, not that they could care less who wins or loses, but this is their method of preparation: vegetation meditation. Numb your mind before you actually use it. And when the clock runs out on the game, Oscar sweeps an arm under the bed one last time and finally extracts . . . his other shoe! And they make the long trip downstairs, through the halls, past the river—

"There's ducks in that pond," Oscar says.

"Ducks?" Shawn says. "Where the ducks? You crazy. Ain't no *ducks* in there."

"Right there," Oscar says. He points toward an amorphous blob underneath a brackish patch of vegetation. Shawn squints at it. Nuh-uh. No way. Ducks? In a hotel?

"Yo, ducks ain't down there."

"Yeah, they are."

"Ducks are *mad* retarded, yo. They were down there, they'd get hit by one of them boats."

"*You're* retarded."

"Whatever."

Catalina Foothills High School, founded in 1992, is set on forty-six acres on the outskirts of Tucson in the midst of what was once a sparse desert and has become yet another thriving suburban American community. In 2003, Robby Adamson, a FIDE Master who also works full-time as a lawyer, took over the school's chess program—or what there was of it—and began recruiting the best young talent in the area. Many of his top players came from Orange Grove, a nearby middle school with a venerable chess program started by a master named Will Wharton, who won multiple national championships in the mid-1980s. But just as Eliot Weiss was bequeathed the gift of Sal Bercys, Adamson also had a minor miracle drop into his district: A few years earlier, Landon Brownell and his brother, Bryant, both of whom are home-schooled, moved to Tucson. They live there during the school year and spend their summers in Oregon. (Their father, Roger, is also working as an official at this tournament.) So Adamson brought in the Brownells, and he found Sean Higgins, a brilliant student whose mother happened to be a teacher at Catalina Foothills (she has since quit and taken a job at Raytheon, a defense contractor and one of the area's major employers), and he found Christopher De Sa, a math and engineering whiz who took to the game like a natural, and he found Pavel Savine, another brilliant student, and he found Vaishnav Aradhyula, who had been playing since kindergarten. And then he began to drill them, once a week after he got through with work, and in private lessons on the weekends, and whenever he could, all on his own. The school pays him twelve hundred dollars a year for his efforts; the money to pay for this trip came from the kids' own families. So he spends all this time essentially doing pro bono work, analyzing championship scenarios and going over games and building up their mental toughness and their self-assuredness. "The school doesn't get it," Adamson says. "They just don't care. They want the chess club to be just like the sewing club. But I'm competitive, man. I want to win."

The students at Murrow refer to their out-of-state competition at these tournaments in the vaguest of terms: One year the threat came from *Texas,* another year from *Philadelphia.* Often, it is the same schools who are up at the top with Murrow, over and over again, but this *Arizona* team—this is a new one.

"We beat Arizona," Mr. Weiss says, "and we'll beat everyone else."

♛

"I think he's preparing for me," Sal whispers.

Not that it would make much of a difference at this point. That Sal's opponent is twenty minutes late to the board won't mean a thing because now that he's drawn a game (*How* did that happen? Carelessness! A moment of overconfidence slipping in, perhaps . . .) and Lenderman has lost a game and the outcome is in doubt, Sal has a purpose. He's the coolest kid in the room, strolling back and forth from board to board, kibitzing with officials, chatting up Hikaru Nakamura (who's strutting between the aisles looking in on the games), and continuing to upset the woman whose job it is to enforce order in this room. It seems likely that Sal is largely responsible for the signs that have gone up around the hangar, growing more restrictive by the hour: NO WALKING IN THE AISLES, NO SPECTATORS IN THE FRONT OF THE ROOM, NO TALKING TO PLAYERS DURING GAMES. But if Sal can't talk, he'll mime. He'll empty his pockets and dig out a reminder card for his last orthodontist appointment and then crumple it up in his fist as a display of strength. And he'll wait, and he'll wait, tightening his grip like the dentist does every month with that goddamn hardware in his mouth, and when the moment is right, poor Arturo Garcia, an 1883 from Texas, won't even know what hit him.

♛

Round Five is something of a return to form: Sal and Alex both win easily, and Nile, Oscar, and Ilya all win too, and although Willy can't pull off another upset over Blake Phillips, an apple-cheeked 2001 from Oregon, Dalphe upsets Jason Kalivas, an 1829 from Oklahoma who insists on wearing Ray-Bans from start to finish. All of a sudden it's Dalphe, with four points, who's taking on a crucial role in the scoring, who seems to have rediscovered the promise that carried him through middle school. He set a trap, let the kid with the sunglasses fork his queen and his rook, then sacrificed his rook and attacked hard with his queen.

Problem is, Arizona keeps winning too. They're up by a point, 16.5 to 15.5, as Shawn's game drags on deep into the evening. He's playing a girl, a *cute* girl from Oklahoma, with long blond hair and narrow cheekbones, and no doubt this is distracting, because when you're a teenaged boy and you've been playing competitive chess for twelve hours how can it *not* be distracting? They exchange queens, and at twenty minutes past nine, the girl offers a draw. Shawn doesn't want a draw, because this girl (named Destiny Sawyer) is only a 1661, three hundred points lower than him, but a couple of minutes later he realizes he has no choice. And he accepts. And heading into the last day, Murrow finds itself half a point short, and Eliot Weiss cannot help but go to sleep thinking of 2000 and 2001, of those two consecutive years when a half point stood between his team and first place.

♛

Sunday morning the hangar suddenly seems much smaller, and the oxygen in the biosphere feels more stale, and the atmosphere is tighter and quieter. Round Six begins at 9:00 A.M., and the players are greeted by yet another new restriction: PLAYERS TALKING TO COACHES OR TEAMMATES WITHOUT PERMISSION WILL LOSE CLOCK TIME AT THE DISCRETION OF THE TOURNAMENT DIRECTOR. There have been anonymous accusations of cheating, as there always are, and now that they are in the final rounds, there is no more kibitzing, no more hovering over others' boards, no more bullshit permitted. Today, Hikaru Nakamura has been denied special access to walk among the top boards. Today, even Sal is muted. Today is different. The silence is overbearing.

The paranoia is heightened. Today is as much about one's own fortitude and inner peace and self-discipline as it is about hard knowledge.
It is, as Robby Adamson has told his players, an endurance test.

"The thing about being a good player is you can't be hypocritical,"
says Josh Waitzkin, who won a national high-school championship in
1991. "Under the pressure, if you have some psychological bubble,
something you haven't dealt with, it's going to come up. If you're ad-
dicted to comfort in any way, you can't be a good chess player. You
have to be at peace with chaos."

Some, like Sal, who dispatches Kazim Gulamali, a 2203 from Georgia, without much trouble, seem to embrace this disorder. Others, like
Alex, who can manage only a draw against Robert Brady, a 1911 from
Virginia, have lost their way temporarily. It happens, in the way a golfer
can lose his swing on the final day of a major tournament. It's happened with Willy, too, who draws with Ran-De Rogers, a 1334 from
New York's Hunter High School, the kind of kid he could crush at a
Right Move event but can't seem to find a way to beat here, on the
last day of the nationals, with the pressure bearing down on him.

As usual, when Shawn stares at the board, his face is blank, even
here, even now, on the last day of the national tournament, having ex-
tracted himself from a position that seemed hopelessly lost. No way he
could win this game. But this kid, Nathaniel Boggs, a 1635 from Indiana with a flannel shirt and a preternatural beard . . . well, let's just say
he missed his chance. He missed *several* chances. He was crushing
Shawn and he blew it, and now that this game has generated into
something entirely unpredictable, something chaotic, Shawn has discovered a way back.

By half past noon, it's becoming clear that if Shawn loses, Murrow's deficit heading into the final round will be almost insurmountable, at least one and a half points. There is no room to play for the
draw, even, which means Shawn must go straight at this kid. And he
does. Playing with white, Shawn flanks his queen and traps his king
in a corner and the kid's time dwindles down under a minute, down
under thirty seconds, down under fifteen, down to eight seconds.

That's when Shawn unveils a wicked combination, and in a matter of seconds, he takes a queen, takes a bishop, takes both rooks, and forces his opponent to resign. It is 12:59 in the afternoon and Murrow is still alive, and so is Shawn, who's wobbling a little but trying to play it cool. Up the stairs he ambles, keeping an eye out for ducks in the artificial river. He rides up a couple more floors in the elevator and bursts into the room where his teammates (who, instead of watching the final hour of his game, went upstairs to continue their latest round of Stupid) are assuming that he's brought bad news with him.

"I won," he says, nearly swallowing the words.

"What?" Sal says. "You *won*?"

"How did you win?" Oscar says.

And Shawn tells them. The kid fucked up, he says, and then he fucked up again, and finally he fucked up one too many times. Into the room comes Mr. Weiss, who, moments before, according to Oscar, had been "mad tight," who now sees a glimmer of hope for one more national championship.

Sal puts down his cards. He shakes Shawn's hand. "You're a hero," he says.

"A *fat* hero," Oscar says.

"A meatball hero," Mr. Weiss says.

It's Shawn who laughs hardest of all at that one. They can call him anything they want right now. At this moment, maybe for the first time in his life, he has realized his own capabilities.

The cream cheese is gone by now, and in its place is a half-eaten sliver of overpriced cheesecake, covered in plastic wrap and left to its own devices. There are practice SAT tests strewn across the floor (Ilya—who else?) and there are several dozen empty cups, a case of Coca-Cola, an open bottle of Scope, and a half-eaten bag of doughnuts on the nightstand. There are boxes of congealed cold pizza on the bed, and Oscar is indulging in one of these pieces, even though it has sat out all night, because what's the difference, really? Pizza is pizza. And into this chaos comes Alex, who apologizes once more, this time because he's "the only one who's not playing well."

Sal says nothing. No doubt, part of him enjoys seeing a little humility from Alex, but a bigger part of him does not want to lose here. A couple of minutes earlier, Sal had turned to Shawn and, after dealing him in for the next round of Stupid, said, "Shawn, please don't play bad this round. You know we need a solid game."

"There's nothing better to prepare for a game than playing Stupid," Shawn replied.

"Yep," Sal said. "Nothing like losing your money."

Something's happening here. In the past twenty-four hours, this has become Sal's team. The petulant superstar who didn't want to waste his time meeting the president, who seemed entirely disinterested in the concept of chess as a team sport, is now in charge. And why? Because he remembers what it was like, all those times he *should* have won, back in Lithuania, and didn't win. Because there's no excuse for bad play, and there's no reason this team *should* lose to a bunch of nobodies from a remote desert in a state Sal couldn't begin to locate on a map. "We're leaving here at fifteen minutes to two," he declares. "Because by the time we get down there it's gonna take, like, ten more minutes."

His last game had not been as easy as he made it look; his opponent is an expert at Bughouse chess, and it took quite some time for Sal to figure out a way to dispatch him. He's tired, but that doesn't matter right now, and though he'll be playing at the top table this round, he doesn't seem concerned about this anymore either. When Ilya looks up the Round Seven pairings on his laptop and Sal sees he's playing Ruixin Yang, a 2152 from Virginia, he can hardly contain himself.

"I'm going to *crush* him," Sal says. "When I go for the win, I go for the win."

A housekeeper knocks on the door at 1:45. This is their cue. They leave, and she takes their place within this petri dish, trying to stifle her horror. On the way down, the elevator stops at every single floor. The last time this happened, Willy says, everybody won their game. So maybe it's a sign.

They exit, and walk past the river. No ducks. Even if there were, Shawn is too preoccupied to look for them. "My head is spinning, man," he says. "This is, like, too much. Last round of Supernationals."

"I haven't been this nervous since, like, the *first* round," Willy says.

♛

The deficit is a single point, the difference between one victory and one loss: Catalina Foothills has 19.5, Murrow 18.5. The good news for Murrow is that they have easier matchups: Four of Arizona's six team members are facing higher-rated players. "We got *nailed* on those pairings," Robby Adamson would say later. Sal and Alex are both playing down, and while Shawn and Dalphe are playing up, Willy (facing Deepyman Datta, the 2058 from Texas who drew Sal) and Oscar (playing down against Daniel Pflughoeft, a 1521 from Wisconsin) are the wildcards. The individual scores look like this:

Murrow (current top four):
Sal, 5.5
Alex, 4.5
Shawn, 4.5
Dalphe, 4.0

Willy, 3.5
Oscar, 3.5
Ilya, 3.0
Nile, 2.5

Catalina Foothills (current top four):
Landon Brownell (2007), 5.5
Sean Higgins (1940), 5.0
Christopher De Sa (1912), 4.5
Pavel Savine (1796), 4.5

Vaishnav Aradhyula (2071), 4.0
Bryant Brownell (1826), 4.0

"I'm playing Weinstein?" Shawn says. He hadn't looked at the pairings when Ilya pulled them up on his computer back in the room. He's seeing only them now, and he's seeing his name listed across from Josh Weinstein, Stuyvesant, and he's thinking, Christ, why couldn't I be playing a stranger (and preferably a stranger who isn't rated a hundred and fifty points higher)?

"Yo, you can beat him, dawg," Oscar says. "*Willy* beat him." Which isn't true, of course, although it's almost true, since Willy *should* have beaten Weinstein at states before he *didn't* beat Weinstein. And Ilya *did* beat him, after all, so maybe Weinstein is merely the roadblock each member of this team has to defeat in order to break through. Maybe this is Shawn's moment. Except he can't help but be scared half to death; after all, here's this handsome and articulate and gregarious and popular and well-connected kid sitting across from him in his Princeton hoodie, representing everything that Shawn is not and probably never will be, and if that's not a mindfuck, then nothing is.

It's not pretty, what transpires over the next hour. Shawn is overwhelmed from the beginning. He'll be fifteen years old in a couple of weeks and nothing in his life has ever felt like this; never before has he been counted on in this way. Weinstein's playing loose and free, because he's a senior, because this is his last game, because Stuyvesant's on its way to finishing somewhere in the top ten but nowhere near Murrow. He's eating saltines and drinking Powerade and kibitzing with Sal between moves. By 3:15, Shawn has lost his queen, and he's up and walking around and shaking his head and covering his eyes with the black baseball cap he's been wearing all week. It's a lost game. And Dalphe, playing Brian Kostrinsky, an 1884 from Georgia, has a losing game as well.

"Go win your championship," Weinstein whispers at Sal, when they both get up to stretch their legs and pass each other in the aisle.

"We can't win," Sal says. "Our third and fourth boards are losing. We can't win."

"What about the individual championship?"

"I don't care about that," Sal hisses back. "That title sucks."

♛

Within fifteen minutes, Shawn has resigned, and Dalphe's in trouble, way down on material, his arms crossed in front of his face, his head down on the table, and those huge eyes staring straight through the board. No chance. It's over. "This sucks," Sal says. "We are *done*."

It would seem not to matter that Oscar is going to win, and is going to break his own record for best performance at nationals by finishing with 4.5 points. And it would seem not to matter that Willy, while playing for the draw, has wound up losing. And it would seem not to matter that the kids from Arizona are just as tight as the kids from Murrow, that one of them, Christopher De Sa, is chewing on a voluminous wad of toilet paper to calm his nerves, and another, Sean Higgins, has masticated his pen cap to shreds. It's over, as far as Sal is concerned. Murrow is *done*. At 5:00 P.M., with his game hopelessly entangled and his mind beginning to wander, Sal does the unthinkable: He offers a draw. His opponent, who is much more concerned with the material notion of an individual national championship, has to stop his clock and leave the table and attempt to find a tournament director, who can explain exactly how the tiebreak system works, and whether if, by drawing this game, he can still finish tied for first place.

"I had a dream like this," Sal says. "That we'd go to nationals and place second."

He sighs. What he does not realize—what he cannot possibly realize—is that just by dreaming of such a moment, just by caring enough for such angst to creep into his subconscious, he has left behind the old Sal, the overconfident Sal, the Sal who, with his inscrutability and his self-regard, could not help but evoke the image of a young Bobby Fischer.

"Now," Sal says, "my dream is coming true."

Ten odd and anticlimactic minutes later, Sal's opponent agrees to the draw. And now, it would seem, there is no hope. After Alex defeats Rory Wasiolek, a 1984 from Pennsylvania, Murrow's top four now looks like this: Sal 6.0, Alex 5.5, Shawn 4.5, and Oscar 4.5, for a total of 20 points. After De Sa takes a draw and Aradhyula wins, Arizona *already* has 20 points, with two games still remaining, at adjacent boards: Landon Brownell is playing up against Kazim Gulami, a 2203 from Georgia, and Sean Higgins is playing up as well. If either of them wins—if either of them even manages a draw—then it's truly and completely over.

As an educator, this is a repellent situation to find yourself in, actively rooting for children to lose. But at this point, there is nothing else for Mr. Weiss to do. All the Murrow kids are upstairs, drowning their sorrows in poker wagers and bad television, and their coach sits in a plastic folding chair at the end of the aisle, watching the action on boards 203 and 204. When Brownell resigns, Weiss shakes his head. He says, "This is the same feeling I had those years when we lost by half a point."

There is one game remaining now, and it is all on Sean Higgins, a ruddy-faced sophomore in a T-shirt and cargo shorts, rated 1940, playing black against Thomas Gossell, a junior from Missouri with a blond brushcut, rated 2189. Time pressure is digging into Higgins, and that pen cap he's been chewing looks like its been set upon by a pack of rabid Dobermans. He's down under ten minutes, and the position is still complex enough that Higgins cannot ask for relief through the principle of insufficient losing chances.

Gossell plays queen from b2 to b7, taking a pawn and threatening Higgins's knight. (See diagram on the following page.)

This is it: If Higgins moves the knight, Gossell can move in for checkmate. And Weiss sits there in his chair and watches the clock run down, and he watches this poor frantic boy from Arizona and tries not to think of anything, all while he's thinking: *Move the knight. Move the knight.*

Higgins moves a rook.

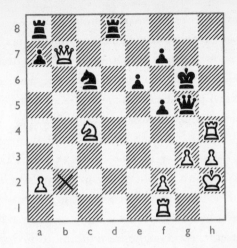

And yet it's enough to set off a chain reaction. Higgins takes a knight, Gossell takes a rook. Higgins's clock is under two minutes. "That should be it," Weiss says. It's 5:50 in the afternoon and Sean Higgins has a losing position, and he offers his hand . . . *he's resigning!!!* The national high-school championship will come down to . . . tiebreakers. But nobody seems to know what the tiebreakers are, or how they work. There's nothing in the program about this. There's no one in the room who has the answers to these questions.

So Eliot Weiss bursts out the doors, skips up the stairs, and heads straight to the office of Chess Control, the tournament's nerve center, which is where he asks a man behind the desk if, by any chance, he would happen to know what the tiebreakers might be for the high-school section. The man says he believes the first tiebreakers are cumulative, which, according to a clause in one tournament manual, means something like this:

Cumulative

In the event of a tie, compute each tied player's cumulative tiebreaker by adding together the player's total score at the end of each round. This should be easy for you to do, since you have already written this information down on the player's pairing card. A player who scored 3 points by winning the first 3 rounds and losing the final game will have a cumulative tiebreaker of $1+2+3+3=9$. A player who scored 3 points by losing in the first round and then winning the remaining three games will have a cumulative tiebreaker of $0+1+2+3=6$. The player with the higher tiebreaker number wins the tiebreaker.

After all that mental labor, all those hours of preparation, this whole season comes down to a math problem: *Accumulate the cumulatives of your top four.* It is silly, and it is anticlimactic, but this is the problem with chess, and one of the reasons why it's never found a more widespread audience: Its entire existence is grounded in an understanding of minutiae. The only other way to settle this would be for the teams to play a series of speed matches, and while that might be more exciting, it would raise a whole other set of concerns, like whether it's fair for a tournament based on endurance and longevity to be decided with a series of split-second decisions, and so on.

Instead, it comes down to math. And because Eliot Weiss has spent the last twenty years of his life doing math problems in his head, he thinks he has this one figured out. He thinks his team has won. He does not say this to the man behind the desk, when the man, in a pleasant voice, asks him what's happening with the high-school section. He simply says that it's come down to a pair of teams, one from New York, and the other from Arizona.

"Catalina Foothills," the man says. "That's my son's team."

For the first time, Eliot Weiss looks at the tag on the man's lapel.

His name is Roger Brownell.

♛

Up in the room, Shawn is trying to purge from his mind any memory of the past few hours. All he wants, at this moment, is to somehow be vindicated, to hear Mr. Weiss knock on the door to their room and walk in and tell them that they've won first place.

And then it happens, just like that: Mr. Weiss knocks five times, and is let in, and tells them that, as far as he can figure it, they've won.

"We *what*?" Sal says. "How is that *possible*?"

The reaction in the room is subdued, almost incredulous. Some handshakes, a couple of muffled cheers, and then back to the card games. There is still one hour to go until the awards ceremony, until the results are made official, and no one can quite believe, after a performance as ragged as this one, that this championship truly belongs to them.

♛

He had done the math once, and he had done it again in the hour between six and seven, while he waited for the official numbers to come down. But even math teachers miscalculate, and what Mr. Weiss had neglected to take into account was the fact that in the final round, his top four players, the four whose scores counted toward the cumulative results, had changed. Oscar was now in his top four, and because Oscar had struggled early on, his cumulative scores are not as high as Dalphe's or Willy's, and because of that the numbers have undergone a seismic change.

The awards ceremony for the K–12 section is held in Presidential Ballroom D, in an overcrowded corner of the biosphere. The room is full, but the standings still haven't been posted. Nobody knows what's going on for ten minutes, for fifteen minutes, and when the numbers go up, the people gather round and box each other out and no one can see anything and finally Mr. Weiss gets his head in there and feels the bile creeping up in the back of his throat. It's not quite like 2000 all over again, not quite like 2001 all over again. This is altogether different: This time, Murrow has lost on the "cumulative" tiebreaker. The margin is four points, 88 to 84.

"Officially," Mr. Weiss says, "we're cochampions."

But no one's buying it. Especially Sal. He knows how this works. He's been on the short end before. He knows there's no such thing as a "cochampion" in chess. You win or you lose, and you abide by the tiebreakers, however esoteric they may be. Downstairs in the K–8 section, the same thing happened to I.S. 318; after several of their top boards accidentally slept through this morning's round, they lost on tiebreakers, by two and a half points, to a team from Middle School 118, in the Bronx.

So officially, both I.S. 318 and Murrow may declare themselves cochampions, yet according to the hard numbers, they've failed. It may sound cruel, but this game is rife with unkind possibilities, and coming to terms with one's identity as a chess player involves coming to terms with one's own shortcomings, not to mention the shortcomings of society itself. "I see parents all the time whose kids will lose and they'll say, 'You played really well,'" says Bruce Pandolfini. "But if you have a lot of ability and you know you didn't play well, then you're going to see right through that."

So they pose for photos, and they force smiles, and Robby Adamson, the coach at Catalina Foothills, says of Murrow, "The toughest thing we've had to do in our lives is beat that team." He says, "As far as I'm concerned, the national championship shouldn't be determined on tiebreakers, so we *are* cochampions," and it's all very cordial, but inside, they're dying. "I can't believe we make it this far," Shawn says, "and then we lose on tiebreaks." All they want is to get as far away from this room as possible and break the seal on the biosphere and taste fresh air once more.

While there are not many long-held traditions on this team, there is one that has continued unbroken for more than a decade now at the conclusion of every national tournament in every city, whether it ends in a win, or in a loss, or in a muddled haze of numbers. Already, the calls have been made and reservations at the restaurant have been confirmed, and eight boys pile back into the white Econoline van with their coach and his family. They crack open the windows and gulp unfiltered oxygen for the first time in days, and then they make a beeline to the nearest Chuck E. Cheese, so they can act like children for a little while longer.

FIFTEEN

SUMMERTIME

THOSE LAST FEW WEEKS OF SCHOOL DRAG ON AND ON AND *ON*, AS THEY always do when the weather completes its slow turn to spring, and the students imprisoned in Room 446 for Eliot Weiss's last cycle of math classes stare out the window and daydream of hitching a ride on the B train to Coney Island. Once his advanced class has taken the AP exam, Mr. Weiss holds their attention by reviewing casino-game odds and teaching them rudimentary card-counting techniques. Attendance at the Thursday after-school chess club meetings dwindles to a level somewhere between sparse and nonexistent and the flyers taped to the walls carry reminders of graduation and spring theater productions. And in his office on the first floor, one of the last members of the Murrow administration's old guard is contemplating retirement. Four thousand students roam the hallways this spring, so many that the school has run out of lockers, and after twenty-eight years at this school, the last twenty-four as an assistant principal, Ron Weiss just can't see things getting any easier.

"In a school like this, with this type of environment, we cannot function with four thousand kids," he says. "It's not beneficial."

In the meantime, Murrow remains hopelessly overcrowded. The transfer policy, now stringently controlled by the Board of Education, has made it difficult for Eliot Weiss to keep recruiting good chess players with questionable report cards. (At one point, Willy and Shawn confronted their coach with a rumor that metal detectors were being installed near the front doors. For the moment, at least, it wasn't true.) What's happening at Murrow is endemic to American society in the early twenty-first century: How do you curtail certain freedoms and keep others in place? "At a certain juncture, the concept of Murrow would no longer be Murrow in its current philosophy," Ron Weiss says. "We may have changed the whole structure of what Murrow is about and what it represents."

And these things that Murrow represents—that you can succeed in granting civil liberties to a large student body, that you can emphasize creativity and individuality without sacrificing self-discipline, that you can produce a national championship chess team in a school that is not a private academy and is not bounded by exclusivity like Stuyvesant or Bronx Science or Hunter—are the embodiment of Ron Weiss's career as an educator. They're the reasons he's stayed all these years. And now what? *Numbers, numbers, numbers.* Where is Saul Bruckner's vision headed today, in an era when education is defined quantitatively, by test scores and classroom hours and pass/fail percentages? With all this emphasis on small schools, on specialized schools, isn't there something to be said for a place like Murrow, which has *nine* art teachers, all with a separate area of expertise?

"It may continue, but it won't be the same caliber, and it won't be the same quality," Weiss says. Maybe some of this is lingering bitterness because, despite widespread support from the school's teachers, he was passed over for the principal's job when Bruckner retired (Lodico, an outsider, was hired instead), but there are times when he feels like a useless appendage. Sometimes, when people ask him what he does for a living these days, he tells them he's the city's highest-paid doorman. A few weeks after this school year ends, he will finalize his plans to retire and leave Murrow to the members of the new regime, who may do with it as they wish. "As people like Eliot and myself and Saul Bruckner move toward retirement, you can replace people, but when you lose that genre of thinking and that belief in education, you can never replace it. What does Eliot get for all his work with chess? *Nothing.* He does it for the kids. He's so happy to get these kids some notoriety; you see his face, and he lights up with this stuff. For someone in private industry who had accomplishments like this, he'd be getting massive bonuses. But that feeling, that *belief,* is something you have to create. One of the things I prided myself on was never saying no to the kids. And I'm sure it will go on, but it won't be the same."

♛

The newspapers and the politicians know nothing of such things as *cumulative tiebreaks.* The newspapers and the politicians recognize yet another feel-good story when they see one, and when Eliot Weiss calls them up to say that his little public-school dynamo had won another national championship—if only, technically speaking, through a tie (never mind telling them that the tie was broken through numbers)— this was good enough for them. So the photo cutline in the "Your Neighborhood" section of the *Daily News* declared that Murrow "won the 2005 National High School Championship" and the story in the *Brooklyn Skyline* began, "They did it again," and in late May, they make another of their regular visits to City Hall to be honored by their local congressman and the City Council. Along with a few of the newbies— including the foursome of Rex, Renwick, Robert, and Adalberto, who had begun this year with a vision of making the traveling team— only four of the regulars bother to show up: Dalphe (who brings a turkey sandwich with him), Willy (who is trying to finish *Angela's Ashes* so he can pass one of his classes), Ilya (who has taken the SAT once, and done well enough, but wants to take it again), and Oscar, who insists that he has given up on gambling altogether.

A few weeks earlier, Oscar had been outed. A *Daily News* reporter had called Mr. Weiss, looking to see if he knew any kids who were into online gambling, and so Mr. Weiss passed them along to Oscar. A reporter from the paper interviewed Oscar and his family and then ran an in-depth front-page story, headlined, ONLINE AND HOOKED:

> When Oscar Santana gets home from school everyday [sic], the Brooklyn teenager dutifully does his homework, then boots up his computer for an evening of Texas Hold 'em.
>
> For Oscar, and a growing number of students, playing the popular poker game online is swiftly becoming a new American pastime—with potentially dangerous consequences.
>
> "I could spend a good two hours playing poker on the computer," said Santana. . . .
>
> But the soft-spoken member of Edward R. Murrow High School's national championship chess team insists he's got his game-playing under control.
>
> "I can tell myself when to stop," he said. "Since I have been playing, I haven't lost. I really don't worry about getting addicted. I just love playing." . . .

The story included five "warning signs" to detect if your child is gambling, and a number for a twenty-four-hour gambling hotline. It quoted Oscar's mother, saying she didn't mind as long as he wasn't playing for money, and later quoted the chairman of a gaming commission in Montreal, who said most underage gamblers are "sanctioned by their parents," and that "parents still rule their children—supposedly."

It wasn't just the ambush of the article that led Oscar to cut back on his gambling. It was the fact that in six months he would be eighteen years old, and he wanted to graduate high school by then. He didn't want to be stuck at Murrow forever. He wanted to live up to his father's expectations. By December, he was hoping, he could make up enough schoolwork to take the GED exam and then he could, finally, channel his considerable brainpower and his endless curiosity into something both legal and moral.

And what about Willy? He turned nineteen in March and he still isn't sure what he's doing with his life. He's trying to make it through the last cycle at Murrow without failing another class, and he's thinking that he'll be able to make up the rest of his classes in the fall and get his diploma and figure it out from there. "I've been lazy," he will admit several months later. "I didn't do the work." And then, in the next breath, he will admit that he skipped class the week before because it was raining outside.

But right now he's thinking of other things. Right now, in the catacombs of City Hall, he's jawing with Oscar about the NBA playoffs. He likes Miami to beat favored Detroit that night. Not only that, he's thinking the Heat's Dwyane Wade will score forty points. "You're crazy," Oscar says, but this is Willy, always pulling for the underdog, living life according to his own unique and complex rhythms. So, yeah, maybe it's true—maybe Willy's a little, shall we say, *out there*. Maybe it'll take him a few years to get his head straight. But every time you underestimate him, every time you think that maybe this kid is lost in the stratosphere and ain't never coming back, he surprises the hell out of you.

That night, the Heat beat the Pistons. And after making a layup in the final seconds, Dwyane Wade finishes with exactly forty points.

♛

After all that has transpired this year, after all they've been through, it's hard for anyone to muster much enthusiasm for the Brooklyn borough championships, which are conducted in a dimly lit gymnasium on the campus of the New York City College of Technology in downtown Brooklyn. Neither Sal nor Alex shows up, and Shawn is not supposed to be there either; Mr. Weiss has grown weary of his antics, of his refusal to show up at class and put in an effort. He didn't register Shawn for the tournament and didn't include him in the orders for the boxed lunches the tournament directors are giving away. But Shawn comes anyway, wearing his black Yankee cap and an Oakland Raiders jersey, and since the tournament is free and sponsored by the Chess-in-the-Schools program, he signs himself up. "You're on your own for lunch," Mr. Weiss tells him.

That's fine with Shawn. He's not here for the free food. He's here because this is the one place where he feels like he belongs, where he can mingle with the only people his own age who can relate to his addiction, and who can understand why he values this game more than he could ever imagine valuing an hour in an algebra class. Here, among chess players, his opinion matters. He can express himself. He can be wry and he can be cynical. He can tell Dalphe that the new Batman movie is going to be garbage, and when Dalphe says, "You think everything is garbage," and then picks up one of his black pawns and says, "You probably think this piece is garbage," Shawn can say, "That's *racist*. You a little racist." And everyone will laugh.

Nobody knows what to do with a kid like Shawn, who can unveil such brilliant combinations over the board but can't seem to muster any energy away from it. Yet here's the question his teachers keep asking themselves: Where would Shawn be *without* chess? What would his life be like then? Would he be just another confused kid roaming the streets without purpose? "Without chess, Shawn wouldn't have either chess or school," says Jennifer Shahade, who worked with him at I.S. 318. "It's not like it's chess that's keeping him from going to school."

♛

"I keep saying I'm going to study," Dalphe says. "But I never do."

"If I studied, I'd be a twenty-two hundred, easy," Shawn is saying. "I'd be a senior master. Bercys, if he *really* studied, would be a GM. Or at least an IM."

"If I studied, I'd be past seventeen hundred by now," Dalphe says. "But that's the thing about studying. It's *hard*. Anyway, you play on the Internet all the time, and that's *like* studying. But I don't play on the Internet to study. I play on the Internet for fun."

"I don't even play on the Internet anymore," Shawn says. "I play outside. I play in the park. That's where it's at now."

♛

The newbies show up at City Tech as well, although they can hardly be called newbies anymore. They have come a long way (Rex wins three of four of his matches in the novice section this afternoon), but they have started to hit a wall. They are discovering the infinite possibilities of this game, and they are realizing that unless you are willing to give over a great deal of your identity to it, there is only so far you can go.

"You have to be serious about it," says Bruce Pandolfini. "Not serious in a debilitating way, but wanting to give it your all. If you approach it with a halfhearted effort, you're not going to be a champion."

Over the summer, Adalberto will move away to South Carolina, and the whole notion of playing competitive chess will begin to seem more daunting than enlightening. The three who remain will stop showing up regularly for the Thursday club meetings, and when Mr. Weiss is asked what became of his quartet of promising newcomers, to the kids he had hoped to shape into traveling players, he will shrug and admit that he has no idea. ("For me it was a combination of having a really busy junior year, and just not having as much interest as I did last year," Robert would write in an e-mail the following spring. "Mainly I just had other more important things like the college process going on that I needed to take care of, and even though I was still interested in chess, I just wasn't as interested as last year.")

Anyway, it's not Mr. Weiss's job to keep track of anyone, or to force them into anything. You either fall in love with this game, usually early in life and with an almost inexplicable passion, or you find that you cannot, or do not want to, deal with the burden it exacts upon your synapses. Life goes on. Maybe someday, Robert says, when he has more time, he'll pick up chess again. Until then, there are other things to take care of if he wants to become a functioning adult.

♛

"I hate that word," Josh Waitzkin is saying. *"Prodigy."*

It's been six years now since Waitzkin has played competitive chess, since he found himself fighting off an unbearable sadness while trying to scratch out a living by playing chess tournaments in Europe, where the money is far better. He went back to the temporary home he'd taken in Slovenia and he sat for two weeks and pondered these essential questions: What if I did this for another six or seven years? What if everything went perfectly? What if I became one of the best players in the world? Would I be happy?

And the answer was no.

A couple of decades earlier, his father had written a memoir about Josh, and the memoir had been turned into a movie, *Searching for Bobby Fischer,* and the success of the movie and the subsequent movement of thousands of American children toward chess had rendered Waitzkin into something he never could have imagined he'd become: He was the closest thing the game would ever have to a rock star. And this wasn't such a bad thing, because Waitzkin had always been remarkably mature, because the publicity guaranteed him a certain financial freedom that most chess players—especially those in the United States—are not privy to. He lent his name to a computer game called Chessmaster, and he found a place on the European circuit, which is not always an easy thing for an American to break into, and he tried to become an ambassador for the game.

But after a while, as so often happens with those labeled as prodigies, the game ceased to make him happy. He had taken courses in Buddhism and Taoism at Columbia, and he found himself pondering things on an existential level. To Waitzkin, chess is a mirror of the psyche: If you're quiet and introverted, you can play the game like an Abstract Expressionist. If you're aggressive and excitable, you can play like a rattlesnake. If you're dealing with emotional issues, those issues will carry over into your chess game. It is all about surviving amid struggle, about subsisting within a cerebral bubble, about being able to withstand all the noise that this eternal struggle creates inside one's head. "When I think back on my career," Waitzkin says, "I just remember the losses. Every big loss is crystal clear to me. The lifestyle is one of getting constantly bludgeoned over the head. And I reached a moment where I realized external success had nothing to do with happiness."

So Josh Waitzkin, child prodigy, eight-time national chess champion, and arguably the most famous American-born chess player since Bobby Fischer, quit playing competitive chess. As a substitute, he took up the Chinese martial art of Tai Chi, and in 2004, he became a world champion.

He is fast approaching thirty years old, and he insists he has never been happier.

♛

So what's the point, really? What possible reason could there be to keep playing this excruciating and exacting and infuriating game, when the only financial rewards to be gained are at exclusive tournaments in faraway places, when no one in your own country could give a damn about it, when spelling bees and hot-dog-eating competitions get nationwide television exposure but chess tournaments never do? What hope is there for chess in America when the greatest player in the world, perhaps the greatest player of all time, can walk the streets of New York City and go completely unrecognized?

This is Garry Kasparov, of course, the exception to every rule, the highest-rated player of all time, according to Arpad Elo's near-foolproof system. For two decades, Kasparov, born in Azerbaijan in 1963, a prodigy who won the Soviet Junior Championship at age twelve and the World Championship at age twenty-two, has been the number-one-ranked chess player in the world, his rating approaching 2900. He has taken on computers (his match against IBM's Deep Blue, in 1996, was one of those rare and fleeting moments when chess penetrated mainstream American culture) and he has written books and delivered lectures and started his own chess foundation, based in New Jersey, whose mission is to expand in-school and after-school chess programs. He is outspoken and charismatic and he is the most universally respected chess player in the world, almost *too good* for his own good at times. "He lacks the artistic purity," Pandolfini says. "You don't know what he's doing. You just know it works."

But in the spring of 2005, even Kasparov threw up his hands, frustrated with the bureaucracy of the international chess federation and with the lack of challenges, and announced his retirement from competition in order to reform the Russian political system.

So why bother with chess when even Kasparov himself doesn't see the point anymore? Why bother with chess when you can do what an ex–chess player named Howard Lederer did—namely, make a small fortune riding the trend of Texas Hold 'Em poker? Lederer dropped out of Columbia to play chess, discovered a poker room in the back of a chess club, and by 2005 had won nearly three million dollars. The same revelation struck Jennifer Shahade's brother Greg, an International Master who taught at 318, took up online poker a few years back, recently moved home to Philadelphia to play poker full-time, and is doing better financially than he ever has before.

Compared to chess, the calculations involved in poker look like remedial math. By the spring of 2005, the game was constantly televised, and its best players, like Howard Lederer, had become minor celebrities, and the money . . . well, compared to chess, the money was a goddamned windfall. Poker is less of an emotional investment, a more shallow mental investment, and a far better financial investment. Anyone (even the underaged like Oscar, with the proper front) can join an online service and start playing. You learn the basics, you learn when to bluff and when to fold, you use a brain that's already been wired for such skills through years of chess training, and you can make easy money. You don't spend hours studying a single opening that might never come into play. "You don't feel bad about yourself as much when you make a mistake," says Jennifer Shahade, who traveled with her brother to the World Series of Poker in Las Vegas in the summer of 2005. "If I do something bad in chess, I feel really bad about myself. But poker, it's not the same psychological depth. Of the chess players I know, almost every one of them plays poker."

And why wouldn't they? The top prize in the main event at the 2005 World Series of Poker was $7.5 million dollars, with $4.25 million for second place and $2.5 million for third. And what is the top prize at this year's World Open of chess, held in Philadelphia in early July? Eleven thousand dollars, with $10,500 for second place (the loser in a tiebreaker), and $1,825 for third.

By chess standards, of course, this is a monstrous payoff, which is why the World Open consistently draws the nation's top talent, and which is why Sal makes the trip there in early July, and Alex goes too, and even Ilya makes the two-hour trip, trying to make a run at the $10,000 first prize in the under-1800-rated section. And while Ilya finishes out of the money, both Sal and Alex wind up winning $900, which might seem like a good amount for a couple of high-school juniors-to-be, but consider the entry fee, and the cost of the hotel, and the cost of food, and the cost of transportation, and what are you left with?

Already this summer, Hikaru Nakamura, the best young player in America and the defending U.S. champion (who winds up tying for third place at the World Open), is hinting that he might take a break to attend college instead of continuing to play chess. And why shouldn't he? If a kid like this can't get anyone to sponsor him, and can muster only a small measure of national publicity, then what point is there in trying to make a living of it? And Alex and Sal have both come to understand this; it's the price they pay for leaving their home countries and coming to America. In fact, the more he thinks about it, the more Sal starts to consider taking that chess scholarship he won from the University of Texas at Dallas, one of the only colleges in the country to offer such a thing. At least then, the game will have given him *something* tangible.

"But you know what? They've already *gotten* the value," says Bruce Pandolfini. "Their lives have already been made much better. They're already better problem-solvers. They're already tougher mentally. They're already more creative. They have more things to draw on to get them through the difficulties in life. The benefit will last for the rest of their lives."

Besides, it's not always easy to let this game go. It is a cerebral parasite; it burrows inside you and stays there.

Shawn is an unexpected visitor at the World Open as well. He and his friend Angel—*Tweedledum and Tweedledee,* as the teachers at I.S. 318

used to call them—caught a ride with one of the guys they've gotten to know by playing in the parks this summer. On Thursday night they sleep on chairs in the lobby. Shawn says one of the park guys volunteered to pay his $280 entry fee (presumably, anticipating he'd get a cut of Shawn's winnings), but Shawn's stepmother wouldn't allow it to happen. So now he's here, with no money, and only vague intimations of where he might stay (a friend from Chess-in-the-Schools eventually allows him and Angel to crash on his floor), and he spends the next couple of days in the Skittles Room, where an entire subculture of park players have camped out with no intention of entering the actual tournament. They're here for one reason, and one reason only: They're here to hustle. They'll play blitz. They'll play cards (exhibiting blatant disregard for a sign on the wall, prohibiting, in order, Smoking, Drinking, and Card Playing). They'll play backgammon. They'll roll dice. Whatever it takes to hook a fish, they'll do it. And because Shawn has no summer job (he filed his working papers too late, he says), and because he has nothing else to do, he's become fascinated with the lifestyle. That week at the World Open, when Elizabeth Vicary asks him what went wrong at school this year, he says, "I've been hanging out with the wrong crowd." For Shawn, that doesn't mean what you think it might. That doesn't mean drinking, smoking, doing drugs, or macking on girls. For Shawn, hanging out with the wrong crowd means hustling chess games in the park with young and middle-aged men of indeterminate backgrounds who do this for a living. They do it at a park called Mount Olympus, near the Brooklyn Museum of Art, and they do it in Harlem at St. Nicholas Park on 145th Street, and of course they do it in the Village, in the southwest corner of Washington Square Park, where two decades earlier, Josh Waitzkin discovered the game of chess.

August in the city is unbearable, and in the snake pit of Washington Square there is no respite from the heat. It slices straight on through the shade trees and chars the asphalt and beats down upon the chessboards and then just lies there. A man saunters past tugging a listless mutt tethered to a makeshift leash and a cooler full of cold drinks stacked on a dolly. *"Water one dollar, Snapple a buck fifty,"* he is saying, and on a day like this it seems like as good a deal as you'll find in the entire city. So the hustlers, some shirtless, some homeless, get up from their tables, clutching wrinkled dollar bills, while Shawn Martinez, bored by the lack of action, keeps letting go with a whistle. It is a soft warble that escapes from between his teeth with a sound like a malfunctioning smoke alarm.

The whistle is Shawn's feeble attempt to attract attention to his chessboard without actually moving, his way of reeling in a fish and getting a game going and making some money. But it's Wednesday afternoon, and most of the people wandering through the park are either curious tourists more interested in gawking at games in progress or NYU coeds, who provide the scenery but present no real revenue potential. The boards are arranged in a circle broken by a series of footpaths, and a college-aged kid wearing sneakers and blue shorts wanders through the radius of the circle chirping, "Che-*essss,* che-*esss,* che-*esss,*" his voice rising and falling on largely deaf ears.

"You ain't gonna make money doing that, just repeating that over and over again," says Angel Lopez. Angel's here to visit Shawn, and he's here because he just took a lesson from a master at the Marshall Chess Club for sixty bucks, money that Shawn doesn't have.

"Che-*ess,* che-*ess,*" the college kid says.

Angel would like to go home. It's hotter than hell and he's hungry and he sees no reason to stick around here, but Shawn's got himself a board within the circle (something that takes a little resourcefulness, since the regulars "reserve" certain boards) and he'd like to make some money today, and a lot of the best players come out here in the evening after work. So he ain't going nowhere. He's rooted on the bench at his spot, wearing a pair of denim shorts that fall below his massive knees, his plastic chess pieces and his game clock all set up and ready to go.

"I ain't staying till nine o'clock," Angel says.

"Why not?" Shawn says.

"Because it's whack, dude. Because you re*tah*-ded to do that."

"You re*tah*-ded. Go get me a McChicken. You staying over at my place tonight?"

"I dunno," Angel says.

Because there's nothing else to do, they start playing blitz against each other. They're rated nearly the same, in the 1900s, and they're laughing and calling each other *ducks* and *patzes,* short for "patzer," the nickname for a novice player made famous in the outdoor scenes in *Searching for Bobby Fischer,* which were filmed in this same section of the park and have made it perhaps the best-known outdoor chess space in the world. It has become both a tourist attraction and a place of business for the regulars, who claim their tables within the circle and sit there all day, smoking blunts and staring at the sky and listening to *Kind of Blue* on a boom box and living for those moments when they can show some poor fish just how the game is played out in the streets. The game is cutthroat out here: The trash talk comes in a steady stream, and cheating is common, if not expected (it isn't so hard, in a speed game, to nudge a piece to another square when no one's looking, or to slide your bishop down the wrong diagonal to capture a piece). And just as street basketball has its sad and cautionary tales of great talents who never lived up to their potential, so does Washington Square Park have its share of brilliant head cases who can break down complex lines of attack but can't hold down a full-time job.

"Who's the best player here?" Shawn says. "In blitz, right now, it's me." But in longer games, over-the-board games, it's the Russian guy over at the far end of the circle. Nobody here would dispute this. The man is the prototype of a hobo; he has a flea-bitten gray beard and his belongings are stacked on a pushcart next to his seat, and there is an empty carton of orange juice at his side. He's sitting alone for the moment, jotting notes on a scrap of paper and muttering to himself like a Dostoevsky character. "Dude comes with crazy stuff," Shawn says. "He's homeless. He, like, basically *lives* here. He sleeps here. That's why he gets the same table every day. And he don't play for money. He charges *you* to play *him*."

Shawn's learned all of this because he's spent his entire summer playing outdoors. Until a couple of weeks ago, his regular spot was in Brooklyn, at Mount Olympus, but the action got tired there. Not enough competition. Not enough money changing hands. The games would go on late into the night, the scene eventually shifting to the back tables at the Wendy's down the street, but Shawn craved something more. He wanted to make some money, since this is the only financial conduit he has. The past few weeks, he's been coming here at ten or eleven each morning, depending on whether his mom lets him go, and then staying through the evening, surrounded by questionable characters with questionable motives and questionable ethics. "My mom don't mind," he says. "She minds me playing for money, but what's she gonna do?"

Beyond the question of whether this is the best atmosphere for any impressionable teenager, there is a split among chess teachers as to whether speed games and blitz games, the kind of lightning-round chess you see on ICC and in the park, are good for a burgeoning child's development. The countervailing argument, of course, is that speed chess prepares you in all the wrong ways, that it's the equivalent of running sprints to train for a marathon. But then, isn't running sprints, or playing in a pickup basketball game, better than doing nothing at all?

"The fact is, if you want to be a good player, you've got to be a fighter," says Josh Waitzkin, who spent a large part of his formative years playing in Washington Square. "Playing at the park can really toughen you up. You have to deal with all the banter, figure out how not to get hustled; it's good for concentration too."

Josh Weinstein—who, like Waitzkin, learned to play chess at Dalton, and then grew disenchanted with the private-school atmosphere—has been coming here since his dad brought him in the sixth grade. Soon after, his father started bankrolling a few of the regulars, buying them meals in order to keep his son safe. One guy in particular, named Earl, has been looking out for this little Jewish kid for years now. He still lets Weinstein use his table, and now that he's on his way to Princeton, as an aspiring congressman, he thought he'd do something . . . well . . . *diplomatic* with his last summer. He's got a flyer he's giving out to the fish who approach him:

Welcome to my table!

> My name is Josh Weinstein, recent graduate of Stuyvesant High School and I will be attending Princeton in the fall. At Stuy, I was captain of the chess team, one-time state high-school co-champion and one-time national speed chess (5-minute) high school champion.
>
> I have come up with a crazy idea to give out free chess lessons to any and all passerby and accept donations on behalf of a charity of my choice. At the end of the summer, I will give all the money I have earned to New York Cares. . . . My acts of volunteerism and community service stem primarily from boredom, a desire to teach/expose chess, and raise money for a needy cause.

According to his tally, Shawn, who's his own needy cause, made over three hundred dollars last week. He plans on giving a cut of that to his mom, if she'll take it. Last Friday and Saturday—the weekends are the best time, obviously—he fended off a steady stream of challengers. He beat a couple of masters, some Filipino IM yesterday and another guy the day before who said his rating was 2250. He beat a few Irish tourists. He beat some Wall Street suit, a CPA or something, taking in ninety dollars from him in the course of an hour. Afterward, the dude mentioned something about sponsoring Shawn so he could take lessons. But now, a few days later, Shawn can't even remember the guy's name.

It takes a couple of idle hours, but at seven-thirty, with the sun falling and the heat loosening its grip, Shawn hooks a fish. Dude—get *this*—is wearing a Day-Glo orange ensemble, the hat turned backward and paired up with the oversized T-shirt. They play blitz, three minutes to a side on the clock; it takes Shawn one minute four seconds to checkmate him. The Day-Glo man asks for a rematch, this time with no clock. Shawn mates him once more. They play blitz again; this time, Shawn puts one minute on his clock and gives Day-Glo man three minutes. Shawn queens a pair of pawns and mates him again. The after-work crowd threads through the radius of the circle, carrying their briefcases and their book bags, folding pizza crusts into their mouths, shrugging off the come-ons from the regulars in the snake pit. At the next table, three men are smoking Newports and finishing off a contentious game of dominoes.

Right then, Nile wanders into the circle, looking for Shawn. He's got a summer job working for his dad's friend at a real-estate office in downtown Brooklyn, but he's been playing in some adult tournaments in Brooklyn Heights with Shawn (ten dollars, ten-minute games, and Nile and Shawn have each taken home about forty bucks for a first-place finish), and he's already elevated his game, and by the end of the summer he'll be up above 1700 and on his way above 1800. Nile can't stay too long out here, anyway; he's got a curfew, and he's far too introspective to really fit into this scene. He's here because Shawn's here, because Shawn's his mouthpiece.

When it's over, when the Day-Glo man finally concedes and moves out of the circle, Shawn has won ten dollars in the course of fifteen minutes.

"Certified chess hustler," he says. "That's me."

♛

Nobody's seen Willy for most of the summer because Willy's been in Martinique visiting his father and his aunts and uncles. It's the first time he's seen his dad in twelve years, since they left the island to come to New York. He kept saying he'd make it up there one year around Christmastime, but he never did, so Willy's mom has sent him down there alone (his sister was supposed to go, too, now that she's back living at home, but her green card doesn't arrive until a week after Willy departs). He'd never traveled anywhere by himself; he'd always been with a chess team. He'd always spend the whole flight playing cards with Oscar, but this time, he watches the in-flight movie and he watches cartoons and he sleeps, and when he wakes up everyone is yammering away in French. And because Willy has a French passport, all the flight attendants start speaking French to him too. For the first time in his life, he's on his own, lost in a strange new world.

♛

That same week, in the town of Belfort, France, Alex Lenderman, playing at the same World Youth Championship event that had torn down Sal's ego the year before, in the under-sixteen division against the best young players in the world, becomes the first American in recent memory to win a gold medal. The achievement lands him on the cover of *Chess Life,* the U.S. Chess Federation's monthly magazine, and wins Alex a new level of renown. ". . . Lenderman's victory is a real cause for celebration, a long-awaited sign that Nakamura may have some company in his ascent up the ratings charts," writes David R. Sands, the chess columnist for *The Washington Times.*

When Sal hears of this, he is appalled. He is indignant. He refuses to accept that such a thing could have occurred without certain improprieties. "The year I played," he says, "it was *much* tougher."

A short time later, Alex delivers a lecture about his victory at the Marshall Chess Club. When Sal shows up with a friend of his to watch, Alex says, "I guess this means you respect me." And this only inflames things further. Respect is not something you *get,* Sal wants to tell him. Respect is something you *earn.* And Alex keeps inflaming his anger, keeps saying that Sal is badmouthing him to his friends, that Sal is conspiring against him, and Sal says Alex keeps insulting *his* friends, that in the wake of his victory he's the one who's gotten too cocky and overconfident. "He's done a lot of stuff," Sal says. "I can't even remember how much stuff he did."

In the months to come, Ilya will take regular lessons from an SAT tutor, and he will apply to several of his dream schools, including Georgetown and MIT. He will appeal to both George W. Bush and Michael Bloomberg, the New York mayor, for letters of recommendation. He will improve his board scores to 1890 (710 math, 600 verbal, and 580 on the writing exam) and he will write several application essays about his experiences as the captain of the best chess team in the nation. He will travel to Vermont with Willy to play in the Green Mountain Open, which will turn out to be a "complete disaster." He will go to Boston for a second interview with MIT and get just as far along with Georgetown, and then in March of 2006, after all those months of waiting, of hoping like hell that he's finally found his ticket out of Brooklyn, he will receive a pair of thin envelopes in the mail thanking him for his application, but the numbers were overwhelming, more applications every year, etc., etc. One of his friends at Murrow, whose grades are not as good, will wind up with scholarship offers at both Columbia and NYU's Stern Business School, and another of his classmates, a social misfit who goes around *licking the floor*—"Really," Ilya says. "He literally licks the floor"—will get accepted at Brown. But Ilya will get only one offer, a full scholarship at Baruch College in Manhattan, part of the City University system. It is a well-respected school, but it is not MIT, and it is not Georgetown. For many of the kids who wind up at Baruch, it is a safety school, and this is what bothers Ilya the most: Here he is, intelligent, hardworking, meticulously prepared, and willing to do whatever it takes to succeed in this nation, and he'll wind up in class next to some kid who slunk through a mediocre high school with a C average and somehow got accepted to Baruch as well.

As always, Ilya will take a pragmatic approach to his failure. In a year or two, as soon as he can, he figures he'll try to transfer. Until then, he'll have to deal with his disappointment by making self-deprecating and (and vaguely morbid) jokes about his plight. From his time working amid the daily drudgery at Washington Mutual Bank, he will say, he has learned that there are two types of people in this world—the annoying customer and the disgruntled employee who must deal with the annoying customer. So he'll study business, even though he hates business, because he still can't see any way to make money by studying physics, and maybe someday, if all goes right, if everything works out perfectly . . . well, then he'll become the disgruntled employee. After he says this, he will laugh, presumably at the starkness of his own vision. All these years immersed in the game, all these ups and downs, and he is just now learning to come to terms with defeat. "None of the colleges that I wanted have accepted me," he'll say. "But that's life, I guess."

And just as it does at Edward R. Murrow High School, one cycle leads directly into the next. Soon enough, someone else will become the captain of this team, and someone else will be charged with holding together this disparate band of eccentrics, and amid the shifting environment at Murrow High School, Eliot Weiss's quiet little club will soldier on through its third decade of existence. In the fall, another group of newbies will gather in Room 446 for the first of the Thursday-afternoon meetings, and Eliot Weiss will assure them that they are in the right place, that yes, this is chess, and if they give themselves over to it, this game will change their lives.

EPILOGUE

USCF ratings:

Alex Lenderman	2452
Sal Bercys	2451
Shawn Martinez	1954
Nile Smith	1849
Mikhail Furman	1765
Ilya Kotlyanskiy	1715
Dalphe Morantus	1697

The 2006 National High School Chess Championships were held in late April in Milwaukee, Wisconsin, sharing space in the city's downtown convention center with a Harley-Davidson executive training session, a concurrence of events that led to some surreal interminglings in the elevators of the adjacent Hilton. Once again, Eliot Weiss treated his team the day before the tournament by exposing them to the vagaries of the alcohol-fermentation process, this time at the Miller Brewery, where Sal would later claim to have nearly suffocated on yeast fumes. Once again, the tournament came down to the final moments of the seventh and final round, and once again, it came down to Edward R. Murrow High School of Brooklyn, New York, and Catalina Foothills High School of Tucson, Arizona. And once again, Eliot Weiss found himself watching a boy he had never met play a game of chess against another boy he had never met, with his program's reputation dependent upon the result.

Twice in five minutes, a pair of overly fastidious tournament officials had come along and ordered Mr. Weiss to move his feet back several inches, behind the line of masking tape demarcating the rows of chess tables from the area reserved for spectators. (It happened so often that weekend that some of the parents in the room took to calling the tournament director, the same copper-haired woman who had policed the room the year before at Supernationals, by the nickname of "Mrs. Hitler.") But Mr. Weiss did not oblige them by moving back. Instead, like the New Yorker that he was and had always been, he leaned in farther, to get a better look at the clock. Sixteen seconds remained on the side of Vaishnav Aradhyula, a sophomore in an Arizona Diamondbacks cap who was the last of the Catalina Foothills players to finish his game. Because Murrow led by one point, the only way for Catalina Foothills to salvage a tie in the team competition, and to win once again on tiebreakers, would have been for Aradhyula to somehow keep on making moves within the five-second delay on his clock and salvage a victory from a game that appeared, by all accounts, to be a dead draw.

After what had happened the year before, after what had happened in 2000 and 2001, to have the win and then lose it *three times* this decade, Mr. Weiss was braced for disaster. Aradhyula's opponent, Cameron Donis, a sophomore from Elkhart, Indiana, had nearly half an hour remaining on his clock, and he was playing with the white pieces, and all he had to do was avoid a stupid mistake in the endgame, ensure the draw, and Murrow would win by half a point. "Protect the pawn. Protect the *pawn*," said Dalphe, standing next to Mr. Weiss. "Take your time. Take your time."

♕

That they'd made it this far was perhaps Murrow's finest achievement in all the decades Weiss had been coaching. Catalina Foothills had only gotten stronger, and arrived in 2006 as the unquestioned favorites, with four of its top players rated above 2000. And Murrow showed up without Oscar (who, improbably, was serving as a *chaperone* for the five dozen Chess-in-the-Schools students who came here to play—he was working at CIS on a regular basis and planned on attending a local community college in the fall) and without Willy (who, while technically still a student at Murrow—he was working on getting his GED so he could attend a vocational college—had already played at four national tournaments and had used up his eligibility here). In their place was Mikhail Furman, a freshman who greeted his teammates with an incessant array of handshakes and flitted about the room like a hyperactive character in a Disney film.

Certain things hadn't changed: They were still petulant and rebellious, and Sal still resented Alex, except now he wasn't alone anymore, after Alex took that gold medal at the World Youth Championships the previous summer. The word was that Alex had started playing tentatively afterward, that he was too content to take easy draws and had descended into a moral gray area, offering prearranged draws to other GMs so he could finish in the money at certain tournaments. And while Murrow had no trouble winning its fifth consecutive city championship, Alex struggled, weighed down by expectations and resentment. When he lost in the fourth round to an opponent rated 400 points lower, the Schadenfreude was palpable. It simmered all around him. *This is how the Allies must have felt when Germany fell,* someone said, and Sal, who could now avoid a rematch with Alex, who could avoid the temptation to beat him instead of taking another draw, thought that quote so clever that he wrote it on his hand. Then in the fifth and final round, Alex snapped at his father, shooing him out of the room, and he lashed out at another player, accusing him of talking during his game, of conspiring to cheat, and the kid jawed right back, saying, "You think I'd stoop down to *your* level?" Afterward, the whole thing degenerated into a shouting match in the hallway, everyone coming down on little Lenderman, with Sal taking pleasure in the whole fine mess. "I don't get in physical fights," Alex said when it was over. "Only mental fights."

Sal exorcised some of that ongoing frustration with Alex at the 2006 U.S. Championships, which were held the same week as the state championship in New Rochelle (the competition was so lackluster at states that Murrow didn't even need its two top boards to win). At the U.S. Championships, in San Diego, Sal beat Alex in forty-three moves—no more gentlemanly draws—and yet even afterward, their fates remained intertwined: Heading into nationals, Alex's rating eclipsed Sal's by a single point.

Funny, though, how all of this animosity faded once they got to Milwaukee. The memory of what had happened in Nashville still tugged at them, and nobody wanted to endure the indignity of a tie again. But there was more to it than that. By now they had been on enough trips together, had been trapped in enough cramped carpools together, that they *understood* each other. When they traded insults, as when Shawn referred to Ilya as "The Nose," there was a certain grudging affection behind their words. When someone told a vaguely racist joke and Dalphe and Nile both laughed and Mikhail took offense, Sal had to explain to him how it worked: that this was the way they talked to each other, and that nobody should take anything personally. When that kid fell into a shouting match with Alex during a match at the city championships, it was Shawn, of all people, who was quick to stand up for him.

Without Oscar's enterprising influence, they were more studious this time around. Alex, in an uncharacteristic display of leadership, declared a moratorium on late-night card playing, and his teammates appeared to have taken him seriously. Even Shawn was less distracted, and a win in the final round gave him 5.5 points, tied for fourteenth place in the championship section among a field of 365. A half hour after Shawn finished, wearing an oversized T-shirt promoting an album from a hip-hop artist named Tone Kapone, his palms were still damp and his forehead was glistening and he made a revelatory confession. "I think it was easier this year," he said. "I didn't make any blunders in my games. Even the game that I drew, I *saw* the win."

Perhaps this was the miracle everyone had been waiting for. Perhaps

Shawn Martinez was finally coming to terms with his impending adulthood. He'd been placed in a special program at Murrow, a more strict curriculum that mandates class attendance and is meant to help its students earn promotion to the next grade. He still looked upon his classwork with contempt, and a few weeks earlier at that high school in New Rochelle where Murrow won its seventh consecutive state championship, Shawn had stayed up so late the night before doing god-knows-what that he'd fallen dead asleep in his chair during one of the morning games. But who knows? The past few hours had unfolded like an epiphany—maybe it was time for Shawn's epiphany as well.

Because Sal and Alex each lost games to inferior opponents in earlier rounds, Murrow trailed by a full point heading into Round Seven. But then Shawn won, and Alex somehow salvaged a victory over a 1920 from what appeared to be a dead draw, and Sal, going head-to-head against Catalina Foothills' Christopher De Sa, rated at 2012, played the sort of brutal, ego-crushing chess that had propelled Fischer to the world championship in 1972. De Sa chose to give up some of his time to prepare for Sal, and he showed up twenty minutes late, setting down his backpack, languorously removing his jacket, and playing his knight to the f3 square. Sal did not hesitate; he played pawn to c4. An hour later, Sal was suppressing a grin and De Sa kept leaving the board to get another drink of water and to attempt to salvage what remained of his dignity. Sal checked with his queen, then checked with his rook, then captured a bishop, then another check, and then finally De Sa resigned with a helpless shrug. Facing the most important match he had ever played at Murrow, Sal did not just win; Sal performed a ritual emasculation. "My God," he said when it was over. "That was beautiful, wasn't it?"

In the end, each of Murrow's top four scorers (Sal, Alex, Shawn, and Mikhail) and six of Murrow's top seven (including Dalphe, who had sublimated chess for hip-hop dancing, and who was performing regularly at New Jersey Nets games with a troupe of youth performers) won their final-round games. In the end, with six seconds remaining on his clock, Aradhyula recognized the futility of his efforts to pull out a victory, and he accepted the draw, and at 5:45 on a Sunday afternoon, Eliot Weiss removed his toes from a line of masking tape, hurried upstairs to his hotel room, and got on the phone to the newspapers. His team had won the national championship by half a point, the sixth in school history and the third in a row, if you counted last year (and who would argue if he did?). Either way, the local Chuck E. Cheese was already anticipating their arrival.

♛

Later that evening, they waited in the back of the room for their names to be announced, so they could pick up another cheap trophy they'd have to squeeze into the overhead compartment on the plane ride home. They were all here, gathered around their coach, though Sal kept wandering off to flirt with some girls he'd met and Ilya was doing one last interview, over the phone, with a reporter from the *New York Post*.

It would all continue to change when they got home: the makeup of their team, the makeup of Murrow itself. Within a few weeks, Dalphe would transfer to a small high school closer to his new home in New Jersey, choosing his dance career over his chess career (in June, he would land a bit part in a Disney film). And that same month, a notice would appear on Murrow's Web site, reflecting a citywide change in policy:

Message Regarding School Safety Scanning
April 2006

Dear Parents:
  We are committed to provide a safe, secure learning environment for all students in our school. The New York City Police Department has assisted us in achieving this goal and in implementing a coordinated approach to school safety. As part of the safety initiative for New York City Schools, Mayor Bloomberg has announced that on some days

students will be asked to go through metal scanning machines like the kind used to screen airline passengers for the purpose of detecting weapons. These scanning devices, deployed by the New York City Police Department, will identify not only weapons but other objects that are never permitted in our building and will help us to keep everyone safe in our school. . . .

These days we often hear that added security measures are "a sign of the times." In our school, however, I see this additional security resource as a sign that placing students and staff in a potentially unsafe situation is unacceptable. We must all commit to ensuring the safety of everyone in our community. . . .

Sincerely,
Anthony R. Lodico, principal

This was not Lodico's idea. This was a citywide initiative, and he had no choice but to post the letter and send it out. As of the end of the 2005–06 school year (when Ilya and Willy became two of the 660 members of that year's graduating class), the scanners had yet to show up at Murrow. But it was there, lingering, as a warning and a threat to the precarious balance Lodico is expected to maintain between a safe school and a free school, between a disciplined student body and a creative student body. "Most of the students come up to me and say they don't notice any difference from the changes we've made," Lodico said at the end of his second year as Bruckner's heir. "In a way, it's a very positive change that's very subtle. After we closed the courtyard, I had *two* kids come to my office to complain."

Times have changed since the 1970s, since Bruckner's vision first came to life. And that's all Lodico is trying to do, is adjust to these times, to keep his school both safe and productive, to keep kids from waking up during their senior year, like Oscar and Willy did, and realizing how much more they could have done.

For now, the chess team remains a constant at Murrow, the school's most potent public-relations tool: Every time Lodico attends a citywide principals' meeting, his colleagues come up to him and say, *Edward R. Murrow. That's the chess school, yes?* Someday in the not-too-distant future, of course, Eliot Weiss will take that teacher's pension and he will leave Murrow to the next generation. What happens then is anyone's guess: This is *his* team, *his* legacy, and where it goes when he goes is a question that cannot be answered any more easily than the question of whether chess will ever be able to penetrate mainstream American culture.

But for one moment, at least, Weiss wasn't caught up in all of the vagaries of the future. Sitting in that chair in the back of the room in Milwaukee, waiting to pick up another national championship trophy, he permitted himself a certain measure of satisfaction. He had done all he could, had transformed an after-school club into a national dynasty. He had done as much for the reputation of a single public high school as any teacher in New York City, and he had done it all for free. There was nothing left to accomplish. There were no more milestones.

Were there?

"Hey," he said. "You guys want to go meet the president again?"

AFTERWORD

More than 1,400 players participated in the 2007 National High School Chess Championships at the Hyatt Regency in Kansas City, a record-breaking number; but as had been the case in years past, the two top seeds both came from the same school: Alex Lenderman and Sal Bercys. They were were playing as teammates for the final time.

By this time, Alex and Sal were seniors, and they appeared to have reached an understanding: They were still not friends, but they had matured enough to fashion a method of co-existing. Alex, his rating at 2471, spent the week before the nationals preparing. When he arrived, he went to bed at midnight, and ordered eggs from room service before each morning round. He won six games, drew one, and took the individual championship on tiebreaks. Sal, his hair long and shaggy, his bangs nearly trailing over his eyes, his rating at 2491, drew twice and finished with 6.0 points, tied for fourth place. Shawn Martinez, his rating at 2009, finished with 5.5 points, and three others, including Nile Smith (1792) and Mikhail Furman (1696), finished with 4.0 points each.

Once again, Catalina Foothills High School had more depth. Their top four boards, Landon Brownell, Christopher De Sa, Vaishnav Aradhyula, and Sean Higgins, were all rated over 2000, and their fifth board, Pavel Savine, was at 1923. For much of the weekend, Catalina Foothills led and appeared as if it would win the championship outright, but things turned in rounds five and six. Heading into the seventh and final round, Murrow led by a point. In the end, Nile Smith, facing Ben Marmont, a 2000-rated player from another Arizona High School, needed nothing more than a draw for Murrow to win outright. Mr. Weiss insists that he tried to signal to Nile, to catch his attention, to get him to offer a draw, but Nile, so fixated on the win, didn't process the directive. A couple of errant moves later, Marmont won the game, and as in 2005, the teams tied for first place, with 22 points each. Again, Catalina Foothills won on a technicality—the cumulative tiebreak. This time, says Mr. Weiss, the teams agreed to share the championship.

A few weeks later, trailed by a pair of documentary filmmakers, the members of Murrow's latest championship team—the seventh in the school's history—met with the governor of New York, Eliot Spitzer.

♛

In May, for the first time in recent memory, with Sal and Alex and Shawn and Nile all absent, Murrow High lost the high school division of the Brooklyn borough championship tournament, sponsored by Chess-in-the-Schools. They did not lose to another high school, however. They lost to Intermediate School 318, coached by John Galvin and Elizabeth Vicary. Already that spring, 318 had won both the elementary (K–6) and the junior high school (K–8) national championships; so Galvin decided to challenge his team at the borough championships by pitting them against Murrow. A couple of days later, *The New York Sun* ran a story headlined "I.S. 318 Youngsters Dethrone New York Chess 'Kings.'" Mr. Weiss was not entirely pleased at the implication ("It'd be sort of like Michael Jordan playing with a bunch of three-year-olds," he told the paper), but he conceded that 318 had constructed a dynasty.

By summer 2007, Vicary had finished her masters thesis ("Encouraging Middle School Girls' Success and Involvement in Chess") and had also begun playing competitively again. In the fall, she planned to begin teaching full-time at I.S. 318, no longer working for Chess-in-the-Schools. Already, she has established herself as one of the better female players in the country; in July, she was one of ten women to compete at the U.S. women's championship in Stillwater, Oklahoma. She finished ninth, although she did win a "brilliancy prize" for one of her games. A Murrow graduate, Irina Krush, finished first.

♛

The loss at the borough championships, however contrived, might have served as the symbolic end of Murrow's own dynasty, at least in the near future. Sal was headed to the University of Texas at Dallas, having accepted a chess scholarship that he once scorned; Alex was moving on to Brooklyn College, also with a scholarship, and planned to study to become a math teacher. (He gives a number of simultaneous exhibitions and lessons through the Internet Chess Club.) The other fixtures of that 2005 team were long gone: Ilya was still toiling at Baruch, and hoping to transfer; Oscar was still working at Chess-in-the-Schools and attending a local community college; and Willy had moved out of his mother's house, still on the verge of getting his GED and starting school. Nile had started college at Lincoln University in Pennsylvania. They'd mostly lost touch with Dalphe after he'd transferred from Murrow to the much smaller Satellite Academy in Manhattan and embraced dancing and acting over chess. And Shawn? Well, no one quite knew what would happen to Shawn. In April 2007, shortly after this book was published, a reporter named Timothy Williams wrote a feature article about Shawn, headlined "Teenage Riddle: Skipping Class, Mastering Chess," which appeared on the front page of *The New York Times*. By then, Shawn was spending most of his time hustling chess at an atrium on Wall Street. "It wasn't weeks [of school] that I missed, it was months," he told Williams. In the aftermath of that story, Mr. Weiss says, he received dozens of e-mails offering Shawn help, with a job or financial assistance or a starring role in a documentary. Whether Shawn responded to those e-mails, Mr.

Weiss could not say. He was supposed to start a GED program at some point, Mr. Weiss told me, but when that would actually happen—or whether that would ever happen, or whether Shawn might return to Murrow to enroll in a GED program at the school—he could not say.

♛

With Sal gone, and Alex gone, and Shawn almost certain not to return to school because he rarely showed up in the first place—he had somehow earned three credits in three years, and how he even earned those remained a mystery—Mr. Weiss would be forced to rebuild, to await the next aspiring master who might land at Murrow from some faraway land or some nearby middle school. No longer was I.S. 318 proving a reliable pipeline: The school's academic reputation had grown to the point that many of its best players were now able to gain admission through competitive examinations to other elite schools, such as Brooklyn Tech.

So in July, when Mr. Weiss held the annual team picnic at his home on Long Island, there was a certain amount of resignation in his voice when he discussed the future. He had no idea what would happen next, but this day was a celebration of what had come before. As the day wore on, he gathered the entire party of current and former players in his living room and subjected them to a piano recital by his children, Julie and Ben; he had even printed out programs for the occasion. And very soon this man, who has an uncanny ability to convince anyone to do anything, had cajoled a group of teenagers and young adults from Ukraine and Martinique and St. Petersburg and Brooklyn into singing a cacophonous version of "New York, New York."

Michael Weinreb
August 2007
Brooklyn, New York

ACKNOWLEDGMENTS

THE FIRST TIME I VISITED THE MARSHALL CHESS CLUB, I MET A MAN wearing rose-tinted glasses, a fedora, and a camel-hair blazer, who looked like he was on his way to a dress rehearsal of *The Front Page* at an off-Broadway theater. He was one of those people who hold your gaze for a moment too long, which may have been an intimidation tactic honed through years of playing competitive chess, or it may have been because he found me unworthy of his trust. This man was an author as well, of instructional chess books, and the first thing he asked me was whether I planned on playing in the tournament that night. I told him that I didn't really play chess. I told him I was a novice. "A *novice*?" he said, and he stared at me for so long that I thought he might be having a mild cardiac infarction. Then he walked over to the board where Shawn Martinez and Angel Lopez were preparing to begin a blitz game, and he showed me a trick that Bobby Fischer had purportedly played on a novice when he was living in exile in Hungary. Fischer's opponent had memorized some complex opening, but didn't notice that Fischer had checked his king with his bishop.

"And we all know that you don't actually have to *say* 'Check,'" Bruce said. "So the boy keeps at his opening, and"—Bruce toppled the king with his bishop. It fell with a thud. Shawn rolled his eyes. Angel stared at the floor and stifled a giggle—"that's that."

I learned about the Murrow chess team while working as a sports-writer at *Newsday*, when one of Eliot Weiss's ubiquitous faxes ended up on my desk. I knew nothing of Edward R. Murrow High School since they had no athletics, and I knew virtually nothing about competitive chess. Over the course of two years I trailed Mr. Weiss's team from one borough to another, from one city to another, from one state to another. Several times, while lingering over the chessboards at various tournaments and taking notes, I was asked whether I might be abetting some sort of elaborate cheating scheme. What these people did not know, what they could not have known, is that most of the time the words I kept writing in my notebook, over and over again, were—and I will paraphrase here—"What just happened?"

Because of this, then, I am grateful to the many people who did their best to educate me on the finer points of the game. (In addition, a number of books and magazine articles, which I have listed in a separate bibliography, proved indispensable.) I start with Eliot Weiss, who, from the beginning, when I was merely a strange newspaper reporter outlining a nebulous project, did not hesitate to share both his time and his knowledge. From there, I met Elizabeth Vicary, who is not only a deeply committed teacher and an outstanding chess player herself, but is also a wonderful storyteller. Without her help, this book would have been much less interesting. I am also grateful to John Galvin, Jennifer and Greg Shahade, and the administration at I.S. 318; to Fred Goldhirsch, Doug Bellizzi, Kofi and Najee McGreen, John McManus and the other employees and volunteers at the Right Move; to the management and staff of the Chess-in-the-Schools Foundation, including Marley Kaplan and Sarah Pitari; to Josh Waitzkin, Lev Khariton, Robby Adamson, Josh Weinstein, Irina Krush, Marty Grund, and Bruce Pandolfini, for providing so much background; to Saul Bruckner and the current administration at Murrow High School; to Joan DuBois and the United States Chess Federation; and to all the other tournament directors and organizers and teachers and volunteers and competitors who allowed me to eavesdrop on their events.

I am grateful to my agents, Jane Dystel and Miriam Goderich, for nurturing this project from the time it consisted of a single sentence, and for finding it a good home. Brendan Cahill at Gotham Books (along with his boss, Bill Shinker) undertook perhaps the largest gambit of all, putting an absurd amount of faith in an unknown writer before departing temporarily to get married and then departing the business to attend graduate school at Wharton, of all things. I will be proud to say I knew him before he became a media mogul. In Brendan's absence, his assistant, Patrick Mulligan, was accommodating, congenial, and meticulous, and is certainly a much better chess player than I will ever be. On the other side of the Atlantic, Beth Coates at Yellow Jersey Press was a supporter from the start, and Michael Bourret with Dystel & Goderich deserves credit for finding her.

Several friends and colleagues, including Adrian Wojnarowski and Dave Hollingsworth, talked me through the middle game. Of course, I bear a certain bias toward my own personal in-house copy editor, Cheryl Maday, who has an uncanny ability to talk me through anything in this world.

Most of all, I am grateful to the small group of teenagers and their parents who entrusted me with their secrets, both on the board and away from it. I did my best to portray both aspects of their lives as faithfully and compassionately as I could. I may still be a novice, but I will miss those days of peering over their shoulders at those sixty-four squares and attempting to read their minds.

GLOSSARY

Annotation: A written commentary on a game or a specific position.

Bishop &: A chess piece that can move only diagonally; worth about three pawns.

Blitz: Speed chess in which each player usually gets about five minutes on his clock.

Blunder: A major error.

Book player: Someone who relies heavily on published theory in his play.

Bughouse: A variation of chess where teams play on two or more boards, trading captured pieces back and forth for use on their own boards.

Bullet: Speed chess in which each player gets one minute on his clock.

Castle: The only time a player can move two pieces on a single turn (the king, which normally moves only one space, shifts two squares, and the rook is positioned on the other side of the king). Castling is permitted only once per game, and only if certain conditions are met, most notably that the king and rook cannot have moved yet, and the king cannot be in check. **(See page 48)**

Check: To make a direct attack or threat on an opponent's king. In competitive chess, check does not need to be verbalized.

Checkmate: The end of a chess game, when an opponent's king has no legal move to extricate itself from check.

Development: The process of advancing one's material into strategically advantageous squares early in the game.

Draw: A tie game. In competitive chess, each player receives half a point for a draw.

Endgame: The third and final phase of a chess game, when most of the pieces are off the board.

Exchange: To trade pieces with one's opponent.

Fork: A move where one piece attacks multiple pieces.

Gambit: A sacrifice made in the opening, often in order to gain a positional advantage.

Grandmaster (or GM): The highest title conferred in chess; based on one's ELO rating and three favorable results (or *norms*) in tournaments involving other GMs. Usually rated at 2500 or above.

Hang a Piece: To leave a piece unprotected or exposed, allowing one's opponent to capture it without getting anything in return.

International Master (or IM): The second-highest title a chess player can earn, one step below grandmaster. Usually rated around 2400. A National Master, usually rated between 2200 and 2399, is one step down.

Internet Chess Club (or ICC): One of the most popular chess sites online.

King ♔: The focus of a chess game, it can move one square in any direction, as long as it is not moving into check.

Knight ♘: The only chess piece that can jump over others; it moves either two squares up or back and one to the side, or one square up or back and two to the side. It is worth about three pawns.

Lost, or Lost Game: A game that one would appear to have no chance of winning, if one's opponent plays it correctly.

Material: The collective name for one's pieces and pawns.

Middle Game: The second phase of a chess game, after the opening and before the endgame.

Opening: The first phase of a chess game, and the name for any sequence of moves commonly used in the beginning of a game (i.e., the Ruy Lopez Opening).

Patzer: A novice or weak player. The word means "bungler" in German.

Pawn ♙ : The weakest of all the units on a chessboard. Pawns can move forward two squares on their first move and one square thereafter; they can capture pieces only by moving diagonally. If they reach the opponent's back row, they are "promoted" and can become any other piece, most commonly a queen.

Pieces: Any of the units on a chessboard with the exception of the pawn.

Pin: To attack an opponent's unit that happens to be shielding another, often more valuable piece.

Queen ♕ : The most powerful piece on the chessboard, the queen can move any number of spaces, in any direction. Worth about nine pawns.

Rating: Refers to one's ELO rating, a four-digit number that signifies a player's strength. Competitive games that affect one's rating are referred to as "rated games." (**See page 32**)

Rook ♖ : One of the strongest pieces on the board; can move in straight lines in any direction. Worth about five pawns.

Sacrifice (or "Sack"): To give up material in order to gain an advantage in position or to further an attack.

Simultaneous Exhibition (or "Simul"): A demonstration in which a high-rated player competes in a number of games, with a number of separate opponents, at the same time.

Skittles Room: The designated area at a chess tournament where talking (also known as "kibitzing") or recreational play is permitted.

Stalemate: A draw in which one player cannot make a legal move without forcing his king into check.

Strategy: An overarching plan for attack in a given position.

Swiss System: Commonly used pairings method for tournaments, in which players with similar results and ratings are paired against each other, usually alternating between the black pieces and the white pieces.

Tactics: The methods used to carry out a specific strategy.

BIBLIOGRAPHY

Ashley, Maurice. *Chess for Success.* New York: Broadway Books, 2005.

Berube, Maurice R., and Marilyn Gittell, eds. *Confrontation at Ocean Hill-Brownsville: The New York School Strikes of 1968.* New York: Frederick A. Praeger, 1969.

Bohm, Hans, and Kees Jongkind. *Bobby Fischer: The Wandering King.* London: B. T. Batsford, 2003.

Brady, Frank. *Bobby Fischer: Profile of a Prodigy.* New York: Dover Publications, Inc., 1973.

Chernev, Irving, and Kenneth Harkness. *An Invitation to Chess.* New York: Fireside, 1945.

Cockburn, Alexander. *Idle Passion: Chess and the Dance of Death.* New York: Village Voice/Simon and Schuster, 1974.

Edmonds, David, and John Eidinow. *Bobby Fischer Goes to War.* New York: Ecco, 2004.

Fatsis, Stefan. *Word Freak: Heartbreak, Triumph, Genius, and Obsession in the World of Competitive Scrabble Players.* New York: Penguin Books, 2001.

Fischer, Bobby. *My 60 Memorable Games.* London: Faber and Faber, 1969.

Fischer, Bobby, with Stuart Margulies and Donn Mosenfelder. *Bobby Fischer Teaches Chess.* New York: Bantam, 1972.

Hallman, J. C. *The Chess Artist: Genius, Obsession, and the World's Oldest Game.* New York: Thomas Dunne Books, 2003.

Hoffman, Paul. "Chess Queen." *Smithsonian,* August 2003.

Hoffman, Paul. "The Pandolfini Defense." *The New Yorker,* June 4, 2001.

Horowitz, I. A., and P. L. Rothenberg. *The Complete Book of Chess.* New York: Collier Books, 1969.

Lasker, Edward. *The Adventure of Chess.* New York: Dover Publications, Inc., 1959.

Nabokov, Vladimir. *The Defense.* New York: Perigee Books, 1964.

Nimzovich, Aron. *My System.* New York: David McKay Company, Inc., 1947.

Pandolfini, Bruce. *Pandolfini's Ultimate Guide to Chess.* New York: Fireside, 2003.

Pandolfini, Bruce. *Chess Thinking.* New York: Fireside, 1995.

Ravitch, Diane. *The Schools We Deserve: Reflections on the Educational Crises of Our Times.* New York: Basic Books, Inc., 1985.

Shahade, Jennifer. *Chess Bitch: Women in the Ultimate Intellectual Sport.* Los Angeles: Siles Press, 2005.

Waitzkin, Fred. *Searching for Bobby Fischer: The Father of a Prodigy Observes the World of Chess.* New York: Penguin Books, 1988.

WEB SITES

U.S. Chess Federation: www.uschess.org

Chess Base: www.chessbase.com

The Right Move: www.therightmove.org

Chess-in-the-Schools: www.chessintheschools.org

The Daily Dirt Chess Blog: www.chessninja.com/dailydirt

National Scholastic Chess Foundation: www.nscfchess.org

Continental Chess Assocation: www.chesstour.com

Internet Chess Club: www.chessclub.com

Chess Cafe: www.chesscafe.com

Inside Schools: www.insideschools.org

Edward R. Murrow High School: www.ermurrowhs.org

Online Chess Database: www.chessgames.com